Merchant Capital and Islam

MERCHANT CAPITAL AND ISLAM

by Mahmood Ibrahim

University of Texas Press, Austin

First Edition, 1990

Requests for permission to reproduce material from this work
should be sent to Permissions, University of Texas Press, Box 7819,
Austin, Texas 78713-7819.

∞ The paper used in this publication meets the minimum require-
ments of American National Standard for Information Sciences—
Permanence of Paper for Printed Library Materials, ANSI
Z39.48-1984.

Library of Congress Cataloging-in-Publication Data

Ibrahim, Mahmood, 1948–
    Merchant capital and Islam / Mahmood Ibrahim.—1st ed.
      p.   cm.
    Bibliography: p.
    Includes index.
    ISBN 0-292-75107-9 (alk. paper)
      1. Islamic Empire—Commerce. 2. Merchants—Islamic Empire.
3. Mecca (Saudi Arabia)—Commerce—History. 4. Mecca (Saudi
Arabia)—Economic conditions. 5. Economics—Religious
aspects—Islam. 6. Islam—Economic aspects. I. Title.
HF3756.I27   1990
332'.041'0917671—dc20   89-14635
                                                  CIP

To Nancy, Arwa, and Adnan

Contents

Acknowledgments

Many points discussed in this book were originally raised in my PhD dissertation, "A Biography of Muʿawiya ibn Abi Sufyan." I feel it is not inappropriate to thank the members of my PhD committee, Profs. Michael Morony, Afaf Marsot, and Seeger Bonebakker, for their support and encouragement.

In the course of rewriting, revising, and updating this work, I had the invaluable comments of colleagues to whom I owe a great deal of gratitude: Prof. Fred Donner of the University of Chicago, who read the manuscript at different stages and who readily offered comments that ultimately focused the discussion; and Prof. Peter Gran of Temple University, whose suggestions helped clarify the methodological approach and thus helped me raise several theoretical issues. Words cannot express the debt I owe to Prof. Rifaat Abu el-Haj of California State University, Long Beach, a friend and a colleague who has been involved with this work from the very beginning and who has displayed an untiring readiness to offer critical thinking and encouraging comments as well as love and support. This he did individually and as a member of Halqatu al-Arbiʿa (the Wednesday Study Circle), whose other members I duly acknowledge for their discussion of the work and for their helpful comments: Dr. Mahmud Abu Swa, Dr. Dina Rizq, Dr. Hala Fattah, and Edward Mitchell. I would also like to thank Mehdi Abadani and Mehdi Estakhr for the use of their libraries, and Thamsanqa Ngubeni for the use of his library as well as for his technical assistance.

I would like to thank my colleagues at Birzeit University: Prof. George Giacaman, for his constant concern and encouragement; and Prof. Lisa Taraki and Dr. Rita Giacaman for the use of their libraries. I would like to express my deep appreciation to Birzeit University, my home institution. It strives to deliver outstanding education to its students against incredible odds, and gave me support and time to complete the final draft during a critical period in the history of the university.

Finally, I would like to acknowledge Arwa and Adnan, my children, who may have suffered the absence of my attention during periods when I was writing this book. I was confident all along that they had the attention of Nancy Halpern Ibrahim, my friend, colleague, and wife, whose love and sense of and commitment to justice keep us together even in my absence. Thank you all. I only hope that my family, friends, and colleagues suffered for a worthwhile endeavor, any shortcoming of which is my responsibility alone.

Introduction

The Semitic race is to be recognized almost entirely by negative characteristics. It has neither mythology, nor epic, nor science, nor philosophy, nor
fiction, nor plastic arts, nor civil life; in everything there is a complete
absence of complexity, subtlety or feeling, except for unity.

—Ernest Renan

European attitudes like those expressed by Renan began to take on intellectual currency with the beginning of the nineteenth century. Martin
Bernal, discussing intellectual changes in Europe during the era of colonial expansion, shows that by merely shifting a model, Europeans changed
their views on the Afro-Asiatic origins of Classical Greece. And according
to the new Aryan model, Egypt's "long and stable history, which had
been a source of admiration, now became reason to despise it as static
and sterile." [1]

An important component of the Aryan model was Orientalism. The
negative characterizations of the Semites and the sterile and static concep-
tions of their history were accommodated in that branch of Orientalism
that devoted itself to the study of Islam and Islamic civilization. Theodor
Nöldeke, a leading philhellenist Orientalist, could declare toward the end
of the nineteenth century that the sum total of his work as an Orientalist
was to confirm his "low opinion" of the Eastern peoples. [2]

One might expect that such unscientific views would have changed,
given the advances in the social sciences and the change in the balance of
forces in the contemporary world. Yet, with the twentieth century nearly
at an end, Patricia Crone echoes these same views when she describes
Arabia's history as "one of tribal immutability: there is not much to tell
between the Arabia of the Bible and the Arabia of [19th century] Musil's
Rawla." [3]

Yet between A.D. 600 and 661 Arab society changed very quickly. Islam was founded in Mecca, a state structure was established, Arabia was
united under Medina, and the state quickly firmed its control over much
of western Asia and northern Africa. The caliphate was initiated some-
what spontaneously after Muhammad's death to lead the Muslim com-

munity. The caliphate, its orientation, and its functions continued to develop into a complex political structure articulating the broader social and economic transformations brought about by Islam. What were those transformations and what were their consequences? What were the conditions under which those transformations occurred, and, if Islam provided their moral base, what was their material base? How were they perceived and which perception dominated the caliphate? Finally, were those transformations part of a continuing historical process or were they the immediate result of Islam alone? These are the general questions that this study will address.

As one might expect, the issues related to this period have been explained by traditional Muslim historians and Orientalists within a diffusionist framework consistent with the Orientalist outlook already described. Two general themes have been utilized: divine intervention, and nomadism. Both, however, see external factors as responsible for change.

Within these two leitmotifs, several kinds of interpretations have been offered by traditional Muslim historians and by Orientalists. In the first, the rise of Islam is usually explained in terms of divine providence. As explained in the Qur'an, God revealed His command to Muhammad out of His mercy and justice. All that is contained in Islam—doctrine, rituals, and institutions—therefore, was externally generated; the society had no creative input save its acceptance of the divine command. These scholars attribute the Arab/Islamic expansion to the zeal imbued in them by the new faith. The expansion is regarded as Jihad, a fulfillment of religious duty to propagate Islam. The Fitna, the civil war between A.D. 656 and 661, was seen as a religious conflict between those who were devout believers and those who were not.

Some Orientalists, on the other hand, attribute the rise of Islam to the diffusion of outside cultural influences.[4] The Islamic expansion is generally seen as being caused by nomads driven by hunger conducting their "habitual" raids for plunder.[5] There has been hardly any discussion of the state that emerged in Medina, and the few exceptions have discussed it in terms of power that it did not possess or in terms of its relations with the nomads.[6] The civil war is seen variously as a religious conflict, as a dispute between northern and southern Arabs or between the nomads and the sedentary, or as a nomadic reaction to the growth of a centralized state.

Although the above interpretations are helpful to some extent for understanding this period, they are generally ahistorical and tend to minimize the role of social forces; internal forces, their formation, their interests, and their relations with one another, become irrelevant in the face of external factors, which then become the yardstick by which the achievements of Islamic society are measured.

Reliance on external and nonmaterial forces has left a gap in our understanding of this complex period. The emphasis of Muslim historians and Orientalists on external factors, however varied or even radically different from one another, has produced similar results: Islam was viewed apart from its historical past as appearing in an isolated historical moment caused by outside intervention, whether divine or not.

The logical extension of denying Islam its historical antecedents is also to deny its relevance to the conditions of its rise and those of succeeding generations. Again, Crone exemplifies this sterile and static view by saying, "Rarely have a preacher and his followers lived in such discontinuous environments: what made sense to Muhammad made no sense to Mu'awiya, let alone 'Abd al-Malik."[7] Agreeing with the notion that external factors were responsible for change, Crone and Michael Cook suggest that Islam was born out of a conspiracy hatched between Jews who were expelled by the Byzantines from Edessa in A.D. 628 and the Arabs, dubbed the Hagarenes, as they were descendants of Hagar, Abraham's wife. It was only after the success of this conspiracy that anything Islamic began to appear. The Arabs, backing out of the conspiracy, disassociated themselves from the Jews. So as not to rely on Christianity, the Arabs then concocted an independent religion and molded it out of "Samaritan calque." Being based on a Samaritan model, the Ka'ba, the Hijra, Muhammad's prophethood and his teachings, as well as the Qur'an, were mere afterthoughts.[8]

Within this view, Crone and Cook consider the Islamic expansion the outcome of the conspiracy of Judaic values and the barbarian force of the Arab tribes.[9] Islamic polity fell victim to this conspiracy, and the Arabs became their own jailers, because the ideological outcome "had caught and fused the alienation from civilization of both the ghetto and the desert," and because "the old tribal hostility towards the alien and oppressive states of settled societies went well with the alienation of the rabbis and the result was that the political imagination of Islam remained fixated on the desert."[10] Fixated also on the past, Islam and Islamic civilization, the authors believe, were not only forgeries and an outcome of cultural expropriation, but also immutable and intransigent, dead and irrelevant from their very inception. In this civilization, which is held to be peculiar, history became not a progression of events and the development of a creative social force, but a retrogression where creativity, if there was any, lay in projecting backward toward an immutable and destructive past. While this approach might pose interesting hypotheses and parallels, it remains fundamentally flawed, since it completely ignores the conditions of internal social, economic, and political relations; Islamic history is frozen in time and then compared and contrasted to "others" across time and space. Consequently, Islamic history is not understood on its own terms, but only in mythified relation to an outside world.[11]

In supporting the view of "discontinuous environment," the history of pre-Islamic Arabia has been stripped of its internal dynamics. One is usually confronted with the notion that Arabia lacked organized internal structures and that it was merely a way station in the commerce of the ancient world. Its inhabitants are depicted as tribes engaged in perpetual conflict and its merchants as merely transporters and exchangers of commodities produced elsewhere. This perceived limitation has resulted in the ideological tenet that Arabian society lacked the capacity to produce a surplus of its own. This lack has been attributed either to the absence of resources (unproductive land, deserts) or to the inability of society (disconnected units, tribes, nomads) to organize and to institutionalize production and extraction of surplus. Therefore, for reasons that must be seen as instrumental in the formation of the political culture of the so-called western/modern world, the peninsula and its inhabitants could be dismissed as historically unimportant. Arabian society is thus placed outside history and in the backwaters of civilization.

A major role in the perpetuation of this distorted and ahistorical perception of Arabia's past was played by early Muslim chroniclers, who insist that the pre-Islamic period—*jahiliyya*—was a period of ignorance and lacked creativity. Although their original intention was to characterize pre-Islamic society as one that did not have a "revealed book" and was thus ignorant of the divine command, the notion was later corrupted to mean uncivilized, uncultured, barbarous, with the intended meaning that pre-Islamic society was incapable of producing Islam with all of its contributions to the transformation of society. This interpretation of the concept was motivated merely by the desire to demonstrate the miraculous and divine nature of Islam, but modern scholarship has assimilated the *jahiliyya* view of Arabia and elaborated it, either for the traditional Muslim historians' reasons or because of cultural bias. This ultimately has reinforced the erroneous belief that Islam, in the words of a leading Orientalist, is rootless and without a historical tradition.[12]

To come to a better understanding of this formative period of Islamic history, we should begin to examine aspects other than nomadism, religious factors, and outside conditions. And even if we suppose for a moment that Orientalists have produced scientific studies, even though we know that their views have been influenced by specific national configurations, it would defy science to accept their framework and their conclusions as immutable. In fact, knowledge, as Thomas Kuhn shows, is advanced only by the restructuring of our thoughts according to new paradigms that allow us to posit new hypotheses and to ask our sources different questions than have hitherto been asked.[13]

Historians of this period are generally in agreement on the commercial importance of Mecca, especially on the eve of Islam.[14] This study will examine the influence of merchants and merchant capital on social development. It will highlight their role in shaping social, economic, political, and religious conditions in Mecca, the very conditions that brought about Islam. I shall also discuss this role in the period before and after the rise of Islam. This examination of merchants and merchant capital will allow us to follow the transition of Mecca from a relatively insignificant stopover in the caravan trade to a major religious, commercial, and political center in western Arabia. Such a framework refocuses our attention onto internal social forces and their relations and allows us to examine how these changed in an unfolding historical context. Far from the redundant and archaic notions of sterile and static history, this approach indicates a history that is creative and dynamic. Only then can we understand the rise of Mecca, the development of its institutions, including those found in Islam, and the foundation of Islamic society within a perspective of historical continuity conditioned by the demands of merchants and merchant capital.

Merchant capital is that fraction of capital that is generated purely through exchange, whether merchants controlled the means of production, as in Yemen, or not, as in Mecca. It is the earliest form of capital and "appears to perform the function *par excellence* of capital."[15] Merchant capital in the Meccan context also meant power—political power in the sense that merchants harnessed their wealth in the mobilization of force to influence the course of events and social relations in a manner to suit their interests. The development of merchant capital largely depended on the human element, since, after all, exchange was between a buyer and a seller of artisan-produced commodities. Perhaps this factor distinguishes merchant capital from other fractions of capital (for example, industrial capital, which reduces the importance of the individual and emphasizes mass and robotic production). There is, however, a clear connection between merchant capital and industrial capital. Therefore, it is with the growth of merchant capital that Michael Tigar and Madeleine Levy begin their account of the rise of industrial capitalism in eleventh-century Europe: *"pies poudreux,* 'dusty feet,' he [the merchant] was called, for he took his goods from town to town, from fair to fair, from market to market, on foot or on horseback, selling as he went. In the great halls of the feudal lords, the merchant was an object of derision, scorn, and even hatred. Lyric songs celebrated knightly robbery of merchant bands, as well as knightly valor in battle and knightly cuckoldry." [16] This characterization seems to be a continuation of the constraints that were placed on merchants in the Roman world, where landowners constituted the governing class, which formulated laws that eventually thwarted the merchants' accumulation of any substantial political and economic power.

Thwarted in the Roman world, accumulation of merchant capital developed freely in Arabia, where the genesis of merchant capital is more ancient and much more deeply rooted than in Europe. Other than occasional insecurity, Arabian merchants did not suffer the same conditions of their European counterparts, because they were nurtured and protected by the state. By the sixth century in Mecca, merchants were the honored and feared leaders of their society and continually introduced mechanisms to enhance their economic interests.

The power to introduce similar mechanisms was gained only slowly by European merchants, who had to challenge laws and customs designed to protect the feudal landlord. The Crusades helped them take perceptible strides toward power and accelerated the rise of industrial capital. As a result of the Crusaders' contact with the Islamic world, European merchants adopted such well-tried mechanisms as the campagna, the commenda, and contracts. Through the Crusades, the Europeans discovered "Arab science, including medical learning. They discovered, and we know that they brought back, a system of mathematics based upon nine numbers and zero, which replaced the cumbersome Roman numerical system. A bit later they brought back rudimentary double-entry bookkeeping. . . . The traders who returned from the East brought Roman law, too, or at least a more systematic and commercially usable version of it than had survived anywhere in the West." [17]

The European Crusaders contacted a sector of Islamic society that Rodinson defines as "capitalistic," and it is with the early history and the formation of this sector that this study is concerned. The specific question that Rodinson tackles in *Islam and Capitalism* is not addressed here, but it will become evident that this study supports his conclusion that Islam, as a religion, did not hinder capital accumulation and that it is not responsible for the nondevelopment of industrial capital in the Islamic world. Rather, industrial capital did not develop (if, indeed, it is an inevitable and natural development) because of social, economic, and political factors. (In the epilogue, I offer specific conditions that determined later political and economic developments.)

The Islamic capitalistic sector began in Mecca. Meccan merchant capital provides a classic example of the growth of this fraction of capital. Its accumulation depended on the adoption of a wide range of institutions and institutional practices that formed an important component of an ideology that supported and facilitated the material dimension of society. The basic institution on which the Meccans built their wealth was that of the *haram*, the sacred area and the sacred time, where and when individuals enjoyed security of life and property and thus were provided the opportunity to trade. Commerce was organically linked to the religious institution of pilgrimage. As they did not own the means of production at the time, Meccan merchants merely bought and sold their merchandise, accumulating profit as they increased commercial activity and enlarged the area of their market. This was done by constructing an institutional framework that facilitated pilgrimage to Mecca, such as *siqaya* (supplying water to pilgrims). They also facilitated their access to a wider market by entering into outside alliances (*hilf*). Although a distinction could be made between *siqaya* as a religious institution and *hilf* as political, both became part of an ideology and contributed to the same end: the increased wealth and power of the merchants. It was in introducing institutions that were relevant to their needs that Mecca's merchants played a leading role in the transformation of Meccan society and, later, that of the rest of Arabia.

Chapter 1 puts forth a view of pre-Islamic Arabia that differs from that permitted by the notion of *jahiliyya*. Arabian society was varied and complex and, aside from nomadic groups, there were pastoral and settled communities organized in states that were centered in the surplus-producing southern and northern regions. It will be shown that, by virtue of their control of the means of production, the landlords (the royal families, temple officials, and tribal chiefs) monopolized state structure and the distribution of surplus wealth. They also became the nucleus of the merchant class. It will be argued that the state served their interests not only in preserving and maintaining their control of the land and of productive forces but also in facilitating and safeguarding their commercial activities.

Chapters 2, 3, and 4 discuss how Mecca developed into a major commercial center and how the accumulation of merchant capital transformed its internal social, economic, political, and religious structure, creating in the process a set of conditions favorable for the rise of Islam. There was an organic connection between Mecca's sacred institutions and its commerce, and the demands of merchant capital transformed the society from a relatively homogeneous one into a differentiated structure in which ownership of capital became the basis of social relations. This transformation led to problems that began to hinder the aspirations of Meccan merchants. It will be argued that Islam, growing in a merchant economy, introduced relevant solutions to these contradictions by providing an ideological and institutional superstructure that led to transformations of the society in a manner advantageous to the merchants.

These transformations will be the subject of chapters 5 and 6. It will be shown that Islam allowed for the rise of a state that easily spread its dominance over all of Arabia prior to the extension of its hegemony to the surrounding surplus-producing regions of western Asia and northern Africa. Arab Islamic expansion will be discussed from the point of view of its relevance to the merchants' needs; they consolidated their political and economic control by monopolizing the state, its administration, and its resources, by initiating a process of urbanization in which the cities served as markets and as an instrument of political control, and by distributing surplus wealth, which enlarged the social base of the capital-owning class, giving the merchants added legitimacy and security.

The outcome of this expansion and of the ongoing distribution of wealth was the emergence of a new segment of Arab/Islamic society that acquired wealth and political power for the first time. This segment will be referred to as the New Segment to differentiate it from the sector that was wealthy and politically powerful prior to the rise of Islam (the Traditional Segment, made up largely of merchants). But as the caliphate came under the monopoly of the merchants, especially as the policies of the third caliph, ʿUthman, took effect, a perceptible conflict between the two segments slowly emerged. They began to compete for a larger share of the political and economic structure. The discussion in chapter 6, therefore, highlights the drama played out between the two segments by explaining ʿUthman's policies and why the New Segment opposed them. Analyzing the conflict in this manner will depart significantly from the usual religious or tribal explanation and will provide better comprehension of the factors behind the revolt against ʿUthman, which led to his murder and set the stage for the first civil war in Islamic history.

Chapter 7 will discuss the course of the civil war. It will be argued that the New Segment came to power represented by the fourth caliph, ʿAli ibn Abi Talib, but that this segment was unable to consolidate its hold over the caliphate, mainly because of the challenge posed by the Traditional Segment headed by Muʿawiya ibn Abi Sufyan. He reestablished the power of the Traditional Segment by inaugurating the Umayyad caliphate, which, for nearly a century, maintained the political and economic hegemony of the Arab merchants.

A Note on the Sources

The sources used for this study are the ones traditionally utilized to study the period, such as the works of al-Tabari, al-Baladhuri, Ibn Saʿd, and Ibn ʿAbd al-Hakam. Chapter 1, however, utilizes evidence from archaeological remains as found in the various studies of inscriptions from southern Arabia. While the evidence found is sufficient to force a revision of our understanding of pre-Islamic Arabia, this chapter does not constitute an exhaustive study. In addition, it should be mentioned that a few Arabic sources have so far been underutilized, such as Muhammad ibn Habib al-Baghdadi's *Kitab al-Munammaq fi Akhbar Quraish*. This book, similar in style to his *Kitab al-Muhabbar*, contains information about Mecca and the Quraish that has added to our knowledge, particularly of the evolution of different political factions and the transformation of Mecca's fortunes. Another book is Nasr ibn Muzahim al-Minqari's *Kitab Waqʿat Siffin*. Still, the present study does not claim to have dug up new sources; rather, it constitutes a reinterpretation of the facts of early Islamic history through a rereading of the sources in a new framework. This has allowed the integration of significant information that has been, for one reason or another, glossed over by previous scholarship.

It is well known to those who approach the sources critically that they will find a considerable amount of confusion and contradiction, which resulted from the methodological styles of the chroniclers, who would collect several reports regarding a single event and thus provide variations and different emphases. This has led some scholars either to doubt the authenticity of the reports or to reject them as evidence. More than that, some scholars have even denied the events of early Islam altogether. They approach the sources rather inflexibly; if there is any contradiction or confusion regarding an event, the event itself is questioned rather than the forces and factors behind the variant reports.[18]

Contradictions, confusion, and varying accounts regarding a single event in the sources should not be dealt with by purely textual analysis, which leaves discussion of historical events aside. The more correct approach is to determine the nature of the confusion regarding the event, the various social forces involved in that confusion, and the different backgrounds and aspirations of the interested parties. It is only then that the event itself can be appreciated within its historical context rather than for what it meant for a particular group. We can easily differentiate between a given objective phenomenon and the variant colorings that may have been given it because of political or religious considerations. Isolating the historical event from the ways in which it was reported should produce a more objective account than that which is produced if we try to champion one report, a process that ultimately will result in the same confusion that we set out to correct in the first place.

At any rate, the confusion that appears in the sources is of two kinds. The first concerns numbers (for example, how many were at the Battle of Yarmuk or, for that matter, at any battle), dates of events (did al-Qadisiyya take place in A.D. 636 or 637?), and names of participants, whether individuals or groups. For a demographer, debating the number of Muslims or their adversaries in Yarmuk, for example, is relevant and important, but for this kind of study it is not.[19] What is a clear and objective truth is that the battle took place and that the Muslims won, allowing them to gain mastery over Syria. Studying the sources from the point of view of textual analysis of Yarmuk reveals several contradictions, the pursuit of which might be useful in another context. But these contradictions do not negate the fact that the battle took place.

The second kind of confusion is more problematic and usually concerns reports of an anachronistic nature. The most evident is the plethora of reports, largely Hadiths ascribed to Muhammad, that either foretell events or deal with specific issues or personalities relevant to generations that lived years after his death. For example, Hadiths extolling the way of the Sufis abound. They make Muhammad the ideal mystic, that is, concerned only with the Sufi life-style. Some Hadiths exhibit a clearly political bent, such as the report that Muhammad once said, "Whichever party kills Ammar is the sinner," or that the Prophet cursed Muʿawiya as a sinner or praised him as a leader. These reports are immediately recognizable as political statements serving the interests of one group or another. One must see them within the framework of the chroniclers; it was important to later generations that they be positively associated with the Prophet in some way, because, in Islamic terms, Muhammad's life represents the ideal, the most correct, the only legitimate one.[20] Reports of this nature, while they indicate the sentiments of the reporters and might prove useful in a different line of research, cannot be considered "evidence" for this kind of study, since they appear to be fabricated. They do not report facts; rather, they are a means of legitimation.

This ahistorical and anachronistic reporting has led to the rise of another form of confusion—projecting the present onto the past. For example, the chroniclers may have projected the hostility engendered by the struggle between the Shiʿa and the Abbasids onto al-ʿAbbas and Abu Talib, the progenitors of the two factions. We find that al-ʿAbbas lent Abu Talib some money, which he could not repay. Because the loan was made on usurious terms, Abu Talib lost his fortune. We may be led by the report to believe that the hostility between the Shiʿa and the Abbasids stemmed from this event, but the objective social analyst will reject this event as an explanation of the above struggle. I cite this event in this study not to explain the hostility between al-ʿAbbas and Abu Talib or between the Abbasids and the Shiʿa, but to illustrate the perceptions of usury in Meccan society, since usury is an objective fact as far as merchant economy is concerned in general and as applied to Mecca in particular. What happened to Abu Talib happened to many others in the same social context. What is relevant to this study, then, is to isolate the historical event from the intentions of its reporters and then to evaluate and interpret it within the framework of the study.

A final and simple case in point is ʿUmar's establishment of the Diwan. Was it inspired by Sasanid practice? Was it done on the urging of al-Mughira or anyone else? Was it prompted by the return of Abu Hauraira with an enormous amount of money that ʿUmar did not know how to distribute? While relevant and important in another context, these questions, representing variations, confusion, and contradiction, do not figure in this study. What matters here is the objective fact that a Diwan was established. We can then quickly investigate its relevance to the state and to the society, and its effect on the social structure.

The objectivity of the chroniclers in collecting and citing variant reports does not merit the attacks that have been heaped on them of late. Despite their methodological shortcomings in today's terms, these sources contain a treasure of information that awaits evaluation according to different hypotheses and frameworks, as has been attempted in the present study.

A Note on the Transliteration

Transliteration of Arabic into English has been simplified to show only the glottal stops of the hamza (ʾ) and the ʿain (ʿ).

1. Pre-Islamic Arabia

The existence in Arabia of tribalism as a type of social formation and of the desert as a material condition cannot be denied, but in view of current research and recent archaeological discoveries, it is inaccurate to generalize this view to all of Arabia. Recent literature on pre-Islamic Arabia, especially its southern part, points to a more dynamic history than that based on the "static and sterile" notion of *jahiliyya*. Arabians were socially and economically diversified and had many life-styles—nomadic, pastoral, and settled. Arabian societies were socially structured to include slaves, serfs, peasants, artisans, merchants, and landlords. An agricultural surplus was produced in Yemen, Oman, Bahrain, Najd, and in many of the scattered oases in the interior. Yemen, with the most rainfall, produced the largest surplus, which allowed for human settlements and encouraged state formation earlier than in other regions. This surplus was based on agricultural production (of frankincense, myrrh, wheat, vine, dyes, and spices) and animal husbandry (cattle, sheep, and camels). Enough surplus facilitated the rise of a cottage industry for the production of such commodities as leather goods, metal products, cloth, perfumes, and other aromatics. This surplus was exchanged in local and international markets, where the location of Yemen, near the main land and sea trading routes, facilitated the rise of merchant capital and helped nurture a merchant class.

Production of the surplus, its collection and its distribution, as shown here, were organized by states that slowly emerged out of the conditions of ancient Arabia, where land was the basis of wealth and power. Those states remained in the hands of the landowners, who extracted the surplus from the producing classes, slaves, serfs, peasants, and artisans through taxation and rent. These landlords grouped themselves around royal families and temple officials (who were landowners themselves) and constructed an institutional framework that allowed them to perpetuate their monopoly of the governing institutions, whether civil or religious, and of the wealth and resources of the area. Furthermore, these land-owners, royal families, religious officials, and tribal chiefs participated (either directly or through agents) in the exchange of this surplus. It was this wealthy class and its agents who formed the embryo of the Arabian merchant class. The organic link between political control and commerce closely associated the development of merchant capital with the develop-ment of the state.

The Period of Antiquity (to A.D. 300)

It is hard to locate precisely the area where the political control of the Yemeni states reigned effectively, since boundaries always fluctuated ac-cording to the strength or the weakness of the central government, whether in Ma'rib, Tamna', Shabwa, or Zafar.[1] According to the South Arabian geographer al-Hamdani (who died in San'a in A.H. 334, A.D. 945), Yemen constituted the southern half of the peninsula, as it included the region bounded on the south by the Arabian Sea, on the north by Najd, on the east by the Persian Gulf, and on the west by the Red Sea.[2] Al-Hamdani, who was able to decipher ancient South Arabian inscriptions,[3] provides a picture of southern Arabian states that at their height held under their sway several surplus-producing regions, including the most important ports of Arabia. In addition, Yemeni states often controlled several stra-tegic islands at the mouth of the Red Sea, the island of Socotra, and portions of the opposite coast of Somalia. Furthermore, to facilitate their commercial contacts with northern neighbors, Yemeni states estab-lished colonies in the Hijaz (for example, Dedan) and in southern Jordan (Ma'an), among other places in the interior of the Arabian peninsula.[4] Therefore, one can immediately recognize the diversity of the land under the control of these states and thus the different life-styles, from the high-lands of Yemen with enough rainfall to support settled agricultural com-munities to isolated oases and steppes where the available resources allowed only pastoral or nomadic life-styles.

Diverse life-styles do not necessarily mean antagonistic. It will become evident that there existed a dynamic relationship between the nomadic and the settled, and each depended on the other. Any hostility between the two stemmed from an imbalance in this relationship, generally at times of political weakness or economic adversity. If the emphasis in the following pages is on settled states, it is to bring their role to light and to integrate them in the development of Mecca, something that has not been studied before because of the overemphasis on nomadism or the constraints imposed by the notion of *jahiliyya*.

The earliest states in Yemen were Maʿin and Sabaʾ. The information related to the first is so scanty that scholars have not been able to agree on the date of its founding.[5] It is generally assumed, however, that Maʿin may have been founded around the first millennium B.C. It was based in the fertile inland area between Najran and Hadramawt. It was thus enclosed by high mountains except for its northeastern side, which was open to the desert of the Empty Quarter. With enough rain falling on the area, Maʿini farmers enjoyed the water of the streams and wadis that flowed down from the mountains. Their major crop was frankincense, an aromatic plant whose product was indispensable to official and religious ceremonies in the ancient world. Frankincense was so important that subsequent states in Yemen built up their wealth and power, as well as their international connections, on its production.[6] Maʿin exported it to Egypt, Syria, and Mesopotamia. Maʿinis were found in different areas of the Mediterranean basin, as illustrated by the Maʿini inscriptions found in Delos, Dedan, and Giza. Moreover, an Egyptian priest who imported frankincense from Yemen in exchange for Egyptian linen was in fact originally from Maʿin.[7]

According to inscriptions found in the capital, Qarnaw, and discussed by Ryckmans, governing institutions in Maʿin were formalized on the basis of landownership. The land was ruled by a king, who was assisted by an assortment of officials, representatives, provincial governors, tribal leaders (themselves sometimes called kings), military commanders, and soldiers. The inscriptions suggest that some of the activities of this hereditary king included the issuing of decrees, the construction of public buildings, the servicing of the temple, and the leading of military expeditions. Important decisions were made by the king after he consulted with members of the royal family, temple officials, city heads, and tribal chiefs.[8] Taxation and land rent provided state revenue. Taxes were collected from merchants, farmers, and artisans, and rent was collected from the peasants who leased lands from the royal landholdings. Sanctioned officials, such as city heads, governors, and tribal chiefs, were responsible for the collection of taxes in their respective areas. They usually kept their share of the taxes before they forwarded the balance to the treasury. The kingdom was divided into provinces, each governed by a *kabir*. Cities in the kingdom, such as Qarnaw, Athlula, Hailan, and Raishan, had a government, a governing council, a god, a temple and a religious hierarchy.[9]

Next to the king, the temple was the richest institution, by virtue of landownership, its tax-collection privilege, access to unpaid labor, and the gifts and offerings of individuals on special occasions, such as after a good harvest, a successful caravan, recovery from illness, defeat of an enemy, or construction of a building or a dam. Thus, the common interest between large landowners resulted in a kind of alliance by which the production, collection, and distribution of the surplus was accomplished. This alliance was instrumental in keeping the balance of power in their favor and was the basis for their continued monopoly of the governing institutions, even if the dynasty or the center of power had changed.

The continuity of this structure is likewise manifest in the kingdom of Saba'. The origin of this state is as obscure as that of its predecessor. Sabaean inscriptions found in Ma'rib, the capital, testify to the similarity of its governing institutions and social structure to those of Ma'in, which had disappeared centuries before.[10] For example, the connection between the king and the temple is clearly evident in many inscriptions, such as [MaMB 188], which says that the descendants of Marba'am offered a female statue to the god al-Maqah for the purpose of securing the "esteem and grace of their lord 'Ilsarah Yahdub, king of Saba' and Raidan."[11] Other inscriptions, such as [MaMB 227] reveal that an individual or a tribe could offer statues or "collect the garden products" of the temple as free labor to vouchsafe the grace of their king.[12]

There is considerably more information about the state structure in Saba' as revealed by these numerous inscriptions. For example, [MaMB 9, MaMB 10] say that a certain Damarkarib, from the family of Shawadabum, who was an administrator for three successive kings, dedicated his children and some of his property (including houses in Yahar and Harur and palm groves in Sawam, Ramdan, and Maqlaman) to the moon god, al-Maqah on the occasion of Damarkarib's appointment as an administrator of the capital city. In this capacity, he was additionally charged with providing war supplies for the king's campaign against a rival in the territories of Qataban to the south of Saba'.[13] Inscription [MaMB 314] tells of yet another dedication by a different family head who had similar duties. Anmarum, master of the house of Salhan, had been charged by a subsequent Sabaean king to assume the security of Ma'rib for a period of five months; the gifts to al-Maqah were occasioned by the successful completion of the task.[14] Another dedication to al-Maqah was made after a caravan station was built. Other inscriptions (for example, MaMB 82, 192, 231, 246) refer to such offices or titles as "equerry of the horses of the king," "treasurer of the rent of the king," high military officials, horsemen, land surveyor, and "camelherd of the king."[15] Other inscriptions [MaMB 137, 212, 219, 270] give numerous accounts of internal revolts. Of the tribal groups mentioned in connection with these rebellions, the Hadramawt, the Himyarites and the Kinda are the most noteworthy. 'Ilsharah Yahdub attacked these tribes because they cooperated with the Abyssinians. Not only did the king lead punitive expeditions against tribal groups but also against such cities as Najran, Shabwa, and Cana.[16] Other inscriptions provide evidence that two families could form an alliance through marriage [MaMB 108], that the king could order his allies to establish military garrisons, and that he expected tribal leaders under his sway to furnish troops to assist in the wars against internal and external enemies [MaMB 182].[17]

Even with so little evidence, it is possible to imagine that the social formations in both Ma'in and Saba' were indeed complex, as illustrated by the presence of a government structure, religious institutions, property rights, accumulation of wealth, and social conflict. The evidence testifies to the existence of a stratified society at the top of which were the landlords, who controlled the state and the resources of the region. The king maintained his authority by means of a government structure that included many officials and tributary allies within his realm and outside it. The surplus generated by the producing classes was exchanged by merchants, whose activity was facilitated when the state secured trade routes, built caravan stations, and established outposts along trade routes and in distant markets. It is also significant that throughout the long history of the two states, and certainly Saba' more than Ma'in, landowners elaborated an institutional structure and institutional practices that maintained them in power.

Similar conditions were found in two other contemporaneous states: Qataban and Hadramawt, with their respective capitals at Tamna' and Shabwa. Qataban was well known for its monopoly of frankincense, but it was in Hadramawt where this plant grew most abundantly. Each of the four neighboring states was concerned with control of the largest share of this trade. Out of this concern and because of competition between those states, Ma'in and Hadramawt formed an alliance to control the eastern half of southern Arabia while Saba' and Qataban allied to control the western half, in addition to the opposite coast of Somalia.[18]

According to this arrangement, Hadramawt and its ally controlled the frankincense province of Zufar in addition to a land route that reached Gerrha in Bahrain, a journey of forty days. This land route became extremely important for the trade in frankincense, making Gerrha the principal port in eastern Arabia for the distribution of frankincense to Mesopotamia and to the Indus Valley.[19]

There is very little information about the state in Hadramawt, and there remains considerable disagreement among scholars about the dates and rulers of this kingdom. We know, however, that Shabwa had sixty temples, which shows that religious officials had exerted an enormous amount of influence on the economy and politics. Hadrami rulers were originally called *mukarrib,* a word that some believe had religious connotations, suggesting that these kings started out as religious officials before they began to specialize in civil authority.[20] A Hadrami inscription [Ingrams 1 and 3] dated to the fifth century B.C. shows that one *mukarrib* had ordered an architect to build a wall, a gate, and other fortifications to guard the road leading to the port of Cana, from which merchants could sail to Omana, India, and Somalia.[21] A late inscription [Ja 910-35] reveals a startling piece of information. On the occasion of the accession of Il'add Yalut to kingship (around A.D. 287), a delegation of fourteen women from the Quraish were present among the many guests at the ceremony.[22] The presence of the Quraishi women and other representatives from Tadmur (Palmyra) indicates that Hadramawt maintained trade relations with northern areas and peoples as far away as northern Syria.

Qataban was interested in keeping an uninterrupted flow of trade between the capital, Tamna', and the port cities on the Red Sea, such as Mokha and Ocelis. Qataban's wealth may have stemmed from the fact that it was based in one of the "most highly developed agricultural areas of southern Arabia."[23] In addition to their interest in the Red Sea, the Qatabanis were eager to secure a connection to ports on the shores of the Arabian Sea, such as Cana and what is now Hisn al-Ghurab. The two ports eventually came under their control. Ships from Cana could sail from Qataban to the rest of the Arabian ports as well as to India and the southern coast of Persia. Ships returning from India anchored there so that merchants could trade with the king's agents such commodities as cloth, wheat, and sesame oil in exchange for frankincense.[24] The most important port in this area, however, was Aden (Eudamon Arabia), which belonged to the Sabaeans, allies of Qataban. Aden was the only safe and shoal-free harbor between Egypt and India, which made it the principal anchor and meeting point for the east-west trade, especially prior to Hippalus's discovery of the pattern of the monsoon winds.[25]

Qatabani inscriptions, like others found in southern Arabia, were commemorative and personal; however, there is ample evidence of tax regulations, laws, and references to commercial activities to suggest similarities with other southern Arabian states. For example, as in Maʿin and Sabaʾ, the king in Qataban decreed laws after they were approved by a council of notables, such as the tribal chiefs, the city heads, and, no doubt, the temple officials, since, we are told, Tamnaʿ had a total of sixty-five temples.[26] A *kabir* was commissioned to collect taxes; some were appointed for a specified duration at the end of which they were replaced.[27]

The Qatabanis were certainly interested in commerce. To foster their commercial network, they built roads and dug tunnels into mountain-sides to facilitate the movement of caravans.[28] There were laws, such as found in the inscriptions (R 4337) known as the Commercial Code of Qataban, to regulate business activities in the capital, payment of taxes, partnerships, travel of merchants to tribal areas, and there were international treaties, which were designed to safeguard the commercial interest of the merchants of Qataban. Indian ships, for example, were bound by a treaty not to enter the Red Sea beyond Bab al-Mandib.[29] It is believed that this restriction was an attempt on the part of Qataban to preserve trade secrets and to ensure its role as a link in the east-west trade. It should not be surprising to find out that the Qatabanis were well aware of the fluctuation of the market and that they used the principle of supply and demand to their advantage. Warmington relates an instance in which a forest fire destroyed some of the cinnamon crop (most likely in India). Qatabani rulers were quick to capitalize on the expected shortage by doubling the price of cinnamon, especially since trade in this commodity was the exclusive right of the Qatabani ruler.[30]

With all of their achievements, Qataban and other states in southern Arabia were overshadowed by yet another state, the first Himyarite state (ca. 115 B.C.–A.D. 300), which was based in the inland city of Zafar. This new capital supplanted the capitals of previous states whose culture and language the Himyarites inherited. It was during this period that Rome sent Aelius Gallus at the head of a seaborne expedition in a bid to control southern Arabia (24 B.C.), and it may have been after this expedition that the Himyarite state was finally consolidated.[31] The Himyarites, who until then had been dominated by Qataban, took advantage of the weakness of surrounding states and of the disorganization that resulted from Gallus's penetration of the Yemeni highlands.[32] The fact that Gallus's expedition was ultimately unsuccessful made it easier for the Himyarites to embark on a course of expansion, sometimes by treaties and at other times by outright conquest.

Alhan Nahfan, who ruled sometime between 135 B.C. and A.D. 160, depending on the chronology one follows, concluded several treaties with Hadramawt and the Abyssinians. Hadramawt was later annexed and Cana and Ma'rib were also incorporated into the realm of the Himyarites during the first century A.D.[33] The Himyarites continued their expansion toward the Red Sea until they took Mokha. Of this city, the *Periplus* says, "The merchandise imported there consists of purple cloth, both fine and coarse clothing in the Arabian style, with sleeves; plain, ordinary, embroidered or interwoven with gold; saffron, sweet rush, muslin, cloaks, blankets (not many), some plain and others made in the local fashion, sashes of different colors, fragrant ointments in moderate quantity, wine and wheat, not much. For the country produces grain in moderate amount, and a great deal of wine."[34] Aden also passed under Himyarite suzerainty and, naturally, played an important role in their commerce.

The Himyarite state was structured very much like its predecessors. A king ruled the land and he minted gold, silver, and copper coins. He was a large landowner and resided in a castle, in Raidan, just outside of Zafar.[35] His powers, however, were checked by what Levi Della Vida calls "a feudal aristocracy that developed alongside the monarchy."[36] This feudal aristocracy was no doubt composed of the innumerable "royal families" and other landowners who had been in control of most of the land and of the state in southern Arabia. Families with royal connections preserved their status by continuous ownership of land. The cultivation of frankincense was a limited privilege, available only through inheritance to some three thousand families.[37] Thus, not only ownership of land was tightly controlled but also the production of the lucrative aromatic.

As in other states, the temple exerted an enormous influence on the governing institutions of the Himyarite state. The temple, again, was the largest landowning institution after the king. Sacred areas and holy months were also known in southern Arabia. Plinny says that the frankincense harvest had to be brought to the temple so that the tithe could be collected before the rest of the harvest was distributed.[38] In this manner, the temple must also have played a sensitive role in the commerce of the region.

Royal families, landowners, tribal chiefs, and religious officials formed the top of a social pyramid. This group nurtured the growth of merchant capital by devising institutions, as we have seen, that governed the production, collection, and distribution of surplus wealth. At the bottom and forming the base of the social pyramid was the rest of the population—the peasants, artisans, slaves, and tribespeople. Peasants worked collectively on the land to which they were bound. And although they were sometimes paid for their labor in the form of fixed shares of the produce, the slaves often received nothing except their food and shelter. In addition, both groups were required to work on temple land without pay as their religious duty.[39] The state also relied on corvée labor to carry out larger projects such as the maintenance and repair of dams, fortresses, and roads.

In support of this complex picture of the social relations in southern Arabia, A. G. Lundin divides Himyarite society into the aristocracy, a council of elders, the *qayels* (intermediary tribal chiefs who were recruited to the landowning class by virtue of land grants), and "the rest of the population."[40] The same division existed in other major cities such as Najran, Nash, and Shibam. Lundin goes on to say that this division was very much the same as that which obtained in the Greco-Roman world.[41]

The tribes were sedentary units and territorially based organizations that were bound by commercial and labor ties. Members were recruited from various classes of society, including serfs.[42] Specialization in the production of one commodity was not uncommon. For example, the tribe of Madhhij, which lived mostly in Saʿda, specialized in tanning, while another tribe specialized in apiculture.[43] It seems logical to argue that specialization, besides increasing production, benefited overall commercial activity, since it led to less self-sufficiency and thus promoted exchange.

In contrast to the varied economic base of southern Arabia, Petra and Palmyra, in northern Arabia, depended mostly on trade. Petra was based in the region of southern Jordan and Palmyra was in the northwestern end of the Syrian desert. The rise of the two states in their respective regions depended on two factors: first was, obviously, their proximity to major trade routes in Syria; second, was the inability of the Yemeni states to extend their direct and effective control to such distant areas from their agriculturally based centers. This inability created a political vacuum in the northern end of the peninsula, a vacuum that was filled by the Nabateans and the Palmyrenes, respectively.

Thus, while southern Arabia enjoyed enough rainfall to irrigate a wide and varied agriculture—which became the basis of its participation in international commerce—northern Arabia received little rain, forcing Petra and Palmyra to exist in a desert or a semiarid environment. Although there was some agricultural production in both Petra and Palmyra, there was no surplus on the scale of Yemen's. Northern Arabian states owed their viability primarily to their geographic location, near major trade routes in Syria.

Petra, capital of the Nabateans, was carved out of solid rock. This made it almost impregnable. Twice were the Nabateans able to resist the attacks of Antigonus, Alexander's successor as king of Syria.[44] Secure in their rock city, the Nabateans were able to extend their control over a territory that stretched from Bosra, south of Damascus, all the way to Dedan. They controlled the Red Sea ports of Ayla, on the Gulf of Aqaba, and Luce Come farther south. It was from this port that Ailus Gallus sailed, with Nabatean help, against Yemen. Through Dedan and Luce Come, the Nabateans were in contact, by land and by sea, with Egypt, Yemen, and other Arabian ports.[45]

This location depended on the proximity of the trade routes and the ability of the Nabateans to control them from their rock center. When the trade routes shifted slightly to the east and to the north, the Nabateans were not able to control them as effectively as before. They began to decline rapidly, and whereas Petra could resist Antigonus before, it was easily incorporated into the Roman Empire by A.D. 106.

The vacuum created by the demise of the Nabateans was filled neatly by Palmyra. Although it was an ancient settlement, it was only after the decline of Petra that it began to assume a greater role in the economic and political life of the region. Palmyra achieved its splendor from A.D. 130 to 270. Just like Petra, it was well connected to international markets: it lay on the western end of the central Asian silk route and was within easy reach of Antioch and other Mediterranean ports. Caravans from Palmyra reached Appologos (known earlier as al-Ubulla and later as Basra), which received ships from as far away as China and India and as near as Yemen and the eastern coast of Arabia. But despite this great advantage, Palmyra suffered the same fate as Petra, since it could not withstand the political and military weight of Rome.[46]

The relatively quick rise and decline of Petra and Palmyra resulted from the advantages that could be gained from commerce. These advantages, however, were limited, since neither had a varied economy or an internally generated surplus. And in addition to the attack of the powerful Roman empire, neither Petra nor Palmyra was able to rectify its deficiencies with durable institutions, as was Mecca. The economic limitations of these states were in direct contrast to southern Arabia, where an internally generated agricultural surplus was the basis of the state and of participation in international commerce. Thus, as long as a surplus was produced, the ruling classes in southern Arabia were capable of regenerating themselves for several centuries.

The Second Himyarite State (A.D. 300–600)

The ability of the ruling classes to regenerate themselves and to continue in a position of political and economic power is most evident in the second Himyarite state. The first declined by about A.D. 300, perhaps because of the decline in the demand for frankincense following the spread of Christianity.[47] The decline might also be attributed to the direct commercial competition offered by the Romans, who reasserted their presence in the Arabian Sea subsequent to Gallus's failed expedition.

Frankincense was gradually replaced by cotton and cloth as the major articles of trade. Cloth was woven from cotton, flax, wool, and silk. Arabia was well known for wool exports, but silk was imported from China in exchange for frankincense.[48] The precise date when the cultivation of cotton and flax was introduced to Yemen is not known. It is certain, however, that by A.D. 500 Najran and other cities in Yemen and eastern Arabia were cloth-producing centers and that the trade in cloth (and leather) formed the backbone of Yemeni exports to other parts of Arabia. Yemeni cloth was the basis for Mecca's later prosperity. And by A.D. 630 (A.H. 8) Najran produced an enormous amount of cloth, as attested by its treaty with the ascendant Mecca, as we shall see later.[49]

Thus, following nearly a century of political and economic stagnation, the Himyarites were able to begin a resurgence under the Tubbaᶜ family. This resurgence was occasioned by the change in their material base, which saw agriculture supplanted by an increase in the production of cloth. The social, political, and economic structure found in previous states continued to exist, but during this period there occurred a gradual shift toward monotheism in the form of Christianity and later Judaism. An inscription [Glaser 389] dated to the middle of the fourth century A.D. had already dropped al-Maqah in favor of the "god of the heavens." Christianization of the Tubbaᶜ dynasty and the construction of churches in cities like Zafar and Aden were the fruits of the work of Theophilus, who was sent there as a missionary by Constantine II. Conversion to a monotheistic religion is significant, since it could better serve the purposes of the state than the multiplicity of religious traditions. It is interesting to note, however, that the adoption of monotheistic symbols did not lead to the eclipse of other gods; these symbols simply became another layer of religious tradition.[50]

As the material base of the second Himyarite state changed from agricultural to commodity production, the Himyarites became more aggressive in expansion than their predecessors. The Tubba[c] line began to pursue expansion for the purpose of direct control of the northern and eastern parts of Arabia. This expansion took place at a time when the Arabian peninsula was experiencing advances in warfare that included the introduction of the horse and a new style saddle.[51] It might also be argued that the objective conditions of previous Yemeni states (i.e., their agricultural base) did not allow them to expand into northern Arabia, aside from establishing colonies along the trade route that linked them with Syria. Sufficient markets were found for their surplus, and their intermediary role in the east-west trade gave them enough markets to ignore other areas in Arabia. But during the second Himyarite state, markets in Arabia were sought to replace those that had been lost as a result of Roman competition.

Some reports about the expansion of the second Himyarite state, such as those expeditions led by Nashir al-Ni[c]am and his son Hassan, are no more than legends. They are said to have led expeditions to northern Africa, Mesopotamia, and Central Asia. They were also credited with founding such cities as Samarqand and Hira. This theme of Himyarite expansion is often repeated in different periods of the history of the state.[52]

Actual expeditions, however, are recorded on numerous inscriptions commemorating the activities of the kings. Several expeditions were carried out in the Tihama-[c]Asir region, where the cities of Najran, San[c]a, and Sa[c]da were most vital in the commercial activity of the Yemeni merchants.[53]

Najran was an important trade center, since it was the terminal point of a trade route that connected it with the Persian Gulf. It also received trade caravans from Hadramawt and Ma'rib. Another trade route came from the ports of the Red Sea via Sa[c]da. Moreover, Najran was connected with Aden through San[c]a and with Syria through Mecca. Najran was an important production center of leather and cloth. At the time of the expansion of the Islamic state, Muhammad demanded from the inhabitants of Najran, as one of the terms of a treaty, two thousand *hillas* (a collection of garments).[54] One *hilla* consisted of a shirt, a *rida'* (an outer garment), an *[c]amama* (a turban), and an *izar* (a sash). Two thousand *hillas* as part of their annual tribute indicate the importance of cloth production in Najran by the early seventh century A.D.

As for Sa'da, where the "wealthy and the merchants gathered,"[55] it was located in the midst of fields of *qarz,* a dye used extensively in the tanning process. The Madhhij, one of the tribes that lived in the city, specialized in the production of leather goods. Leather continued to be an important industry in Sa'da throughout the Middle Ages, and the city was famous for its hides, shoes, and sandals.[56]

San'a was even more important than Najran or Sa'da. It grew to become the seat of royalty and remained the capital of the Himyarites. San'a was situated in the middle of fields of *wars,* a dye important for the cloth industry.

Cotton, *wars,* saffron, henna, and other plants used in cloth production were exempted from taxation by the Muslim state.[57] This exemption might have been a continuation of the practice under the Himyarites, since the Muslims initially modified few of the practices in the areas that came under their control. Such exemption should have encouraged the production of those plants, to the benefit of the cloth industry. Again, at the time of the Islamic expansion, San'a's cloth production was important enough to prompt Mu'adh ibn Jabal, Muhammad's governor, to demand the tribute in the form of cloth instead of corn and barley. Mu'adh argued that payment in cloth "will be easy on the Yemenis and will be more beneficial for the Muhajirun in Medina,"[58] indicating cloth's abundance in Yemen and its commercial value in Medina.

The economic motives behind Himyarite expansion were also evident in other regions of Arabia. Their expansion into Hadramawt, a principal producer of frankincense, had already been accomplished by this time. The pacification of this region led to the migration of different tribal groups toward Oman, which was noted for its excellent ports as well as the production of copper.[59] Omana, according to the *Periplus,* exported various commodities to India, including purple, frankincense, pearls, dates, and wine.[60] Control of Oman was effected after the migration of the Azd under the leadership of Malik ibn al-Fahm.[61] Reports about this migration indicate that the Muhra accompanied Malik until al-Shihr, on the Arabian Sea. The Muhra decided to remain at al-Shihr, which grew to become an important port where, according to al-Marzuqi, Arab and non-Arab merchants frequented the place for the exchange of such commodities as leather, cloth, and the abundant amber.[62] Malik and the rest of his party continued until they reached Oman proper, where some of the Azd stayed at Qalhat, on the shore, while others went to al-Jawf, in the interior. Malik reached an agreement with the Persian *marzuban* (the governor) to share control of Oman.[63] The Banu Julanda, from the Azd, exercised their authority over the port of Duba, where they collected taxes from merchants and carried out their own commercial activities. They were still masters of Oman at the time of the Islamic expansion.[64]

The central Arabian highland of Najd was another area that witnessed Himyarite military activities. The economic importance of this region lay in its command of the roads that connected the four corners of Arabia. Al-Yamama was the major center of Najd. It was known for the production of cereals, especially wheat, among other food products. Tubban ibn Kalkikarib, taking advantage of a local request for support, led an expedition against al-Yamama and thus firmed the Himyarite grip on the region.[65] Several other kings led expeditions against Najd until A.D. 516, when Ma'dikarib Ya'fur attacked Wadi Ma'sil.[66]

Control of Najd and the rest of central Arabia was entrusted to the Banu Akil al-Murar from the Kinda.[67] The Himyarites cemented their alliance with the Kinda, as usual, with marriage ties. Al-Harith ibn 'Amr, of the Banu Akil al-Murar, was the nephew of the Himyarite Tubba' ibn Hassan. Hujr ibn 'Amr was married to a Himyarite woman. Another branch of the Kinda, which controlled the northern part of the Hijaz, was related to the Himyarites, also by marriage.[68]

In their alliance with the Kinda, the Himyarites found easy access to the markets of eastern Arabia and the ports of al-Qatif (Gerrha) and al-Mushaqqar. Al-Qatif was originally inhabited by Chaldean exiles from Babylon, and by the first century it had become a major distribution point of frankincense to Mesopotamia and the Indus Valley.[69] By the fourth century, al-Qatif was used as a disembarkation point for goods to be distributed to Mesopotamia and Syria without incurring Persian taxes.[70] Al-Mushaqqar was frequented by Arab and Persian merchants for the products of the area—swords, pearls, and cloth.[71]

The Himyarites thus satisfied their search for markets by expanding their territorial hegemony in Arabia. They were able to accomplish this by several means, including marriage alliances, migrations, and outright military conquest. But Himyarite control of these Arabian regions was usually temporary and limited and therefore did not produce unified social and political development, even though merchant interests were common. Tribal groups in the interior, for example, were only nominally under the control of the state. In central Arabia, for example, the Kinda suffered a major tax rebellion at the hands of the Banu Asad.[72] This rebellion precipitated the breakup of the Kinda and led to the loss of

Himyarite influence in the region. The vacuum created by the absence of the Kinda and the Himyarites was gradually filled by the rising power of Hira. The leitmotif of the flow and ebb of state power, conditioned by its material base, provided a chance for many groups and cities, such as Mecca, to pursue their own political and economic interests.

Himyarite expansion, however, was not inconsequential. On one level, the temporary unity of the merchants in Arabia brought them in touch with one another under one political unit. This awareness would eventually solidify their interests as merchants and would facilitate the formation of a larger Arabian merchant class.[73] On another level, Himyarite expansion integrated nomadic groups within a state structure by several means, such as coercion, employment in garrisons, or as guards of merchant caravans. Equally important was the recruitment of the tribal chiefs into the ranks of the merchant class by virtue of the rewards they received for services rendered to the state and to the merchants.

The Decline of Himyar

There were many inherent weaknesses in the structure of all of the Yemeni states, including Himyar. This not only limited their political growth, but also meant that the merchant class, whose welfare was dependent on the state, was at times severely disrupted. It has been mentioned that the foundation of the Yemeni states depended on an agricultural base, and that power (civil and religious) was the prerogative of the landowners; therefore, the governing institutions remained their monopoly. The majority of the population worked on the land as slaves, serfs, peasants, or farmers, and most of them did not own any land. Their interests were not represented at any level of the state structure. Slaves and serfs were required to stay on the land and were punished if they escaped. We have also seen that the cultivation of frankincense was considered a privilege and was permitted only through inheritance. Thus, the most serious shortcoming shared by all of the Yemeni states was that upward social and economic transformation was for the most part unavailable to most members of society.

Another weakness was the absence, aside from a growing but vague sense of mercantile interests, of a flexible ideology capable of binding the social fabric, especially at times of diversity. The ideology of the states in Arabia was intractably constructed for the benefit of the landowners, the ruling class. This resulted, if not in the separation of the social classes, in the indifference of the larger sector of the population to the welfare of the state and its institutions and discouraged upward social and economic mobility. In such conditions, the governing class had little contact with the producing classes except in relations of exploitation. It is not surprising, then, to find constant reference to social strife in the form of uprisings, revolts, and punitive expeditions.

Religion, as in any premodern society, could have acted as a unifying force. But in southern Arabia, each city had its own god and its own religious hierarchy, even though the deities throughout the region may have been the same. This multiplicity prevented the growth of a unitary experience. Moreover, the religious institution was part of the ruling class by virtue of its extensive landholdings. The adoption of monotheistic symbols in the fourth century A.D. might have produced religious uniformity, but they were not sufficient to repair the fragmentation of society because adoption was haphazard and isolated.

Fragmentation was evident not only on the local level, but also on the regional level. In the absence of a unifying ideology, force became the state's main instrument for incorporating other regions. But the maintenance of force required a government with a strong social and economic base, a condition that was not constant in southern Arabia. Even though each region was viable enough on its own to produce a surplus, a budding merchant class, and a semblance of ruling institutions, none of these regions were strong enough to force and maintain the unity of all regions.

Because the economic structure changed with only little modification to the social structure, the second Himyarite state began to disintegrate rapidly during the last two decades of the fifth century A.D. On the political level, this disintegration took the form of numerous claimants to the throne. The conflict between them aggravated internal crises and speeded the downfall of the government. Political instability at the center encouraged outlying areas and tribal groups to act independently, threatening the economy with disorder to the detriment of the merchants.[74]

The chaotic political situation, especially during the first two decades of the sixth century, gave the Abyssinians the opportunity to renew their political and economic interests in the region. Prior to their arrival, a certain Lakhniʿah Dhu Shanatir, who was from a "house without any royal claim," usurped power and killed the reigning king, Yaʿfur, who himself had just defeated other claimants to the throne, including his own brother.[75] Dhu Shanatir was not able to contain the situation, however, and the civil war continued. Another claimant, Dhu Nuwwas, killed Dhu

Shanatir and proclaimed himself king. Dhu Nuwwas converted to Judaism and proceeded to attack the cloth-producing center of Najran with its large Christian population (ca. A.D. 523).[76]

This persecution prompted the archbishop of Najran, Dhu Thaʿlaban, to seek help from Christian Abyssinia. The insistence of Dhu Thaʿlaban, the persecution of the Christians, and the long-standing economic interests of the Abyssinians in Yemen provided sufficient grounds for Abyssinian intervention.[77] Consequently, by A.D. 525, Abyssinian troops led by Abraha intervened and occupied southern Arabia once more. Leaders of important Himyarite families, such as Dhu Hamden, Dhu Muʿhir, and Dhu Dhubyan, sided with Dhu Thaʿlaban and welcomed the invading army.[78] With their cooperation, Abraha was able to defeat Dhu Nuwwas and a new Himyarite king, al-Sumaifaʿ Ashwaʿ, was installed to rule in the name of the *negus* (king) of Abyssinia.

The efforts of Dhu Thaʿlaban and the support rendered by leading Himyarite families to the Abyssinian army illustrate how the landlords and other elements of the ruling class preserved their social and economic position. By shifting their allegiance to the victor, they guaranteed their standing as well as the continuity of their economic base and thus ensured the development of merchant capital.

During the reign of al-Sumaifaʿ Ashwaʿ, there was no change in the social relations that precipitated the original crisis; political conflict reemerged. Having been assured of support by leading Himyarite families, Abraha removed al-Sumaifaʿ and ended the Tubbaʿ line on the throne altogether. This revolt was ostensibly in the name of the Yemeni leading merchant and landholding families, as Abraha proclaimed to them, "The time has come for you to be free."[79]

Following the traditional methods of alliance formation, Abraha allied himself with the family of Dhu Jadan when he married Rihana, Dhu Jadan's daughter and, until then, wife of Murra Dhu Yazan.[80] Abraha's takeover, however, was not endorsed by all of the factions in the ruling circles. Dhu Yazan, who had just lost his wife, and Maʿdikarib, son of the deposed king, were among many who resisted Abraha by joining the revolt of Yazid ibn Kabasha.[81]

The origins of Yazid ibn Kabasha are obscure. This might mean that he was not from an ancient family rooted in "royalty" and, like Dhu Shanatir, came to power without any prior royal pretensions. The cases of these two "pretenders" are evidence of the rise of new social forces against the established socioeconomic and political order. These men who had no previous standing in the power circles of southern Arabia thus attempted to assert their newly acquired position by aspiring to the office of the king, as in the case of Dhu Shanatir, or leading a revolt backed by traditional families, as in the case of Yazid. The relatively new formation of these groups, however, worked to their disadvantage, and they were not able to withstand the assault of the more traditionally rooted power circles. Yazid ibn Kabasha, for example, was not able to sustain his revolt, so he ended it, especially after Abraha assured him of high standing.[82]

The socioeconomic order, however, continued to disintegrate as uprisings against Abraha flared up. The constant turmoil had adversely affected the agricultural and commercial life of the area, and it was not until he finally put an end to the uprisings that Abraha could turn his attention to repairing the economic damage of almost half a century of violence. The long-neglected Ma'rib dam was repaired. Abraha left an inscription [Ry 506] celebrating this event as well as many military campaigns that he carried out in and outside Yemen.[83]

As agriculture itself was no longer a viable economic base, his was a vain attempt at repairing an ancient dam, for it collapsed soon afterward, never to be repaired again. In the midst of the upheavals in Yemen, the collapse of the Ma'rib dam at this time could hardly have any significance of its own,[84] except perhaps as a symbol for the collapse of a long political tradition and of an ancient system that was slowly being taken over by a rising power in Mecca.

Mecca with its sacred center, the Ka'ba, had experienced growth throughout this period of turmoil, which enabled its merchants to compete with the Yemenis. To end this competition, Abraha built the Qullais in Najran (or in San'a) as a rival sacred center, hoping to divert the merchant-pilgrims away from Mecca and to lure them back to Yemen. But the Qullais could not match the Ka'ba, and the merchant-pilgrims preferred the Meccan sanctuary. Abraha finally decided to attack Mecca and sack its Ka'ba, but his army fell apart before he could accomplish his task. This event (of which more will be said in the next chapter) is known in Muslim annals as the Year of the Elephant.[85] Abraha retreated with his shattered army to Yemen, where he soon died. Following this defeat, the Abyssinians were attacked and expelled from Yemen at the hands of a Sasanid naval force (A.D. 575). This force, demonstrating Sasanid interests in Arabia as a whole and in Yemen in particular, was sent at the request of the Yemeni ruling class. By then, however, Yemen no longer played an active role in the politics of the region, and Mecca was well on its way to becoming the major economic, religious, and political center in Arabia.

The Lakhmids of Hira

Before Mecca emerged as the strongest center in Arabia, it had to face Hira in the north. Hira's development into a major political and economic center had been long in the making. It was located in southern Iraq, on the western bank of the Euphrates, and it was well connected with the trade routes reaching the Mediterranean through Syria, the Persian Gulf, and central and eastern Arabia. Aside from this strategic location, Hira was close to the fertile areas of the Sawad in Iraq.[86]

During most of the sixth century, Hira's ascendency came at the expense of Yemen. The Lakhmids had begun to replace the Himyarites in Arabia when the Banu Kinda, Himyar's allies, lost at the hands of the Banu Asad. Hira was gradually able to expel the Banu Kinda from central Arabia altogether and thus extend its control over this strategic location.

Hira's expansion, like that of Himyar, was also motivated by economic factors, since the Lakhmids directed their attention to the main production centers and trade routes in Arabia. Thus, the whole of eastern Arabia down to Oman passed into their control, including the allegiance of the Banu Tamim in Bahrain and the Banu Julanda in Oman.[87] Hira also attempted to spread its influence over the Hijaz, perhaps to block Yemeni trade with Syria.[88]

The expansionist aims of the Lakhmids were also manifest in Syria against the rising power of the Ghassanids.[89] In addition to the economic advantages that could be gained from this policy, the Lakhmid/Ghassanid conflict over Syrian markets and trade routes, such as Hira's attack on Antioch, was heightened by the seemingly endless competition between their respective patrons, the Sasanids and the Byzantines.[90]

Like the states in Yemen, Hira was able to sustain a monarchy with a court, tax collectors, governors, armies, and a system of alliances over a long period. Aside from a regular army and an elaborate system of tribal alliances, the institutions of *ridafa* and *Dhu al-Akal* were most important for the integration of Arabian tribes into Hira's orbit. *Ridafa* (literally, being second on a mount) was a hereditary position reserved for tribal chiefs who represented their tribe at the king's court, rode with the king, participated in the decision-making process, and received a fixed share of the spoils.[91] *Dhu al-Akal* was reserved for tribal chiefs of noble lineage (*al-ashraf*), who usually received large land grants from the Lakhmids. Qais ibn Mas'ud, as one of the recipients of this honor, was granted the important port of al-Ubulla in addition to eighty villages.[92]

As a client state of the Sasanids, Hira received enormous land grants in Iraq, both for its own use and to assist the Persians in the administration of those territories. The Lakhmids were thus able to grant land to tribal chiefs, such as the chiefs of the Bakr ibn Wa'il, who guaranteed the security of Hira's trade caravans.[93]

Hira, moreover, acted as an intermediary between the Sasanids and Arab tribes, as happened during the tribal council called by al-Nu'man ibn al-Mundhir in the palace of al-Khawarnaq. This council was called to discuss the new taxes imposed by Khusro Parviz, the Sasanid monarch.[94]

The Lakhmids at the same time developed their independent relationship with tribes in the Arabian peninsula.[95] Arab merchant interests developed greatly under Hira, owing to its advantageous position and to the institutions that encouraged the development of commerce. Merchants were attracted to Hira because of its efforts to secure trade routes and markets, which provided the mobility necessary for the development of capital. As a result, Hira grew into a major center that reflected the three cultural traditions prevalent at the time: Arab, Byzantine, and Sasanid.

But it was the development of Arabic panegyric poetry at Hira that best indicates the achievements of the Arab merchant class.[96] This type of poetry could only have developed at a time when there was enough prosperity, luxury, and, most important, audience to appreciate the achievements of its patrons. Composed in honor of the king and his retinue, the poems were recited at the innumerable markets and fairs, such as at 'Ukaz and Dawmat al-Jandal, and thus were transmitted all over Arabia.

Hira represented, in many ways, an advanced stage in the development of political and cultural institutions in Arabian society. It was able to integrate many tribes within its fold and thus to spread its influence more visibly and concretely than was Himyar over a large portion of the Arabian peninsula. Hira mobilized a greater number of forces, even to the extent of involving them in the imperial wars of the Sasanid/Byzantine conflict. Yet, despite Hira's greatness, it was easily swept aside by Mecca in A.D. 632 (A.H. 10).

Hira's collapse was not sudden, however, but a long and drawn out decline. Just as the Yemeni states exhibited inherent weaknesses, so did Hira. Its involvement in the incessant conflict between the Sasanids and the Byzantines strained its resources and sapped its strength. Hira was sacked at least once by the Ghassanids. As in Yemen, there was no ideological force to support the existence of the state; the ruling family's adoption of Christianity came too late to save the situation.[97]

Hira's decline set in in the last two decades of the sixth century, as Arab tribes began to challenge its dominant position. Hira and its allies suffered a major defeat at the hands of the Quraish in the Fijar Wars fought near Mecca around A.D. 580. This reversal was followed by yet another when several eastern Arabian tribes joined and defeated Hira in the Battle of Dhu Qar (ca. A.D. 602). Although Dhu Qar might not have had the significance accorded it by Arab chroniclers,[98] the Lakhmids were not able to recover any of their prestige and Hira continued on its rapid course of decay. Attempts to revive Hira under a different family headed by 'Iyas ibn Qabisa, from the Banu Tamim, failed altogether, which proves that it was the state and its institutions that were in need of change. It was in providing that change that Mecca was successful and ultimately victorious.

To conclude this brief account, it is obvious that the current understanding of *jahiliyya* is false. Therefore, social, economic, and political circumstances in pre-Islamic Arabia have to be reevaluated so that they can be understood within their proper historical context and so that we can form a clearer picture of the historical antecedents of Islam.

Several conclusions may be drawn. First, political authority in the form of state institutions existed in Arabia, and those states were at one time or another in control of a major portion of the Arabian peninsula. Consequently, the inhabitants of Arabia, whether settled or nomadic, were integrated within a state structure, even though this integration might have varied in duration and in degree.

Second, Arabia should no longer be viewed merely as a depot or a way station in the commerce of the ancient world, since it produced the surplus that became the basis for the participation of its merchants in international commerce. It is worthwhile to remember that the capitals of these states were always in the interior, not along the coast. Royal families, temple officials, and tribal chiefs, by virtue of their control of the land and its surplus, formed the nucleus of the merchant class. The merchants benefited from the state's efforts to safeguard the movement of trade caravans and to secure markets inside and outside of Arabia.

Third, the development of merchant capital was a long and continuous historical process that saw the rise and demise of many states. As one state declined, a new state developed to take its place. Himyar and Hira began to decline together by the middle of the fifth century A.D. This decline, simultaneous with the decline of the Roman and Sasanid worlds, was due primarily to their inability to ensure the constant transformation of their social and political structure. This allowed Mecca to emerge and to develop as an alternative center built on the institutional experience of its predecessors, but with new institutions of its own.

Finally, Mecca's growth and the rise of Islam are organically and historically linked to the events in Arabia, especially those that took place during the sixth century A.D. It is to that stage of Mecca's history that we turn next.

2. The Development of Merchant Capital in Mecca

Merchant capital in southern Arabia, for the most part, was dependent on the exchange of an internally generated surplus from agricultural and commodity production. The situation was totally different in Mecca, for it was located in a barren valley. It was for centuries a stopover for the trade caravans that traveled through the Hijaz, either going north and northeast to Syria and Iraq, or south to Yemen. Mecca's role in the commerce of Yemen is implied in the Qur'anic verse (Saba' 34:18) that says that the Sabaeans were blessed by having a sacred center where their merchants could find succor on their journeys. Mecca had neither an agricultural surplus nor any commodity production of which it could boast. It had, however, one commodity that was very much sought after: water, provided by the water well Zamzam.

Water was so dear in that environment that the territory around Mecca was held to be sacred; thus a *haram* area grew with a sacred enclave called the Ka'ba. Because it was sacred, life and property were secure within the confines of the sacred area, making Mecca a natural place for pilgrims and merchants to find a haven and to exchange commodities with each other. These came to Mecca during the four sacred months of the year, when it was understood that an individual or a group could travel with immunity from attack. Having no surplus of their own, Mecca's merchants thus accumulated capital only through trade occasioned by the institution of the *haram*, providing us with a classic illustration of exchange as the origin of merchant capital.

Starting with the institutional framework that already existed in Mecca, the discussion in this chapter will concentrate on the creation of institutions and institutional practices that had a direct influence on the growth of Meccan merchant capital. I shall show that the merchants transformed Mecca from a relatively insignificant settlement into an economically and politically powerful center in western Arabia. Furthermore, this process was accomplished by enhancing the religious value of the sacred center, which made religious, political, and economic growth part of the same development.

The Genesis

Mecca's early history is clouded with legends. Arabic tradition claims that Abraham (Ibrahim) brought his wife, Hagar, and his infant son Isma'il to the location of Mecca and left them in that inhospitable place. Zamzam is believed to be the direct result of divine intervention on behalf of Isma'il. It is also believed that while the panic-stricken mother walked between Safa and Marwa in search of water to give her thirsty son, a stone (that is, a meteorite, which came to be called the Black Stone) hit the earth, causing the well of Zamzam to burst forth. Abraham later came back to build a *bait* (house) for his family, which came to be known as the Ka'ba. This is the genesis of Mecca and, supposedly, the genesis of its sacredness. Thus, the Black Stone, the travel between Safa and Marwa, and the circumambulation around the Ka'ba were incorporated into rites of pilgrimage performed by those who came to Mecca.[1]

The belief in sacred space and sacred time is ancient and was held throughout Arabia. It is not possible to determine when Mecca acquired its sacredness, but as Saba' 34:18 implies, it was considered sacred for several centuries before the rise of Islam. Therefore, Mecca already provided a safe resting place for the trade caravans thanks to the institutional belief of the *haram*, which, as already noted, provided the time and place for the exchange of commodities and allowed for the accumulation of merchant capital in the area. Thus, it is from the very beginning of Mecca's history that there was a direct relation between the development of its sacredness and the advancement of its economy; the more pilgrims, the more exchange, and the greater the accumulation of merchant capital.

Aside from legends, the evidence available on early Mecca is extremely scanty; thus, little is known with certainty about life there before the Quraish became dominant. The area of Mecca was inhabited by several tribes, and one usually dominated the others. Again according to legend, the first known tribe to inhabit the settlement was known as the 'Amaliqa. This tribe was later dominated by the Yemeni tribe of Jurhum, only for the latter to give way to the Khuza'a, who also were from Yemen.[2] With the present lack of facts, little of value can be said to explain the conditions that led to change of power. What is worth noticing, however, is that several tribes were living in the area and that competing interests were expressed in one's political domination of the others.

Reflecting the interest of Muslim chroniclers, there is more information regarding Mecca after the Quraish took over. Around the middle of the fifth century A.D., when Yemen and Hira started their decline, Qusayy ibn Kilab led several kinship-related clans to form the Quraish and defeated the Khuzaʿa. He then took control of the most important function in the city by assuming the institutional practice of *wilayat al-Bait,* the upkeep of the Kaʿba. As head of the Quraish, Qusayy became the leader of Mecca, giving the various clans under him the opportunity to dominate the affairs of the city. Thus, although Qusayy's leadership of the Quraish was undisputed, the various clan heads shared in the power structure. This power sharing might be attributed to the relatively recent change in the position of the Quraish, which required them to cooperate to defeat their adversaries. Their recent takeover of Mecca and, therefore, their recent full-scale involvement with commerce probably indicates that these clans were not as differentiated as they became in later years and that intraclan competition was not as prominent. These circumstances allowed for their solidarity as expressed in the collectivity of their decision making.

The circumstances of this transfer of power to the Quraish are obscure. Traditional accounts claim that Qusayy was an orphan who lived with his maternal tribe in Syria before he came back to Mecca. It is also claimed that, after his return, he married the daughter of Hulail ibn Hubshiyya, chief of the Khuzaʿa. After Hulail died, Qusayy took over and was able to defeat a branch of the Khuzaʿa that resisted his assumption of power. Following their victory, the clans led by Qusayy moved into the area immediately adjacent to the Kaʿba (the *bitah*) and thereafter were known as Quraish al-Bitah, those of inner Mecca. Other related clans remained in the outskirts, and some moved to Oman and northern Arabia and came to be known as the Quraish al-Zawahir (those who stayed outside Mecca).[3]

The formation of the Quraish must have been long in the making. There is a reference to them as early as 287 A.D. in an inscription left by King Ilʿadd Yalut of Hadramawt. The inscription reveals that, among other guests, a delegation of fourteen women from the Quraish were present at the coronation. Discussing this inscription, Jamme says that the women were acting on their own initiative.[4] The inscription, however, does not answer many questions. We do not know why the reference was exclusively to women and we do not know if the Quraish lived near Mecca. But the reference to the Quraishi women was made in conjunction with one about a Palmyrene delegation, decidedly from the north. At any event, the Quraish were already linked to "royalty," most likely for purposes of trade. Indeed, the word *quraish* is etymologically linked to trade.

The Quraish trace their origin to Luʾayy ibn Ghalib ibn Fihr ibn Malik, one of three brothers. The implication is that he already lived in the area of Mecca. Luʾayy had many sons: ʿAmir, ʿAwf, Khuzaima, al-Harith, Samah, and Kaʿb. ʿAmir had few descendants and they later lived in Mecca. ʿAwf's descendants became part of the Qais ʿAilan in eastern Arabia. Those of Khuzaima (Asad) became part of the Shaiban of the Bakr ibn Waʾil in northeastern Arabia. Those of al-Harith became part of the ʿAnaza in north central Arabia, and those of Samah went to Oman.[5] This outward movement was significant for later Meccan development, since the Quraish of Mecca could easily obtain allies among distant relatives in the various regions.

The most powerful of the sons, Kaʿb, remained behind. He apparently inherited his father's title. His descendants were also the most numerous: ʿAdiyy was the progenitor of a clan by the same name; Husais was the progenitor of two clans, the Sahm and the Jumah. A third son, Murra, inherited the title and was the progenitor of Kilab, Yaqza (Makhzum), and Taim. Kilab inherited his father's title, which was passed to one of his sons, Qusayy, to the exclusion of the other, Zuhra (figure 1).[6]

It is important to remember that all of those clans were related through kinship to a common ancestor and through endogenous marriages among the clans. Kinship relations, no doubt, were instrumental in unifying the clans behind Qusayy. These same relations, however, did not prevent the clans from competing for dominance, as we shall see later. It is also important to notice that "nobility" passed from father to son.

The transformation of the position of the Quraish because of their proximity to Mecca allowed Qusayy to take over Mecca. His assumption of power was certainly favored by the Khuzaʿi chief, thus the transfer of power would have been peaceful had it not been for other sections of the Khuzaʿa who resisted the change. Qusayy, therefore, had to ask for help from his distant "cousins," the Kinana and the Qudaʿa.[7]

But in the absence of reliable information we are left to speculate on the nature of this takeover. Since Qusayy was married to Fuhaira, daugh-

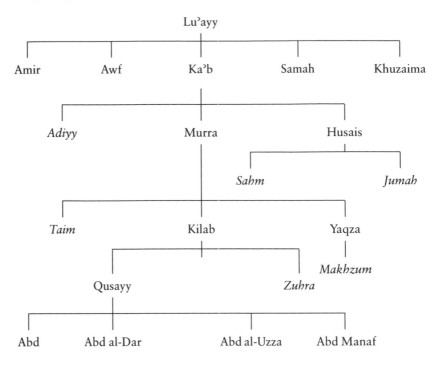

Figure 1: The Quraish at the time of their takeover of Mecca; the names of clans under Qusayy are in italics.

ter of the Khuzaʿi chief, he must have been considered a *kufʾ*, that is, of equal nobility. His marriage to a Khuzaʿi woman shows that the two tribes were already related. Indeed, this relationship might have been an alliance, since marriage between clans or tribes was one way of creating the bond of kinship. The marriage might indicate that the transformation of power was expected, since their offspring would be of noble Khuzaʿi lineage.

The match between Qusayy, a nomadic or a seminomadic chief, and the daughter of a settled chief might also indicate that the Quraish were in a transitional period, most likely due to the commercial advantages they reaped as a result of their closeness to Mecca. The involvement of the Quraish in the commerce of Mecca was achieved by actual participation in the exchange, by hiring out their camels, or by a combination. As these advantages increased after the middle of the fifth century A.D., the inducement to permanent settlement became greater. Thus, one can speculate that participation in the commercial life of Mecca or the lack of it explains the two-way division of the Quraish: those who participated in commerce settled down and became the Quraish al-Bitah; those who did not participate remained on the outskirts until a time when they too moved into Mecca.

Tradition regarding Qusayy credits him with the introduction of institutional practices that eventually became a bone of contention between the competing clans of the Quraish. Those pertaining to the Ka'ba and the sacred center were already in existence, however, so Qusayy merely formalized them. He may have introduced institutional practices related to the internal administration of Mecca that were indeed new and revolutionary to the extent that they set Meccan life on a course of rapid commercial progress: *rifada,* providing food for the pilgrims; *siqaya,* providing water for the pilgrims; and Dar al-Nadwa, a statehouse where clan chiefs met to deliberate.[8]

The formalization of these institutional practices should be understood within the context of the changed political and economic circumstances in Mecca. In addition to *sadaqa* (voluntary alms-giving), *rifada* and *siqaya* formed a system for the distribution of wealth as a way to deal with the economic stratification that was taking place, no doubt as a result of the different opportunities available through commerce. The benefits of this system, naturally, did not go only to the pilgrims but also to the poorer members of Meccan society. And as practices that facilitated the religious and economic transformation of Mecca, *rifada* and *siqaya* played the double role of servicing the pilgrims/merchants and of attracting more settlers to the city. To provide food, Qusayy collected taxes from Mecca's merchants as well as from merchants who came from outside.[9] And to provide water he dug several wells in and around Mecca, an example that was followed by other Meccans as the population of the city continued to grow.[10] Dar al-Nadwa was built near the Ka'ba, thus giving it a measure of sacredness. It functioned as Qusayy's residence and the meeting place of the collective clan heads, who also invested in commerce. Caravans are said to have started out from Dar al-Nadwa and there they returned. Other social ceremonies, such as those pertaining to puberty, circumcision, and marriage, were also performed in Dar al-Nadwa.[11]

The growing sedentarization of the Quraish is also revealed in Qusayy's order to divide the area immediately adjacent to the Ka'ba between his clans. They settled permanently on those divisions and built round structures as their dwellings, perhaps in deference to the square or cubic structure of the Ka'ba.[12]

The alteration in the life-style of the Quraish, as I have said, indicates their involvement in Mecca's commerce. But it also indicates that Mecca was growing in importance, since the Quraish took over at a time when Yemen had begun to experience continuing social and political upheavals, from which it never really recovered. Hira was too involved at this time with its northern neighbors and became involved in the Sasanid/ Byzantine wars, which ultimately contributed to its decline. The growth of Mecca as an alternative haven for merchants was facilitated by the security of the *haram*. The increase in the number of pilgrims and merchants probably motivated Qusayy to excavate wells in the city, something that was not done previously, as well as to formalize the practices for distribution of wealth.

Qusayy's institutional innovations, however, did not remove all of the obstacles facing Mecca's merchants, especially since his efforts were oriented toward the internal organization of the city. This organization facilitated exchange and increased the accumulation of capital but did nothing to secure access to the city by, for example, forming alliances with other tribes or by expanding the territorial hegemony of Mecca. Such actions would have been very important, since there were tribes—the Muhillun—that did not believe in the concept of the sacred time and sacred place as applied in Mecca.[13] These tribes had no qualms about attacking trade caravans even in sacred months.

Unresolved tribal conflict, therefore, still hindered the commercial success of Mecca, and the Muhillun continued to be a stumbling block for the merchants, despite the institutional advantage of the *haram*. Meccan merchants, for example, were hesitant to take a two-night journey to Dubaiq, on the Red Sea, where an Abyssinian ship had docked full of badly needed provisions.[14] This state of affairs is the subject of commentaries on the Qur'anic sura (106) dealing with the Quraish in pre-Islamic times. Having no power outside the *haram*, Meccan merchants passively waited for other merchants to bring in goods and, only after they acquired these commodities, did they have anything to trade with one another or with the tribes in the immediate vicinity.[15] At this time, therefore, the participation of Mecca's merchants in commerce depended on factors beyond their immediate control. This limited their trade, created a high level of competition among them, and forced them to undertake individual ventures with very little cooperation from other merchants. Because of limited trade, accumulation of capital remained on a small scale to the extent that many a merchant was tottering on the verge of bankruptcy. These were the conditions of the genesis of Meccan merchant capital. Let us turn to the conditions of its development.

The Development

The limited accumulation available to Mecca's merchants often led to disastrous consequences. This is illustrated by the events that preceded the introduction of the *ilaf* (a commercial agreement) by Hashim ibn ʿAbd Manaf, Qusayy's grandson. Because of the restricted sphere of their commercial undertakings and because of the organizational nature of their commerce, Mecca's merchants were in constant danger of financial disaster. Financial loss seemed to occur often enough that Meccans, in search of a solution to this problem, were forced to practice ritual suicide (*iʿtifad*). A merchant who lost his wealth was forced to separate himself and his family from the rest of the clan and to starve to death.[16]

This practice, however, did not solve the dilemma of the Meccan merchants. When the Abyssinians were engaged in Yemen and the opportunities for commerce seemed to increase during the first two decades of the sixth century, *iʿtifad* was no longer necessary. As the practice was fading, it was the intention of a man from the clan of Makhzum to commit ritual suicide that gave Hashim the chance to speak against the practice. He pointed out that the attrition rate of Mecca's merchants because of *iʿtifad* was enormous. They, he continued, became less numerous and weaker in the face of other Arabs, presumably other Arab merchants. To regain their strength, Hashim argued for a change in the nature of their undertakings. Simply put, he suggested that if several merchants pooled their capital they would fare better in their undertakings, since, as he declared, "there is strength in numbers."[17]

Accordingly, Hashim argued that the weak and the poor should be allowed to invest in the caravans. This is significant, since it allowed the weaker merchant to rebuild and the poor the chance of upward mobility. The weak and the poor would not have had the means by which to participate in international commerce had it not been for Hashim's innovative perceptions of the needs of Meccan commerce.

This chance for upward social and economic mobility appealed to all Meccans, especially the merchants. Thereafter, Meccans began to carry out their commercial ventures communally and on a large scale. The individual investor was reassured and risks were minimized; *iʿtifad* was abandoned altogether.

But the reorganization of Meccan commerce alone could not redress the situation that obtained during Qusayy's time and that of his immediate successors. A more far-reaching change was needed, especially in Mecca's relationship with tribes outside of the *haram* area. To break out of the confines of the *haram,* a better relationship with other tribes was required so that merchants could be more secure in their travel. Only then could they have access to a wider market area and thus more opportunities for commerce.

Reflecting a newfound strength, Hashim traveled to Syria, where he secured a safe conduct for Mecca's merchants by pointing out that Mecca would provide cheaper cloth and leather to Byzantine merchants.[18] He secured separate agreements with tribal chiefs who lived along the trade route between Mecca and Busra, in the grain-rich Hawran district. This agreement, the *ilaf,* was not an alliance under which the two parties came to each other's aid in times of conflict. Rather, the relationship was limited to providing services for one another. The tribes provided *khafara* (security and protection) for Meccan caravans passing through their territories. In exchange, Meccan merchants carried with them, on consignment, commodities produced by the tribes to be sold in the markets and fairs that the Meccans had begun to frequent. On their way back, the Meccans returned the capital and the profits to the original investors.[19]

Profit sharing as a characteristic of this mutually advantageous arrangement tended to eliminate the thorny problems of safety while traveling and the Muhillun tribes. With the *ilaf,* Hashim mobilized Meccan merchant capital on a larger scale than before and added security. As a response to the demands of merchant capital, the *ilaf* was, by far, a more successful experiment in institution building than *i'tifad* had been.

Thanks to the *ilaf,* Mecca's merchants began to participate for the first time with full confidence in international commerce, especially since it was instituted during a time of favorable political circumstances for the Meccans (around A.D. 520). Yemen was at the height of its social unrest and was yet to recover any measure of stability. Hashim, and many other Meccan merchants after him, began to frequent and trade regularly with Busra, Gaza, and Alexandria, among other markets under Byzantine control. Following the example of their brother, 'Abd Shams, al-Muttalib, and Nawfal opened the road to Abyssinia, Yemen, and Persia, respectively.[20] They led the trade caravans and were in charge of the merchants, Meccans as well as those from other parts of Arabia, who took advantage of the mobility of Meccan caravans and tagged along for the security they provided. These successful operations added to the prestige and influence of the Meccans, beyond what they already had as residents of the sacred center. With the *ilaf* and with their newly expanded commercial network, their prosperity increased.

Another important aspect of the *ilaf* was how it altered the tribes' relationship with Mecca. Through the *ilaf* agreement, Meccans provided tribesmen employment in guarding the caravans, an arrangement similar to that practiced by earlier states in Arabia. Mecca's merchants also utilized tribal livestock (camels) to transport commodities, again to their mutual benefit. More important, Meccans provided a market for tribal products, which encouraged production and thus prosperity for the tribe. Tribal chiefs who were associated with the *ilaf* began to frequent Mecca, thus drawing the tribes into its economic framework either by direct participation in commerce, as agreed to by the *ilaf*, or by raising the possibility of settlement in the city, a process of sedentarization much like that experienced earlier by the Quraish themselves.[21]

Hashim's achievements resulted in the mobility of Meccan merchants and in the creation of a wider network of markets. Mecca gradually became the focal point of this commercial network. Thus, the internal organization of Mecca's merchants affected external relations, since Meccan contacts with tribes outside of the *haram* area increased. These contacts grew in closeness and complexity, and the changed political and economic circumstances made the Meccans ripe for new institutional adaptations.

The most noteworthy adaptation was the incorporation of the concept of *hilf* (alliance) in their relationship with others. These alliances were of the traditional type, in which an attack on one party was considered an attack on the other. Alliances, consequently, supported a closer association between the Quraish and tribes in the far corners of Arabia. They were cemented by the traditional practice of intermarriage, which fostered kinship and gave the relationship a moral basis in addition to its material one. The case of ʿAbd Shams illustrates the point. He was married to women from the Banu ʿAmir ibn Saʿsaʿa in central Arabia, from the Tamim in eastern Arabia, from the Azd in Oman, as well as from the Kinda in Hadramawt.[22] Through his kinship and alliance with each of these powerful and commercially involved tribes, ʿAbd Shams became one of the most powerful and successful merchants and clan leaders in Mecca.

Alliances were formed with tribes near and far and both worked to strengthen the political and economic power of Mecca's merchants inside their city and outside. The alliance with the Ahabish, a tribe on Mecca's outskirts, was formed after two of the tribes that helped the Quraish defeat the Khuzaʿa chose to leave the area. The Meccans felt threatened and sought additional allies. Prompted by security concerns, the ʿAbd Manaf proposed an alliance with the Hawn ibn Khuzaima and the al-Harith ibn ʿAbd Manah. The latter complied and brought to the alliance the al-

Mustalaq and al-Haya tribes. The alliance was formalized near Hubshiyy, a mountain south of Mecca. It is perhaps in reference to this mountain that the four tribes—al-Hawn, al-Harith, al-Mustalaq, and al-Haya—as a coalition were called Ahabish, not because they were mercenaries of Habashi (Abyssinian) origin.[23]

The Ahabish, however, displayed a certain militancy in defending the interests of Mecca, and the Quraish called on them for military help on more than one occasion. This close military cooperation and their name, with its tenuous link to Abyssinia, might have led to the confusion regarding their origins and the nature of their relationship with the Meccans. The militancy of the Ahabish in defending Meccan interests is understandable when we realize that they were defending theirs as well, for they too joined Mecca's merchants and began to trade with Syria and other places.[24]

The Ahabish continued to have a special and a close relationship with the Meccans. The Banu Qariz and the Banu Qara clans even became part of the Quraish and, more specifically, part of the clan of Zuhra. The Banu Qariz achieved this in two stages: first, their alliance with the Ahabish, allies of the Quraish; second, after the Ahabish as a whole grew and assumed greater strength. The Banu Qariz decided to move into Mecca proper and allied themselves with Zuhra, one of the weaker Quraish clans.[25] Zuhra may have been searching for alliances to shore up its position, for clans and individuals could also form alliances.

Another important alliance was concluded with the distant Tamim tribe. The Tamim controlled the port of al-Mushaqqar in Bahrain. They were also on excellent terms with the Lakhmids of Hira and through them with the Sasanids. This tribe seemed the perfect trading partner for the Meccans. Their relationship grew so strong that some members of the Tamim were in charge of certain religious ceremonies in Mecca and exercised some control in the market of ʿUkaz. The details of this alliance have been discussed by Kister,[26] but it is important to remember that through these alliances the Quraish facilitated trade with the various regions of Arabia and provided their merchants with security and access to the important regional markets.

Merchants who frequented al-Mushaqqar began to seek the protection of the Quraishi merchants because of their alliance with the Tamim. Those who went to Dawmat al-Jandal similarly sought the protection of the Quraish. Meccan merchants who visited the port of Rabiʿa in Hadramawt enjoyed the protection of Banu Akil al-Murar.[27] Thus, alliance by association was also respected, so that even though the tribes of Kalb and Tayy, which controlled the access to the market/fair of Dawmat al-Jandal, were from the Muhillun and had no alliance with the Quraish, they did not attack Meccan caravans because they were allied with two allies of the Quraish: the Asad and the Tamim, respectively.[28] It should be clear, therefore, that in their concern to find added security for their caravans and to obtain access to a wider market, Mecca's merchants began to transform the political and economic structure of Mecca and its relationship to the outside just as the practices of *siqaya* and *rifada* had contributed to the growth of the city's religious and commercial significance.

The Rise of Mecca's Power

The system of *ilaf* and alliances allowed Mecca's merchants to increase their commercial enterprises and to accumulate capital on a large scale. Gone were the days when they were afraid to leave the *haram* area and thus accumulated capital on such a limited scale that many were forced into ritual suicide. Thanks to the introduction of new institutions and the adaptation of institutions from other areas, Meccans transformed themselves into rich and influential merchants with international connections. Their new wealth could be seen in the changes they made in their dwellings, since it is said that after the *ilaf* the Quraish began to build roofed square structures, rather than round ones.[29] Besides indicating the use of more permanent building materials, the new construction techniques might have been an attempt to identify visibly with the Ka'ba.

With this growing prosperity, the political clout of the Quraish also grew, no doubt, as a direct consequence of the system of alliances that they cultivated and of the added prestige of their city. Also responsible for this political power was the growing strength of their capital after years of accumulation. A case in point is their relationship with their neighbors, the tribe of Thaqif, in the city of Ta'if.

Ta'if, located in the hills east of Mecca, was a fertile area and commanded important trade routes passing through Najd to southern Arabia. It was the nearest producer of food, wine, and leather. Two main tribes lived there, the Thaqif and the Daws. Both cultivated the fertile area of Wadi Wajj, which, they said, had been developed by their forefathers so long ago that they had used stone tools, not iron ones.[30]

After the introduction of the *ilaf,* the success of their trade, and the development of their network of alliances, the Quraish began to feel con-

fident enough to challenge the exclusive rights of their neighbors to cultivate the Wadi. This challenge was also the Quraish's incipient attempt to
control the resources of this agricultural area so that eventually they
could monopolize production from the area for themselves. The Quraish
demanded the right to acquire land in the Wadi and said that they would
reciprocate by making the Thaqif partners in the *haram*. The Thaqif regarded this demand as an encroachment, however, and argued that
whereas their forefathers were responsible for the development of the
Wadi, it was Abraham (believed to be a common ancestor) who developed the *haram,* and thus the Quraish should not regard themselves as its
sole proprietor. The Meccans' proposal seemed unfair and was resisted.
But the Quraish insisted on the terms and, to give teeth to their demands,
they mobilized their supporters among the surrounding tribes and vowed
to block the Thaqif from the *haram* area. Fearing military confrontation
with a powerful enemy, the Thaqif acquiesced, although it was against
their interests.[31] Thereafter, Meccan merchants acquired property in Ta'if,
invested in land development, and became engaged in moneylending at
usurious rates (*riba*). On the eve of Islam, almost every important Meccan merchant had investments in Ta'if to the extent that it appeared to be
their summer resort, very much like its function today.[32] Investment in
productive land only increased the strength of their capital.

The way the Thaqif were brought into submission reveals that the
Quraish had enough capital to invest in land development and thus diver-
sify their investments. They had also acquired enough military power to
enforce their will. Their investment in the agriculture of the nearest food
producer was exceptionally beneficial to Mecca's merchants, since Mecca
itself did not produce food. This encounter also shows the importance of
the *haram* and the seriousness of being excluded from it, especially if one
wanted to trade.

Intertribal conflict provides another example of the growing power of
the Quraish. This time they deployed their forces effectively against their
adversaries. The Bakr ibn 'Abd Mana ibn Kinana had been expelled from
Mecca years earlier by Qusayy. Apparently the Bakr continued to resent
the expulsion and waited for an opportunity to regain their lost position.
A branch of the Bakr, the Banu Laith, were living in Tihama in an area
between Yemen and Yalamlam, which is on the southern edge of the
haram area and a two-night journey from Mecca. The Banu Qara of the
Ahabish were pasturing their camels in the same area. Their leader, 'Aw-
waf, was at the time an ally of Hisham ibn al-Mughira and al-'As ibn Wa'il

of the clans of Makhzum and Sahm, respectively. It had been a particularly bad year for the Laith, and, in search of provisions, they were forced
to resort to raiding others' property. Their leader, Balʿa ibn Qais, had already set out on one of those raids, leaving his brother Qatada in charge.
One night while Qatada was inspecting the encampment, he spotted a
free-roaming herd of camels, which belonged to the Banu Qara. Against
the advice of two of his clansmen, who warned him that the owner had
powerful allies, Qatada attacked the herd the next morning, killed one of
the guards, and herded off thirty camels. Qatada immediately slaughtered
ten camels and distributed the meat to his hungry clansmen. He divided
the rest of the loot later.[33]

Attacks as a form of social conflict for the distribution of wealth
(*ghazwa*) were not uncommon. Difficult times, like that in which the
Banu Laith found themselves, often forced many a tribe to "brigandage."
Qatada had no reservations about attacking the herd of even a powerful
man so that he might feed the hungry in his clan. An unequal distribution
of wealth and resources already existed in and around Mecca. This unequal distribution thus had the potential to threaten Mecca's prosperity
and to disrupt its network of alliances and trade routes.

Such an attack could not be ignored by the Quraish, and they spared
no efforts to redress the situation. They were concerned not only for their
wronged ally, but also for the security of the Yemeni trade route, which
could have been blocked had the attacks been allowed to continue. Hisham and al-ʿAs tried to resolve the matter first by peaceful means. But the
Laith were unwilling to come to terms. The Quraish then mobilized their
allies and, with a force of about two thousand, headed toward the Banu
Laith, who were waiting with an even larger number. A terrible battle
ensued at Dhat Nakif, near Yalamlam. The Banu Qara, the aggrieved
party, being excellent archers, seemed to have done a good bit to turn the
tide in favor of the Quraish and their allies. The Banu Laith broke camp
and fled toward the *haram*. The Quraish and the Ahabish together decided on the terms and insisted that the Banu Laith should go into exile,
away from Tihama.[34]

The actions of the Quraish against their neighbors and the surrounding tribes show that Mecca had developed economic and political strength
and that it had become much more powerful and influential than in the
days of Qusayy. Meccans no longer timidly waited in their sanctuary for
other merchants to come in with food and other commodities. Due to the
changed circumstances and to the growing demand for their trade goods,

their inadequate infrastructure was reformed by the initiative they took in building an institutional framework to improve their condition. They became more mobile and widened their market; the more mobile the merchant capital and the wider the market, the greater the accumulation. Thus, capital increased to the extent that they could venture into other avenues of investment, especially land development, which increased their control of available resources. The alliances that they formed for the purposes of trade also gave them military and political strength, which they began to field in the expansion and defense of their interests. Mecca's power increased proportionately with the increase in its commerce; wealth and power went hand in hand.

Mecca's economic and political growth, as we have seen, did not occur in isolation. Merchants turned the adversity of others into gains for themselves. Nor did Mecca's growth escape the attention of the Byzantines and the Sasanids. Both powers were already competing with one another over trade routes in Syria and both were eager to use the strategic assets of the Arabian peninsula for their purposes. Al-Qatif, for example, provided Byzantine merchants with cheaper silk, since it was not taxed by the Sasanids. The Sasanids, meanwhile, were at pains to maintain a monopoly in the silk trade to get Byzantine gold in exchange; thus merchant operations at al-Qatif thwarted Sasanid policy. Persian monarchs often attacked eastern Arabia as a result. When Hira was drawn firmly into their sphere of influence, it assumed the responsibility for securing the area. As indicated earlier, Hira was in control of eastern Arabia, including Oman by A.D. 530. Therefore, with the growing concentration of commerce in Mecca, it was natural that each of the two powers would attempt to bring this trading center under its sphere of influence.

The Byzantines attempted it first through their Abyssinian allies, who had already occupied Yemen. Taking into consideration Abraha's policies of reviving Yemeni trade and Abyssinian interests in southern Arabia, there is strong evidence that the Abyssinian attack on Mecca was prompted by the Byzantines. Abraha repaired the Ma'rib dam and built the Qullais in an attempt to revive the economy of Yemen and consequently to compete with Mecca. This policy, however, was not successful in diverting merchants away from Mecca. Abraha then decided to destroy the Ka'ba and thus end Mecca's prestige as a pilgrimage and trade center. He mobilized a mixed army of Abyssinian and Arab soldiers and marched north, subduing all resistance. Having secured the allegiance of Ta'if, Abraha proceeded toward Mecca with an elephant (or elephants) in the vanguard. But while his army was laying siege to Mecca, the army was cut down by smallpox.[35] Sura 105, in celebration of this event, describes the army as "straw, chewed up and left over." With the disintegration of his army and the failure to destroy the Ka'ba, Abraha retreated with the remnants of his soldiers to Yemen, where he lived the remaining few years of his life. However, many of the Arab soldiers who came with him remained behind and began to seek employment in Mecca as shepherds and guards for the livestock of the Quraish.[36]

Mecca's continued growth must have renewed the desire of the Byzantines and the Sasanids to compete again in Arabia. Abraha's failure must have been a signal for Sasanid intervention in Yemen, especially since Dhu Yazan had been seeking Persian assistance. A seaborne expedition was sent to Yemen and was able to defeat the remaining Abyssinians; consequently, a Persian garrison occupied San'a (in about A.D. 575). However, there is no indication that the Sasanids attempted to extend their direct control to Mecca at this time. Instead, they encouraged the Lakhmids to try. But the Lakhmids, already weak, were unable to pursue this policy seriously enough to amount to anything.[37]

From Byzantium's perspective, Persian control of Yemen could threaten Byzantine interests in the Red Sea. In response to this development, the Byzantines attempted to control Mecca a second time, taking advantage of efforts on the part of some Meccans to tie themselves with the Byzantines, most likely through the Ghassanids.[38]

Although the reports about this incident are vague, we know that 'Uthman ibn al-Huwairith, a Quraishi merchant with Syrian connections, attempted to crown himself king in Mecca on behalf of the Byzantines. Many Meccans objected on the grounds that they were *luqah* (autonomous in religious and political affiliation).[39] In the face of Meccan opposition, 'Uthman had to abandon the idea altogether. The Byzantines thus also failed to extend direct political control over Mecca. In fact, each attempt seemed to strengthen Mecca's development as an independent religious, economic, and political center.

Mecca, however, could not have had direct political influence over a large area of Arabia, as it did in Ta'if, especially given the presence of the Sasanids or their clients, the Lakhmids. The wide connections that the Quraish cultivated throughout Arabia were based on purposes of trade and pilgrimage; their political influence had to develop gradually. This growth can be linked once again to the growth of their wealth and also to the political circumstances around them. Thus, while Yemen was insecure and Hira in decline, and while the Byzantine and the Sasanid empires were occupied with one another, Mecca's political influence in Arabia was left to grow without interference.

Mecca's political growth is illustrated by the Fijar War (the wicked or sinful war), so called because it was fought during the *haram* months, in around A.D. 580. The war between Mecca and Hira near the market-fair of ʿUkaz took place barely a decade after the market's establishment or incorporation within the Quraishi sphere of influence after the Year of the Elephant. In fact, this confrontation took place after the Persians (Hira's benefactors) established a garrison in Yemen. Therefore, in their stand against Hira, the Meccans may have been attempting to sever any direct link through Najd between Hira (and the Sasanids) and Yemen. Such a link would be detrimental to their political and economic interests.

The events preceding the confrontation at ʿUkaz are instructive. The war was instigated by a certain al-Barrad ibn Qais ibn Nafiʿ. Al-Barrad had sought refuge in Mecca, where he was allied with the Banu Sahm. He later switched his alliance to Harb ibn Umayya, leader of the Banu Umayya, a wealthier and more powerful clan than the Banu Sahm. It is said that al-Barrad killed a Meccan from the Khuzaʿa and as a result had to flee to Yemen. There is no indication that al-Barrad's alliance with Harb was affected. After a year in Yemen, he traveled to Hira, where, sources tell us, he requested employment from al-Nuʿman ibn al-Mundhir as a guide for the *latima*, a Lakhmid trade caravan on the way to the market-fair of ʿUkaz. Al-Nuʿman, however, refused to employ him, appointing instead ʿUrwa ibn ʿUtbah from the Kilab.[40]

Undeterred by this rejection, al-Barrad and an unspecified number of men tracked the caravan until it halted at Duwain al-Jarib. While ʿUrwa was sleeping in his leather tent, al-Barrad attacked and killed him, dispatching Bishr ibn Khazim immediately with the news of his deed. Bishr, who later led a Meccan contingent in the Fijar War, was instructed to inform such notable Meccan merchants as ʿAbdallah ibn Judʿan, Hisham ibn al-Mughira, al-Barrad's ally Harb ibn Umayya, Nawfal ibn Muʿawiya, and Balʿa ibn Qais from the Bakr, all of whom were already assembled at ʿUkaz. Balʿa had attacked at least two caravans that belonged to al-Nuʿman in the Tihama region, either on their way to Yemen or on their return, which implies a policy of harassing Hira's Yemeni trade.[41]

This quick communication allowed the Meccans to withdraw into the *haram* area, where they began to mobilize their supporters for the impending battle. The Quraish supplied money, arms, and food to all those who gathered on their side. ʿAbdallah ibn Judʿan supplied complete armor for one hundred men. Hisham ibn al-Mughira and Harb ibn Umayya armed and equipped an unspecified number of men. Hisham, moreover, contributed a great deal of money to the war effort. The Quraish, the Khuzaʿa, the Ahabish, a section of the Tamim, and many other clans from the tribal grouping of the Kinana assembled under the leadership of Harb (or perhaps ʿAbdallah ibn Judʿan) and confronted Hira's central Arabian allies at ʿUkaz.[42]

The details of the battle are not altogether clear, but there is some indication that the two sides clashed on at least four occasions (some reports make it seem that they clashed in four successive years). The decisive engagement took place on the fourth meeting, called Fijar al-Barrad. The tide turned in favor of Mecca, and the Umayyad ʿUtba ibn Rabiʿah was able to negotiate a stop to the fighting by proposing that the side that suffered more casualties would receive from the other blood money for the difference in the number of casualties. Abu al-Barraʾ, leader of the Qais and the rest of Hira's allies, agreed to the proposal. He and Sabiʿ ibn Rabiʿah, leaders of Qais, guaranteed the truce from their side while Harb ibn Umayya, Hisham ibn al-Mughira, and ʿAbdallah ibn Judʿan guaranteed the Meccan side. When the dead were counted, the difference was found to be twenty more dead on the side of Qais. Some reports say that Harb paid all of the blood money, while others say that Quraish paid collectively (*trafadu*).[43]

In assessing the significance of the Fijar War in the history of Mecca's external relations, one must keep in mind that the Meccans had reached this stage after more than a century since Qusayy held sway. Although it could never be called a state (or a republic), Mecca had a dynamic social formation in which the merchants were able to introduce institutional practices that generated enough wealth and power to allow them to compete effectively with contemporary Arabian states. Mecca's involvement in the Fijar War shows the degree of the merchants' transformed position—a far cry from the insecurity and the isolation that were their lot before the *ilaf*. They were now able to challenge Hira itself and to cut off its access to Yemen, especially given the presence of a Persian garrison in Sanʿa. The Yemeni route now passed into Mecca's control and must have made the Persian garrison seem more remote than ever before.

The economic results of the Fijar War could be seen immediately in the attitude of some Meccan merchants toward their Yemeni counterparts. Sources report several incidents in which the Meccans refused to deal fairly with the Yemenis and withheld payments or confiscated property.[44] Such unbecoming behavior might indicate the Meccan merchants' confidence in themselves (militarily and economically) and their desire to cut the Yemeni merchants out of the *haram* trade. Mecca was indeed acquiring the requisite institutional and material bases for the formation of a state, and Meccan merchants were gradually acquiring additional political authority.

Culture as Ideology

Abraha's failure to harm the Ka'ba was attributed to divine intervention and thus was a momentous victory for Mecca and its inhabitants, especially those—the Quraish—in charge of the upkeep of the sacred center. His inability to repeat his attack was a clear indication of the precipitous failure of the Yemeni ruling class to mobilize any further military expeditions. Abraha's failure gave added prestige to the Quraish, and thereafter they were revered by others as *ahl Allah,* the people of God, since it was believed that only He could save the Quraish from the calamity that Abraha had in store for the Ka'ba.[45] This year is so significant in Mecca's history that the birth of Muhammad ibn 'Abdallah, the future prophet of Islam, is ascribed to it.

The Ka'ba and Mecca assumed greater significance among the Arabs now that they had been spared by Allah. The enhanced religious position of the Ka'ba, of Mecca, and of its inhabitants was used by the Quraishi merchants to cement further the ideological and institutional framework that they had constructed for their own benefit. The added reverence for the Ka'ba and the Quraish was incorporated into a total system that supported the interests of the Quraishi merchants. As such, respect for the *haram* and the rites of pilgrimage increased more than ever, to the advantage of the Meccans and especially the Quraish.[46]

These advantages were highlighted by the incorporation of two more institutional practices into the system of their beliefs immediately after the Year of the Elephant. The first was the distinction called *hums.*[47] No one had claimed this distinction before, but it appears to have been connected to the recent victory regarding the Ka'ba. The exact meaning of the word *hums* is unclear, but it implies the vigorous application of one's beliefs, and in the case of the Quraish, it would be the application of their religious, political, and economic institutions, since all were bound up with the *haram.*

There were several rituals performed by the tribes that claimed the *hums.* Some of these rituals entailed the endurance of hardship, such as seeking sun rather than shade in Mecca. This "hardship" may imply a new distribution of market space in Mecca, as more merchants would have competed for the limited shade around the Kaʿba. To preempt such competition and to ensure the position of the established merchants, it became desirable to accept shadeless areas to exhibit one's merchandise. Other rituals called for abstaining from eating meat or even from entering the house through the door![48] But these rites may have been a later understanding of the obscure distinction of *hums*, or an effort to upgrade the position of the Quraish by showing the degree of their suffering involved in the practice of their religious rites.

A more original rite was the Quraish insistence that they not leave Mecca to perform the *wuquf* (a pilgrimage rite) on Mount ʿArafa. The Quraish thought that the *wuquf* would detract from the reverence of the Kaʿba.[49] Apparently, they assumed that Mount ʿArafa was less holy. Approaching the Kaʿba thus became the final step of the pilgrimage, the crowning achievement of a holy act.

Aside from elevating the Kaʿba above all other holy sites, this change might be significant because Meccan merchants forced the market to come to them, indicating perhaps their central role in the commerce of the season and the degree of accumulation of merchant capital (and goods) in Mecca. The distinction of *hums* applied to the inhabitants of Mecca, including the Khuzaʾa, and to the important allies of the Quraish.[50] Alliance with the Meccans had proved to be a profitable enterprise.

The *hums* also prohibited the bringing into Mecca of any food or cloth. The sanctity and purity of the Kaʿba would be maintained and enhanced, it was argued, by preventing any defiled food or cloth from coming near it. Those who came for the greater pilgrimage or the lesser one were required to leave all of their "defiled" provisions outside of the *haram*. Pilgrims and merchants then had to clothe themselves with Meccan cloth and had to eat Meccan food. While there are indications that the pilgrims had to buy Meccan food and there are references to pilgrims' seeking food from Meccan vendors, the sources leave the impression that the injunction against foreign cloth applied only to the cloth worn during the circumambulation of the Kaʿba.[51] But, just as with *siqaya* and *rifada*, Meccan merchants were using institutions with religious significance to advance their material interests. And since food and cloth had to be brought in from other areas in the first place, their insistence on the use of Meccan cloth and the consumption of Meccan food was in fact an implied monopoly of the commodities that were available for exchange.

Such cumulative and self-supporting institutional practices were themselves part of the ideology of Mecca's social formation as dominated by merchant clan leaders.

A second institutional practice may already have been in place, but it was only after the Year of the Elephant that it became important, because it was "acquired" by the Quraish, especially after the Fijar War. After A.D. 570 the market-fair of ʿUkaz quickly became *the* market in pre-Islamic Arabia.[52] ʿUkaz was located to the east of Mecca, at the edge of the *haram* area. Trade routes that came from central Arabia toward Mecca and those that skirted their way to Yemen passed in the vicinity. Merchants from all over Arabia began to frequent the market. They brought Yemeni cloth, leather, perfume, and swords and various wares from Egypt, Syria, Iraq, and Abyssinia. Livestock was an important commodity and camels, cows, and sheep changed owners. Arab "royalty" sent their agents with prized commodities to be sold only to those who could afford them, the noblest and the richest merchants. Hakim ibn Hizam, a wealthy grain merchant with strong connections to Syria, purchased such commodities at ʿUkaz, for example.[53]

ʿUkaz was more than a market, it was also a fair with a carnival atmosphere. Poets went there to recite poetry praising their wealthy patrons or celebrating their deeds and the traditions of their tribes. Horse races were held and booths were set up to dispense wine and other pleasures. ʿUkaz was a place where not only capital and commodities were exchanged but also culture. Panegyric poetry recited in ʿUkaz became an impressive literary achievement of the age. The best poems were especially honored by being embroidered in gold thread and draped over the Kaʿba (thus the name al-*muʿallaqat,* the hanging odes).[54] As merchants from all over Arabia visited ʿUkaz, news came with them, and news about Mecca and the rest of the peninsula was carried back. Mecca had gradually become a major center in Arabia, surpassing others in religious and economic significance. Indeed, Yemen had not yet recovered from its political crisis when the country was newly occupied by the seaborne Persian expedition. Hira was already declining; only Mecca seemed to be growing in importance.

By the last decades of the sixth century A.D. and certainly after the Fijar War, the *haram* area of Mecca probably was a huge market. Although ʿUkaz overshadowed the other markets around Mecca, these lesser markets continued to operate. Majanna, south of Mecca, held a market after ʿUkaz, during the last ten days of the sacred month of Dhul Qaʾdah. The market of Dhul Majaz was held in turn, during the first nine days of the sacred month of Dhul Hijja, the last month of the year, before the pilgrims ascended Mount ʿArafat for the ceremonies of *wuquf*. It was where merchant-pilgrims who were late in joining the *mawsim,* the pilgrimage season, engaged in some last-minute shopping.[55] Clearly, the continuation of the three lesser markets points to the increased volume of trade that the Meccans began to handle after their long series of successes.

A final point should be raised about the pilgrimage to Mecca. This sacred center was the object of pilgrimage by pagan Arabs. Certainly, the institutional structure that the Quraish built in Mecca revolved around pagan institutions and beliefs. Deities were worshiped as the incarnation of the divine or as objects that possessed divine characteristics. The idols and the institutions that went with them could hardly have appealed to the Christians, Jews, and Zoroastrians, some of whom frequented Mecca during the pilgrimage season and others of whom lived in Mecca and the surrounding area. Their purpose in coming to Mecca during the pilgrimage season can best be understood in the framework of trade, as clarifying the connection between pilgrimage and commerce. Contacts with the major religious traditions of the region—Christianity, Judaism, and Zoroastrianism—in Mecca and outside, must have made Meccans aware that their religious traditions were different and quite separate from those around them. Thus, their insistence on being *luqah* (independent in religious and political affiliation) can be explained. Their awareness of Persian and Byzantine conflicts could have led them to view separateness as neutrality in the conflict and as independence from either party. Their political neutrality was jealously guarded, for they believed that it was indispensable for the carrying out of trade (as revealed by their argument against ʿUthman ibn al-Huwairith and his bid to attach himself to the Byzantines). Viewed differently, it could also be said that the Meccans were consciously developing wider pagan institutions based on their *haram,* since the wider the appeal, the greater the flow of pilgrims and merchants. This argument is more striking still when we realize that the Quraish attempted to accommodate various pagan deities within the Kaʿba or around it as a show of "universality."

In conclusion, the development of an institutional structure capable of supporting an increased volume of trade transformed Mecca into a major political, economic, and religious center in Arabia. The Quraish, a kinship-related group of clans, took over at a time when Mecca's merchants were weak, insecure, and dependent on a limited market. Building on the *haram* and thanks to other institutional beliefs introduced by the Quraish, such as the *ilaf, hums,* and *hilf,* Meccan merchants became rich through access to an international market and powerful through their alliances. They accumulated capital as a result of the cumulative institution building that they consciously introduced or adapted. Their interests and the demands of merchant capital, therefore, influenced the development of the religious, economic, and political structure in Mecca. This influence grew deeper and became more far-reaching as the merchants continued to lead the development of their city.

3. Merchant Capital and Mecca's Internal Development

As the wealth and power of Mecca's merchants grew and as their external relations became more intricate, the Meccans began to experience significant internal social, economic, and political transformations. In this chapter, I shall show how the growth of merchant capital led to the loosening of tribal and clan ties and to the eventual diversification and stratification of the city's society and economy. The gap between the rich and the poor grew and a social structure based on the ownership of merchant capital began to solidify. I shall also show that as capital accumulated in the hands of a few merchant-clan leaders, the Quraish lost their unanimity, which led to the formation of competing coalitions and the subsequent emergence of a singular leadership.

Social and Economic Differentiation

The inhabitants of Mecca were never homogeneous in the sense that they were members of a single tribe. It has been shown already that other tribal groups lived in Mecca before the Quraish. Some of these groups continued to live in Mecca even after they lost their preeminence. More clans came into Mecca after the Quraish took over.[1] Meccan society, therefore, was made up of several layers of dominating tribal groups all giving way to the others. The Quraish, in their turn, dominated the other tribes in Mecca and, in time, the vicinity. The decline in the position of the Khuzaʿa illustrates that the change in the fortunes of those tribal groups was the result of the existence of relations of power based on social and economic strength.

The population of Mecca began to increase more rapidly as its economic fortunes improved. Several factors made Mecca attractive for settlement. Foremost of these was the *haram,* which had been the destination of merchant-pilgrims from the various parts of Arabia. The institutional practices devised by the Meccans also played a role in bringing more settlers. We have seen that the *ilaf* attracted tribal leaders and tribesmen to Mecca to participate in its commercial undertakings. Alliance formation, whether with tribes, clans, or individuals, also attracted more people. Because rich merchants practiced *rifada, siqaya,* and *sadaqa* (alms collection), settlers were assured of some provisions. Population growth in Mecca is evidenced by the constant necessity to expand the water sources of the city by digging more wells. Such activity was required to meet the demands of the growing number of merchant-pilgrims and residents.[2]

Besides increasing the power of Mecca's merchants and attracting new settlers, alliance formation accelerated social diversification. It became symptomatic of diversification, since the potential outcome of this process was an increase (or decrease) in the relative strength of the social group concerned. Alliances between several clans could end up in the formation of a single tribe, for example, the Ahabish. But for the internal structure of Mecca, the formation of the Banu Fihr serves as another illustration of the point. The Banu ʿAmir ibn Fihr, already living inside Mecca, formed an alliance with the Banu Maʿis, the Banu Taim, and the Banu Muharib. Once constituted as the Banu Fihr, these clans moved into *batn al-wadi,* inner Mecca, where they pitched their tents. The move is a concrete demonstration of their attempt to get closer to the city's source of wealth and prosperity, the Kaʿba. As there was an organic link between the internal and the external relations of Mecca, the Banu ʿAmir's move was completed after Mecca escaped Abraha's invasion.

The importance of this alliance is clear when we learn that the Banu ʿAmir repudiated their already-existing alliance with the Banu ʿAdiyy.[3] It is in this shifting of alliances that the strength or the weakness of a tribe or clan could be affected. The Banu Fihr, becoming strong enough to be on their own, had no need of their *hilf* with the Banu ʿAdiyy. Thus, the shifting or formation of alliances probably indicates a constant realignment of forces and an attempt to secure a better position in the economic and political structure of the city.

Another significant aspect of alliance formation was its tendency to lead to the solidification of a class structure, since an alliance was formed between equals or between business partners. A report by Ibn Habib al-Baghdadi implies that there was some measure of control over who should settle in Mecca. Although he does not give any further information, he says that anyone who wished to settle in Mecca had to seek an alliance with its population.[4] Such a demand was tantamount to requiring citizenship, whereby an individual acquired a license to participate in the commercial enterprises of Mecca. Thus, when Haritha ibn al-Awqas, from the Banu Sulaim, moved to Mecca, he was told that he had to ally with a Meccan. Significantly, he chose ʿAbd Shams ibn ʿAbd Manaf, one of the richest and most influential merchants in the city.[5]

The alliance of Suwaid ibn Rabiʿa from the Tamim and Nawfal ibn ʿAbd Manaf is an example of an alliance between persons with similar business interests. The circumstances behind the formation of this alliance are instructive. Suwaid was married to the daughter of Hajib ibn Zurara, who had close ties with Hira and represented the Tamim at the Lakhmid court. Relations between Suwaid and the Lakhmids took a bad turn when he attacked Malik ibn al-Mundhir, who had been on a hunting trip. Suwaid fled with his family and headed toward Mecca, where he formed an alliance with Nawfal, who had earlier initiated Mecca's trade with Iraq.[6] Hira's relations with the Tamim seemed to cool after this incident.[7] But Suwaid's actions against the ruling family of Hira, his choice of refuge, and his choice of ally seemed to anticipate the decline of Hira and the growing tension between the Lakhmids and the Quraish.

As merchants increased their wealth and as more people came to Mecca to participate in its commerce, the merchants stood apart from the rest of the social order. Social stratification began to take concrete form. In his study of the social organization of Mecca, Wolf says, "Under the impact of commercial development, Meccan society changed from a social order determined primarily by kinship and characterized by considerable homogeneity of ethnic origin into a social order in which the fiction of kinship served to mask a developing division of society into classes, possessed of ethnic diversity."[8] Social status based on wealth became important. The highest in the social ladder was the *sayyid*, the clan leader who at the same time was a merchant. His strength and the extent of his influence depended primarily on his clan and the alliances he could muster, as shown earlier by the example of ʿAbd Shams. The *halif* (ally) of the *sayyid* was similarly in a high position, as exemplified by the alliance of Nawfal and Suwaid. Clansmen, as free members of society, depended for their position on the position of their clan as a whole. They were protected by the clan and they were required to reciprocate by defending it against any adversary. The clan, as a social unit, provided the initial infrastructure for the development of the power and wealth of the clan leader.

The *mawla* was lower in social status than the *sayyid*, his ally, and the clansmen. A *mawla* was often a manumitted slave who was required to remain beholden to his former lord. In fact, a *mawla* was discouraged from seeking the protection of anyone else.[9] The *mawali* in Mecca were of Arab and non-Arab origin. A *mawla* could even be one's kin, indicating that kinsmen could be socially and economically diversified and that social relations that were based on traditional clan or tribal bonds were giving way to relations based on power and wealth. This relationship was retained as another instrument of social control. It was also another means by which merchants could profit. A set of devices was recognized as socially acceptable for changing this relationship. These devices usually required the *mawla* to transfer capital that he earned to his master, thereby concentrating more wealth in the hands of the *sayyids*.[10] When the *mawla* satisfied the terms of agreement, he could move up the social ladder and become a *halif* with little restriction on his social and economic mobility. This is illustrated by the case of 'Imad al-Hadrami. A prisoner of war from Hadramawt, he was sold as a slave in Mecca, where he was able to become a *mawla*. Eventually, he acquired his freedom and lived to become a wealthy carpenter and merchant in Mecca. His descendants were also prominent in later Meccan affairs.[11]

The lowest social class was the slaves, the *qinn*, and their offspring, the *muwalladun*. Slaves could also be of Arab and non-Arab origin. Slaves lost their freedom in various ways, primarily by being captured in war or by being unable to pay their debts.[12] Slaves were either household servants or were employed to generate wealth for their owners. Another set of devices governed the relationship of slaves to their owners, and there were several methods by which slaves could obtain their freedom. Again, transfer of capital from the slave to the owner was the main component of this process.[13] Slave owners had at their disposal socially acceptable methods of freeing their slaves. Hakim ibn Hizam, for example, a wealthy merchant, freed one hundred slaves annually as *sadaqa*, a gesture of goodwill.[14] The status of the slave and that of the *mawla* are indicative of the transformation of the social structure to the point that these members of society were regarded as commodities or as tools for the benefit of merchants.

The changing social structure and the process of differentiation in Mecca was intensified further as tribesmen who were already polarized into rich and poor settled in the city. This process was certainly ongoing in Mecca, for we have seen that the rich came to Mecca either in alliance with rich Meccan merchants or as a result of the *ilaf*. The wealthy came seeking further opportunities to invest excess capital or to hire out their livestock to transport Meccan trade goods. The poor also moved, especially those who lost their freedom as a result of their inability to repay their debts. There is evidence that tribes often forced their poorer members to seek refuge elsewhere, lest they become a drain on the collective livestock of the tribe.[15]

In his observations regarding tribal settlement, Sahlins observes a similar process: "The social arrangements of pastoralists inhibit one's responsibility for others' welfare, and poor families are thus driven by necessity into town before they become a drag on the livestock-capital of everyone potentially concerned." At the same time, he continues, "rich pastoralists are having their own problems. Big herds are difficult to manage, and the owner . . . might be inclined to invest his surplus in other kinds of property."[16] The inward movement of this differentiated population reinforced class divisions in Mecca. The rich, as we have seen, usually identified and sought alliance with their equals. The poor, in addition to their alienation from their own tribe, moved into an environment that was already differentiated according to ownership of capital.

Class division in Mecca resulted from and reinforced the concentration of wealth in the hands of the rich merchants. These merchants began to use their excess capital in another form of banking practice: moneylending. *Riba* (usury) played a significant role in maintaining a diversified social and economic structure. It is difficult to determine when usury became common in Mecca, but since it is bound to the development of merchant capital, it may have started after the introduction of *ilaf* and continued thereafter, especially as commerce grew in volume and in extent. Thus, it could be argued that, with the increased commercial activity and with the reduction of risks involved in such investments, those who had no original capital were encouraged to borrow from those who did, the merchants.

Moneylending thus became another way to increase capital, and many Meccan merchants amassed their wealth through this practice. Merchants who later played a prominent role in Islam, such as ʿUthman ibn ʿAffan, ʿAbd al-Rahman ibn ʿAwf, Khalid ibn al-Walid, and al-ʿAbbas ibn ʿAbd al-Muttalib, were all involved in moneylending and became wealthy as a result.[17] An incident connected to al-ʿAbbas illustrates the effect of *riba* on the social and economic structure. Al-ʿAbbas lent his brother Abu Talib ten thousand dirhams. When Abu Talib was unable to repay the loan as specified, al-ʿAbbas took away the offices and privileges of *siqaya* and *rifada*.[18] Kinship ties, such as those between al-ʿAbbas and Abu Talib, gave way to relations based on capital versus capital, and the stronger usually won, not only in economic terms but also by acquiring a larger share of the ideological symbols, as the passing of *siqaya* and *rifada* to al-ʿAbbas illustrates. This shift also indicates a process whereby merchants shed loyalty to their families in favor of individual accumulation of capital. Abu Talib's loss must have caused a considerable dislocation in his finances, and there came a time when he was not able to afford the upkeep of his children.[19] Many others lost their freedom as they were not able to repay their loans or the exorbitant interest charged on them. Al-ʿAbbas, among others, acquired a huge number of slaves through *riba*.[20] *Riba*, therefore, played a double role in the social and economic structure of Mecca by allowing the concentration of huge amounts of wealth in the hands of a few and by reducing the social status of others. This downward social and economic movement took place concurrently with the erosion of traditional types of social organization.

Social differentiation was not the only feature of a merchant economy. Labor also became diversified and there grew up an infrastructure of craftsmen, laborers, and others in the service sector who supported a caravan economy. Thus, aside from the merchants, who might have wide-ranging or only local markets, there were various types of skilled professionals, some of whom might have been merchants also. Frequently mentioned professions include tailors, carpenters, smiths, arrow makers, veterinarians, and various other shopkeepers.[21] Other professions catered specifically to the caravan economy, such as porters, herders, guides, guards, entertainers, and servants. There are references to those who prepared food and sold it in the streets of Mecca as well as to wage laborers who earned their livelihood daily in the various markets of the city. Finally, there were many who were known to be bankrupt and thus had to depend on the charity of the rich merchants.[22]

It is clear, therefore, that the growth of merchant capital transformed Meccan society on several levels. Some merchants grew wealthier and more politically powerful. Social structure also began to change, and there appeared different social classes and a diversified labor force. More than that, the very basis of the social formation—clan and tribal solidarity—began to give way to social relations based on the ownership of merchant capital.

Factional Conflict and the Rise of the Banu Umayya

Social and economic transformation in Mecca, conditioned by the development of merchant capital, challenged merchants on several lev-

els. On one level, as has been shown, was solidification of a class structure that disrupted clan-based social relations when kinship and clan
ties gave way to relations based on the individual and his ownership
of capital. On another level, because of new alliances or the introduction
of a dependent population, tension and conflict became a constant feature and the balance of power fluctuated. The constant shift in the balance of forces was occasioned by the merchant-clan leaders' competition
for power. In essence, then, the further concentration of merchant capital
in Mecca resulted in the concentration of capital and power within certain of Mecca's clan leaders. Competition between these leaders eventually led to the emergence of a segment represented by clan leaders that
dominated Meccan affairs. It will be argued here that capital accumulation led to the formation of two main factions within the Quraish,
the Ahlaf and al-Mutayyabun. After further accumulation and competition, a third faction formed, al-Fudul. This process allowed the Banu
Umayya to consolidate their position as the leading clan in the city, as we
shall see presently.

When Mecca and the Quraish were not too differentiated, there was
rule by consensus, as all of the clan heads participated in the decision-
making process. However, by all indications, Qusayy was the dominant
figure in Mecca after he defeated the Khuza'a. Before he died, he passed
all of his privileges on to his oldest son 'Abd al-Dar, to the exclusion of
'Abd Manaf and 'Abd al-'Uzza. Although Qusayy's action conforms to
the concept of primogeniture, the sources insist that he singled out his
oldest son because he had not attained the wealth and status of his younger
brothers.[23] It is not clear how long 'Abd al-Dar was able to follow in his
father's footsteps, but some harmony must have existed, for there are no
reported disagreements between the Quraishi clans.

Although Qusayy and his son are represented as the most powerful in
the Quraish, sources imply that the clan heads continued to deliberate
issues of collective interest in Dar al-Nadwa. And even though this choice
of venue betrays a distribution of power in favor of the residents of Dar
al-Nadwa, it did allow for a measure of collective leadership. Therefore,
as long as the balance of power remained unchanged, harmony existed
and the Quraishi clans collectively ruled Mecca.

Whatever the arrangement may have been, it did not prove satisfactory
a little more than half a century later to Qusayy's grandsons Hashim and
'Abd Shams, the Banu 'Abd Manaf. In all likelihood, they began to resent their exclusion from power after they began to accumulate wealth
and influence following the introduction of the *ilaf*, especially since

Hashim and ʿAbd Shams (and their other brothers) were instrumental in developing it.

Sources report that as the numbers and wealth of the Banu ʿAbd Manaf grew, they felt strong enough to challenge the Banu ʿAbd al-Dar (their cousins). This challenge was posed when the Banu ʿAbd Manaf demanded the keys of the sacred building. In effect, they were demanding the office of *wilayat al-Bait,* the highest religious office and a visible symbol of economic and political control. But the Banu ʿAbd al-Dar would not give away such a high office, which led to a disagreement within the Quraish. As a result, they split into two factions: the ʿAbd al-Dar faction, known as al-Ahlaf, and the ʿAbd Manaf faction, known as al-Mutayyabun. The Ahlaf faction was made up of the clans of ʿAbd al-Dar, Makhzum, Sahm, Jumah, and ʿAdiyy. ʿAbd al-Dar was the only clan in this faction that descended directly from Qusayy. The Mutayyabun faction was made up of the Banu ʿAbd Manaf (Hashim and ʿAbd Shams), Zuhra, and Taim. The Banu ʿAbd Manaf were the only descendants of Qusayy.[24] The real struggle, thus, can be isolated further in Qusayy's grandsons, who indeed dominated the two factions. This, however, changed when the Banu Makhzum came to dominate the Ahlaf.

As a result of their disagreement and the loss of their consensus, the two factions faced each other poised for war. War, however, threatened to weaken both, which prompted them to reach a temporary compromise. The Ahlaf agreed to give away some offices to the Mutayyabun, who received the pilgrimage-related institutional practices of *siqaya* and *rifada.* The Ahlaf retained *wilayat al-Bait* and other offices, such as the *liwaʾ,* the standard of war. ʿAbd Shams, it is said, declined the offices in favor of Hashim. This is explained in the sources by the fact that ʿAbd Shams traveled constantly in pursuit of trade.[25]

Thus, the first major split in the Quraish was formalized by the passing of offices. This split affords us a glimpse of the earliest political maneuvering among the heads of the ruling clans of Mecca. It is also instructive to note that this competition took place as the commercial fortunes of the Quraish began to improve after the introduction of the *ilaf.* Furthermore, competition for a larger share of political control was directed at controlling the religious institutions in Mecca. Thus these offices were not merely symbolic but also a source of political and material gains.

The formation of these two factions cannot be understood simply by looking at strict kinship ties, since members of both sides were related. The two factions were actually contending social forces, each backed by an infrastructure of allies, *mawali*, slaves, and other dependents. The two factions were competing for a greater share of the political structure in Mecca. But since this conflict was restricted to the top, between the leading merchant-clan heads, it was an intraclass conflict among owners of merchant capital, a conflict that later concentrated among the clans of Makhzum, Hashim, and 'Abd Shams. Each of these clans, therefore, represented a segment of merchant capital in Mecca.

Intraclan/segment conflict in Mecca is documented through the institutional practice of *munafara*. *Munafara* (from the root $N^aF^aR^a$) was essentially the competition for greater honor and status based on wealth and material strength. It usually started as a dispute between two individuals and then their respective groups became involved. To avoid outright conflict or elimination, the contending groups eventually appointed an independent arbiter. What the sources have left as evidence of *munafara* seems to be nothing more than traces of a legendary past. Nevertheless, even in those traces we can see actual social conflict. By documenting *munafara*, therefore, we could get a closer look at Mecca's internal political dynamic and trace the development of the strongest segment of merchant capital in the city.

'Abd Shams versus the Banu 'Adiyy

An early controversy took place between 'Abd Shams and the Banu 'Adiyy. 'Abd Shams owned a *bukhtiyya* (a rare she-camel). One day he missed it and could not find a trace of it. He offered a reward to anyone who had any information. A man came forward with the information that a certain 'Amir ibn 'Abdallah, from the Banu 'Adiyy, had slaughtered the *bukhtiyya* and that 'Abd Shams could find its skin buried in the man's courtyard. 'Abd Shams mobilized his relatives and supporters and headed for 'Amir's house, where the informant's story was verified. As the action was considered an attack on 'Abd Shams's honor as well as on his property, he took 'Amir hostage, vowing to take all of his wealth and to cut off his arm as punishment. The Banu 'Adiyy interceded and requested that 'Abd Shams only confiscate the man's property and send him into exile. 'Abd Shams accepted this compromise. When 'Amir and his family were about to leave the city, the Banu Sahm intercepted them and allowed them to stay in the Sahmi quarters. It seems that 'Abd Shams did not object to this. An alliance was thus forged between the Banu Sahm and the Banu 'Adiyy that remained in effect until the arrival of Islam.[26]

Umayya Ibn ʿAbd Shams Versus the Banu Zuhra

The leadership of the Banu ʿAbd Shams passed to Umayya ibn ʿAbd Shams, the eponym of the Banu Umayya and later the Umayyads. Umayya became involved in a dispute with the Banu Zuhra as a result of a disagreement about rights-of-way. Umayya passed by the house of Wahb ibn ʿAbd Manaf ibn Zuhra, which seemed to annoy Wahb. After Umayya passed one time too many, Wahb asked him to go another way. Umayya refused and insisted that he would pass wherever he pleased. An altercation ensued in which Umayya was injured. He mobilized his supporters, who began to agitate for Wahb's exile.

Although on the surface this seems to be a trivial dispute, it betrays the existence of latent social conflict. The outcome of these disputes, furthermore, always translated into concrete advantages for the winner. As the Banu Zuhra were less powerful, they could not resist the demands of Umayya's followers, and some of them began to leave later that night. Here again, other parties interceded and the matter was dropped. A compromise similar to that between ʿAbd Shams and the Banu ʿAdiyy may have been reached at this time, for we know that the Banu Zuhra remained in Mecca and that Umayya was able to confiscate some of Wahb's property, namely a house that later came to be known as Dar Safwan ibn Umayya.[27]

Some observations on these two incidents are in order. First, leadership passed from father to son, which concentrated rather than dispersed wealth and power. Second, the clans were differentiated, as some clan members were so poor that they resorted to stealing, like ʿAmir, or so weak that they could be forced to give up some of their property or exiled, like Wahb. It was this differentiation that provided a catalyst for further political competition among the various clans. Third, the Banu Umayya were involved in disputes with clans that were from al-Ahlaf and from al-Mutayyabun, suggesting the presence of competing interests within each of the two larger coalitions of the Quraish. Fourth, each time the Banu Umayya won a dispute, they increased their influence by gaining morally and materially over their adversaries. Finally, just as alliance formation led to social conflict, social conflict led to the formation of alliances, as that between the Banu Sahm and the B. ʿAdiyy.

Harb ibn Umayya versus the Banu ʿAbd al-Muttalib

The Banu Umayya continued to increase their power at the expense of other clans. A dispute between Harb ibn Umayya ibn ʿAbd Shams and

ʿAbd al-Muttalib, leader of the Banu Hashim, is very instructive, since it is directly related to commercial competition. Harb, it is said, instigated the murder of Udhaina, a Jewish merchant from Najran. Udhaina had been in the *jiwar* of ʿAbd al-Muttalib, which allowed him to trade in the region of Tihama. As part of his responsibility in the *jiwar* (neighborly protection), ʿAbd al-Muttalib had to find the perpetrator of the crime. When he learned that Harb was responsible for Udhaina's death, the two appointed a *hakam* from the Banu ʿAdiyy to judge between them. The judge ruled in favor of ʿAbd al-Muttalib, a decision that angered Harb. He mobilized his supporters against the judge, and the Banu ʿAdiyy, supported by their allies, the Banu Sahm, mobilized to protect their clansman. Meanwhile, the Banu Hashim and the Banu Zuhra supported ʿAbd al-Muttalib, but did not join forces with the Banu ʿAdiyy. Military conflict was averted, but it became clear that a realignment of forces within the Mutayyabun faction was due. The *munadama* (close friendship, drinking companionship) between Harb and ʿAbd al-Muttalib was lost forever.[28] The Banu Umayya and the Banu Nawfal came closer together on one side as the Banu Hashim, the Banu Zuhra, and the Banu Taim came closer together on the other. From then on, the Banu Umayya and the Banu Nawfal gradually emancipated themselves from their alliance with the Banu Hashim.

Nawfal ibn ʿAbd Manaf versus the Banu ʿAbd al-Muttalib

The two-way division in the Mutayyabun faction was particularly evident in the *munafara* between ʿAbd al-Muttalib and Nawfal when social conflict, once again, led to the formation of alliances. ʿAbd al-Muttalib inherited some land in Mecca known as al-Arkah. At a certain point, Nawfal ibn ʿAbd Manaf, who was supported by the Banu Umayya, claimed the land as his and granted it to one of his sons. ʿAbd al-Muttalib, not being able to confront Nawfal on his own, asked his relatives for support, but "no one of high stature" offered him any. In search of aid, ʿAbd al-Muttalib reportedly went as far as Medina (Yathrib) and asked the Banu al-Najjar for help, although some sources cast doubt on this connection.[29] He was forced to form an alliance with the opposition group in Mecca, the Khuzaʿa, who until then had been kept from the limelight in Mecca's politics. Seeing the dilemma in which ʿAbd al-Muttalib found himself, a leading group of Khuzaʿi men held a council and declared that "time had healed what had been injured between us [Khuzaʿa and Quraish]."[30] They decided to propose an alliance with ʿAbd al-Muttalib to support him in his dispute. A delegation from the Khuzaʿa approached him with the offer and he promptly agreed. After this initial acceptance, a delegation from each side met in Dar al-Nadwa and hammered out their agreement, which was sealed by marriage. No one from the Banu Umayya or the Banu Nawfal attended this meeting or became part of the alliance, which stood independently from the Mutayyabun faction.[31]

Thus, the influence of the Banu Umayya increased further at the expense of the Banu Hashim, since, for the first time, they were forced to seek an alliance outside of the Quraish against members of their own tribe. The Banu Hashim were slowly edged out of the circle of the ruling elites, as their alliance with an outside party implies. It is also worth noting the existence of several layers of clan and factional alliances, as indicated by the alliance of ʿAbd al-Muttalib with the Banu Khuzaʿa while still a member of the Mutayyabun.

This alliance, however, was sorely needed by ʿAbd al-Muttalib, since he had yet to confront claimants to other property. Like many other Meccan merchants, ʿAbd al-Muttalib owned land in neighboring Taʾif, called dhu al-Haram. Khandaq (or Jundab) ibn al-Harith from the Banu Thaqif claimed the land and began to develop it. The ensuing dispute between ʿAbd al-Muttalib and the man from Taʾif was fought without the intervention of the B. Umayya. Clearly then, it was not in the interest of the B. Umayya to offer any assistance to ʿAbd al-Muttalib, although ostensibly he belonged to the same faction.[32] Again, this offers us an indication of the extent of the competition between merchant/clan heads, even though they could be related by kinship or belong to the same faction. Their material interests seemed to dominate their relations. In this environment, the Banu Hashim lost considerable leverage in Meccan economic and political affairs by allowing the Banu Umayya to consolidate a stronger position in the Mutayyabun faction as well as in the city.

The Banu Umayya versus the Banu Makhzum

Emerging as the strongest segment in the Mutayyabun, the Banu Umayya began to confront the leader of the Ahlaf, now the Banu Makhzum. This competition was more cautious and took shape over a long period. An early source of disagreement between the two clans was the unfriendly relationship between the Quraish and the exiled Banu Laith. Three years after the Quraish had exiled them, bloody fighting between the two tribes broke out again. Al-ʿAs ibn Waʾil and Hisham ibn al-Mughira, from the Makhzum, gathered supporters and appealed to Saʿid ibn al-ᶜAs, also known as Abu Uhaiha, to lend his support and that of the Banu Umayya against the Banu Laith. Abu Uhaiha refused on the grounds that he was maternally related to the Banu Laith. He also harbored a member of the B. Laith, ᶜAmr ibn ᶜAbd al-ᶜUzza, a fugitive who was sought by al-ᶜAs and Hisham.

With no support from the B. Umayya, the Makhzumi force headed toward the B. Laith. When they reached a place called al-Mushallal, fierce fighting broke out, al-ᶜAs reportedly was killed, and the Meccan force was routed. This defeat was aggravated when the Laithi ᶜAmr, who was whisked out of Mecca when his whereabouts became known, returned to kill other Quraishis near the city. Fighting would have resumed had it not been for Abu Uhaiha, who finally managed to bring the two camps to agreement.[33]

The role played by Abu Uhaiha and his clan, the Banu Umayya, was significant, both when he withheld his support from the Banu Makhzum and for his efforts to bring peace. On the one hand, the Banu Umayya were not interested in helping a potentially strong adversary such as the B. Makhzum. Any loss in the latter's power and prestige was a gain for the Banu Umayya, and it must have been calculated as such when the Banu Makhzum were left to fend for themselves, as long as the fight did not involve any others from the Quraish. But when the war came closer to Mecca and when ᶜAmr killed other Quraishis—and thus threatened others besides the Banu Makhzum—Abu Uhaiha stepped in and gained further prestige by bringing peace, not only to the combatants but also to Mecca.

Consolidation of the Position of the Banu Umayya

As social conflict and clan competition did not abate, the Banu Umayya utilized their role as peacemakers to cultivate a stronger position with regard to the affairs of Mecca, this time in relation to the strongest segments in the city, namely the Banu Makhzum and the Banu Hashim. This can be seen in the confrontation of Yawm al-Ghazal in Mecca proper. We are told that the house of Miqyas ibn ᶜAbd Qais, of the Banu Sahm, was a *hanut* (a tavern) that was a meeting place for young men to "drink and spend money." One night after a caravan had arrived from Syria laden with wine, many Meccans were at the *hanut*, including the future Abu Lahab. Two men from the Khuzaᶜa were employed as servants and they poured the customers wine while two female entertainers sang for the audience. Abu Lahab and his friends became intoxicated as the night went on and their funds gradually disappeared. It was then that Abu Lahab suggested to his company that to replenish their funds they should try to steal a precious statue of a gazelle from the Kaʿba. They liked the idea and when no one was about, they went to the Kaʿba and managed to steal the statue. It was taken to the home of the Khuzaʿis, where they extracted the embedded jewels and gold from it and used the money for more drinks.[34]

It was several days before the absence of the statue was noticed. It had been offered to the Kaʿba by ʿAbd al-Muttalib and thus it was the responsibility of the Banu Hashim to find the thief. But it was another man, ʿAbdallah ibn Judʿan, who immediately recognized the potential ill-effects of such a breach of the *haram*. Disrespect of the *haram*, he argued, would bring catastrophe to the Meccans. He spoke so vehemently against the theft that he had to be restrained from further mention of it and had to be reminded that it was the responsibility of the Banu Hashim to carry out the inquiry. Several weeks later the details of the theft became known. Several disagreements led to military confrontation. At the beginning, it seems that the Banu Umayya extended some support to the Ahlaf faction, which strengthened them against the Banu Hashim. After a while, such leaders of the Banu Umayya as Abu Sufyan, Abu Uhaiha, and ʿUtba ibn Abi Rabiʿa held a council and decided to withdraw their support from the Ahlaf. This decision, coming at a critical moment, changed the course of events, and the case of the Ahlaf faction began to weaken. The balance of power changed in favor of the Banu Hashim, but when an equilibrium was achieved in the process, the Banu Umayya forced the warring factions to agree to end the conflict.[35] Thus, the Banu Umayya were strong enough to play one faction against another and impose on both factions conditions favorable to the Banu Umayya; they were able to attain the position of the dominant segment, which could check such disruptive tendencies as internal conflict and would advance its own interests, the interests of the strongest segment of merchant capital in Mecca.

This hegemonic role was translated into action immediately in the Fijar War against Hira and its allies. When either the Banu Hashim or the Banu Makhzum (or any other tribe in Mecca) mobilized the Quraish, they in fact mobilized only their own forces. The Banu Umayya, on the other hand, mobilized the whole of Mecca and even its allies. Thus, the interest of the Banu Umayya became synonymous with the interests of the whole city, an indication of the extent of their influence and position within the competing Meccan political coalitions.

The connection between al-Barrad, who triggered the Fijar War, and the leader of the Banu Umayya has already been noted. It suggests that Harb had foreknowledge of al-Barrad's plans. It is notable that al-Barrad's immediate concern after attacking the caravan was to inform his ally and other influential Meccan merchants. Had Harb chosen not to confront Hira, he would have simply disavowed his alliance with al-Barrad, leaving him to his own devices. But without hesitation or discord, Harb and other Meccan merchants immediately began to prepare for the impending battle. Harb was joined by other members of the Banu Umayya, such as Kariz ibn Rabiʿa, ʿUtba ibn Rabiʿa, and Abu Sufyan, all of whom fought valiantly in the battle (they became known as *al-ʿAnabis*, the lions).[36] Harb supplied weapons and money to a number of fighters who helped the Quraish. He was even mentioned as the leader of the center of the army. It was the Umayyad ʿUtba ibn Rabiʿa who finally was able to offer a compromise to end the fighting. Harb guaranteed the truce and even gave his son Abu Sufyan as a hostage in assurance of his compliance with the final decision. It is also mentioned that Harb might have paid all of the blood money that was agreed to between the warring parties. In short, the war that was started by an ally of Harb ibn Umayya resulted in a great advantage for the Meccans and allowed many members of the Banu Umayya to play a significant role in the victory of Mecca, only to add to their already high prestige.

The preponderant role played by the members of the Banu Umayya suggests that the victory was really theirs. Indeed, their position in Mecca had become so strong that they stood alone (with the Banu Nawfal in the shadow) as an independent faction retaining Hilf al-Mutayyabun. Thus, victory in the Fijar War caused further alignment of forces within Mecca, to the advantage of the B. Umayya. The remnant clans—Hilf al-Mutayyabun, Hashim, Zuhra, and Taim—were thus cast out and were forced to form their own faction, that of Hilf al-Fudul.

This *hilf* was formed right after the conclusion of the Fijar War, whether immediately or three months later is unclear.[37] In either case, the attitude of the Meccans toward the Yemeni merchants is given as the impetus for its formation. As indicated earlier, some Meccans began to cut the Yemeni merchants out of the *haram* trade by carrying out questionable business transactions. But the clans of Hashim and its followers did not want injustice against the Yemenis to go unanswered, so they called for the formation of the Hilf al-Fudul. With this noble aim as the driving force behind its formation, this *hilf* was called the "league of the virtuous."[38]

But, as we have seen, the power of the clans that formed the Hilf al-Fudul was slowly diminishing. In fact, aside from the Banu Hashim, neither of the other two clans ever exercised any considerable leverage in Meccan affairs. Thus, while they may have harbored good intentions, the enforcement of their goals could be easily challenged by more powerful clans such as the Banu Umayya and the Banu Makhzum. Consequently, it is necessary to attempt a different understanding of the Hilf al-Fudul.

It is the etymology of the *hilf* that may have led to the confusion. One meaning of the word *al-fudul* (pl. of *al-fadl*) is indeed the virtuous; thus it could be the *hilf* of those who are virtuous, especially since Muhammad's clan was the one that asked that it be formed and was the principal party in it. The same word can also mean "last, superfluous, or remnant," that which has no primary significance. Given the balance of power in Mecca, this is how the word ought to be understood, especially since this variant is supported by reports such as that of Ibn Habib al-Baghdadi, who says that Hilf al-Fudul "was a *hilf* that came out [*kharaja*] of Hilf al-Mutayyabun and the Ahlaf and it was *fadl^{an} bainahuma ʿalaihima* [an addition, a redundancy] between them and better than them." [39] As we shall see later, the position of the Banu Hashim deteriorated to such an extent that they were boycotted by the other clans of the Quraish.

Having eliminated the Banu Hashim from power politics, the B. Umayya concentrated on the Banu Makhzum. Abu Sufyan and Abu Jahl, leaders of the Banu Umayya and the Banu Makhzum, respectively, were competing for leadership in Mecca while Muhammad was preaching his new religion. It was this competition that allowed Muhammad to challenge Meccan leaders for as long as he did before he finally moved to Medina, in A.D. 622 (A.H. I). Two years later, the Muslims routed the Meccans and handed them their worst defeat. Disaster befell most of the Meccan clans, but especially the Banu Makhzum, who lost Abu Jahl in the battle. Aggravating this loss, a member of the Banu Makhzum attacked and killed Abu Uzaihir, leader of the Daws and an ally of Abu Sufyan. Yazid ibn Abi Sufyan, in the absence of his father, who was attending to business in the market of Dhu al-Majaz, mobilized the Banu Umayya and their supporters and prepared to respond to the attack on his father's honor. Receiving this news, Abu Sufyan set out hurriedly for Mecca to find an extremely tense situation with a military confrontation about to begin. He took the *liwaʾ*, which must have passed to the Banu Umayya after the Fijar War, from Yazid and managed to defuse the volatile situation a little by dispersing the crowd. Abu Sufyan then called on other influential members of his clan to gather and discuss a course of action. In the meeting, he chose to handle the situation by diplomatic means, and his suggestions seemed to have carried the day. He sent a delegation from the Banu Umayya to Abu Uzaihir's family with two hundred camels as blood money (twice the normal amount) to cover Abu Sufyan's responsibility in his alliance with Abu Uzaihir.[40] This gesture was understood to mean that the Daws were left to settle their accounts with the Banu Makhzum in the manner of their choosing. Thereafter, the Daws attacked the caravans of the Banu Makhzum on several occasions and several men were killed in retaliation for Abu Uzaihir's death. The Banu Makhzum were finally obliged to pay an annual sum of money (*itawa, kharj*) to the Daws.[41] Thus, with Abu Jahl dead and with their economic interests threatened by the Daws, the Banu Makhzum lost their significant power in Meccan politics. This left the field wide open for Abu Sufyan to consolidate his position as the unchallenged leader of Mecca and for his clan to become the most powerful clan among the Quraish. Indeed, it was Abu Sufyan who led the Meccans in their subsequent battles against the Muslims and it was he who negotiated with Muhammad the final surrender of Mecca after eight years of hostilities.

In concluding this chapter, it should be noted that the development of merchant capital not only affected Mecca's external relations, but also conditioned the internal social and political structure. The social structure was characterized by the rise of relations based on the ownership of merchant capital. These relations gradually replaced clan-based relations and eventually produced a stratified social structure. At the top were the merchant-clan leaders, the *sayyids*. This rank was strengthened by other *sayyids* who allied with Meccan clan leaders. There were also the free clansmen, the *mawalis,* and the slaves. This stratification was paralleled by a specialization of commodity labor, with the service sector as a dominant character. This service sector catered to a merchant/caravan economy. A stratified social structure was facilitated by the settlement of a large dependent population as well as by a population already diversified. The practice of *riba* also helped concentrate wealth in the hands of the few and caused further disruption of the clan-based social structure.

On the political level, the development of merchant capital conditioned the emergence of singular leadership, rather than collective leadership, as had been the case previously. As merchant capital concentrated in Mecca, competition between merchant-clan leaders took place, allowing for the rise of competing political factions. Three dominant clans emerged, each of which represented a segment of merchant capital in Mecca. By defending their interests, they were protecting merchant capital. The Banu Umayya, as documented through *munafara*, gradually gained precedence over the other two and came to represent the strongest segment of merchant capital. The leader of this segment, Abu Sufyan, emerged as the dominant figure in Mecca's politics.

Through this development, we can appreciate the process by which the merchants consolidated their political power. They were beginning to exercise political hegemony, at least in their immediate surroundings, just at the time when Muhammad began his career as a prophet. However, even though Abu Sufyan was unquestioned leader, these merchants did not resolve the competition for political and economic power, the agitation for a larger share of the ideological symbols, and the nearly feverish pitch of social conflict, a situation that created the need for and facilitated the rise of a social reformer.

4. Merchant Capital and the Rise of Islam

Mecca's economic progress took it beyond what its institutional structure could support. The emergence of a society based on the ownership of capital gradually weakened tribal bonds. Mecca's tribally supported superstructure was no longer viable in the new social environment. The development of merchant capital accelerated this tendency, and the social, political, and economic structure was transformed.

This disequilibrium manifested itself in continuous social conflict, which posed several threats to society, especially to merchant-clan leaders, who had the most to lose from social violence or from a total breakdown of the social order. It is in this milieu that Muhammad appeared as a man singularly inspired, a prophet who articulated the problems of his society and in the process founded a new religion with an institutional framework relevant to the solution of the social, political, and economic problems that impeded the progress of Mecca's merchants. Embodying Muhammad's articulation of the solutions to these problems, Islam became a new ideological and institutional superstructure relevant to the immediate needs of society. It transformed society to the point, in fact, that it was considered "miraculous."

Analyzing Muhammad's contributions within the context of the mercantile society in which he lived should not be construed as a denial of the religious significance of his message. Undoubtedly, most of Muhammad's followers were spiritually moved by his teachings, and as a prophet who communicated the divine command, he was able to capture the imagination of his contemporaries. I have shown that there was always an organic link between religious rituals and social, economic, and political developments; however, no historian of early Islam, whether a believer or a nonbeliever, can deny that Islam grew in a mercantile society. And I have shown that this society faced many problems that threatened its well-being and that these problems were not all of a religious character. Accordingly, solutions, although contained within a religious framework, should be addressed within the perspective of historical continuity. Therefore, the institutional structure provided by Islam will be discussed in the light of the Meccans' experimentation with institution building, just as the *ilaf, hums,* alliances, and other practices have been discussed. Although the mercantile antecedents of Islam are recognized by many, the relevance of Islam to the demands of merchants and their capital has not been sufficiently detailed before.

The historical continuity and the human origin of Islam demanded by methodological consistency might be distasteful to those who believe that Islam was given as an immutable divine message. Yet, to analyze the rise of Islam and the content of Muhammad's message within a historical framework is in no sense a denial of the spiritual content and the validity of that message. Although it is clear that there are many pronouncements in the Qur'an that are relevant to all ages, it is equally true that many were revealed in the context of a specific society in specific circumstances, as the early Muslims well recognized (see, for example, the genre of *Asbab al-Nuzul,* "causes of revelations").

Since most of the rituals found in Islam, such as pilgrimage, alms giving, and prayer, were practiced by many generations before Muhammad, one could say that he merely removed those rituals from their pagan framework and placed them in a different one by giving them divine sanction. There is historical continuity here, as Muhammad built on what his predecessors had constructed. Divine sanction reinvigorated those institutions and caused them to thrive again. What becomes important for this discussion, therefore, is the process of institution building continued by Muhammad and what he added to the accomplishments of previous generations. This chapter, therefore, will analyze the institutional environment in Mecca on the eve of Islam to clarify the significance of those institutions and ideas that Muhammad introduced to or adapted within the body of Islam. The discussion is divided into three parts: (1) how and why Mecca's institutional structure declined; (2) Muhammad's career in Mecca and in Medina; and (3) his triumph over Mecca and Arabia. Islam will be discussed, once again, not as a religion with a set of rituals and beliefs (many studies of this kind are available), but mainly from the perspective of the relevance of its ideological and institutional superstructure to the social, political, and economic demands that were conditioned by the development of merchant capital and that Meccan merchants confronted at the turn of the seventh century.

The Institutional Environment of Islam

Mecca's merchants and their institutions were constantly challenged by the conditions obtaining from the concentration of merchant capital. The most obvious challenge was to their social structure. The population of Mecca ceased to be a homogeneous society, if it ever was. By the time of Qusayy there were several layers of tribes that had lost their predominance and blended into the social fabric of Mecca. Clan solidarity, as the institutional foundation of the social structure, was strong enough to allow the Quraish to become the dominant tribe, but this solidarity gradually dissipated because of the demands of merchants and their capital. The Quraish eventually split into several competing factions. Their collective and cooperative leadership gave way to competition between clan heads and to the concentration of political and economic power in a dominant segment represented by a single clan leader. In addition, clan solidarity was rendered much weaker by the constant inflow of settlers who were already socially and economically differentiated. Those who were poor, or who had been forced out of their own tribe, came without any clan protection. In Mecca, they were known as *al-mustad‘afun*. They were socially weak, since they had no clan backing and no one to protect them from the ill-treatment that they might encounter. Most often, they had the status of a slave or at best a *mawla*. It was this sector among Muhammad's followers that suffered most from persecution by some clan leaders.

The situation, therefore, was not conducive to clan solidarity under the authority of a clan head. As a basis of social organization and social relations, this bond began consistently to give way to relations based on the individual and his possession of wealth and power. For example, the *mustad‘afun* did not pay allegiance on the basis of clan ties either to the clan leader or to the clan as a whole, neither that which cast them out in the first place or that which they were forced to adopt. Rather, their allegiance was based on relations of power that were conditioned by the ownership of wealth. As a socially marginalized population, they were not reintegrated into a clan structure, even if their status improved. With the continued development of merchant capital and the consistent movement of people into Mecca, this marginalized population increased and

visibly limited the authority of the merchant-clan leader, since his juris-
diction did not extend to this population, unless he developed extraclan
justifications.

This was not the only factor that contributed to the decline of clan
solidarity and the authority of the clan leader. Stratification within the
clan itself contributed. *Sadaqa* was initially developed to distribute wealth
within the clan. But this distribution was never intended to make the
whole clan equally wealthy. Stratification within the clan grew in Mecca
as wealth concentrated in the hands of a few merchant-clan leaders.

When confronted with the contradictory demands of merchant capital
and clan ties, where the one demanded concentration and the other, distribution, at least in the form of *sadaqa,* merchants, it seems, chose the
practice of monopoly to protect their individual interests. Given a choice,
they opted for more accumulation at the expense of family ties and social
harmony. There is no better evidence for this than the practice of *ihtikar,*
the monopoly of foodstuffs, especially during times of famine.[1] *Sadaqa*
itself, as a nonproductive expenditure, could strap the merchant's finances
if the dependent part of his clan continued to grow.

The breakdown of clan solidarity can be illustrated by two incidents
related to Muhammad's struggle against the Meccans. The first incident
is the social and economic boycott of his clan, instituted in A.D. 618. By
then, he had been preaching publicly for several years and had been able
to gather a modest following of rich as well as poor individuals from several clans. Mecca's clan leaders failed in their repeated attempts to recon-
cile Muhammad to the established order. They enticed him with wealth
and status but he insisted that they recognize his prophethood. Fearing
the loss of power and authority implicit in accepting him, they rejected
his prophethood, and no reconciliation was achieved. Some leaders even
tortured their *mustad'afun* who accepted Islam.

Muhammad, however, continued to preach and to gain new followers.
In response, his opponents instituted a boycott of the clan of B. Hashim,
Muhammad's clan. Several clan leaders, led by Abu Jahl, decided in a
meeting that they "should not seek them [members of the clan of Banu
Hashim] in marriage or marry them, sell them anything or buy anything
from them." The document containing the agreement was entrusted to
the inner sanctuary of the Ka'ba, and Muhammad's clan was forced to
endure the hardship of isolation in their *shi'b* (quarters).[2]

This measure failed to stop the spread of Islam, since not all of the
Muslims were from the Banu Hashim and thus were not affected by the
boycott. In fact, not all of the Banu Hashim were Muslims. Indeed, Abu

Lahab, Muhammad's uncle, joined the boycott and went on to become a most vehement opponent of his nephew. The boycott was doomed because it was a clan-based response to a nonclan-based social movement. It was lifted after the instigators failed to enforce it.[3]

The deterioration of the clan leader's traditional responsibility to his clansmen is evidenced by the actions of Abu Lahab, as the second incident illustrates. When the boycott was instituted, Abu Lahab was not the leader of the Banu Hashim, so his action in joining the boycott was motivated by personal interests. Soon, however, he became the head of the Banu Hashim, after the death of Abu Talib. Unlike the latter, who had continued to fulfill his clan responsibility even though he did not join Islam, Abu Lahab disregarded his traditional role and did not offer "protection" to Muhammad. Having no protection from the head of his clan, Muhammad had to leave Mecca and then reenter it under the *jiwar* of al-Mut'im ibn 'Adiyy of the Banu Nawfal.[4]

As a social unit and an institution, the clan, therefore, showed signs of strain, as did other institutions that regulated social and economic relations. The *haram*, the source of Mecca's wealth, seemed to have become less enforceable, as evidenced by the many incidents that directly violated the spirit of, especially, justice and commerce. 'Abdallah ibn Jud'an recognized the danger of this trend when he declared that, if blasphemous acts continued, catastrophe would befall his fellow Meccans. This does not mean that the *haram* lost its effectiveness in drawing in merchant-pilgrims, most especially during the *mawsim* (the pilgrimage season), but that "blasphemous" acts would erode the sanctity of the *haram*, and the merchants would lose their source of power.

The *haram* was challenged in other ways, even by Muhammad. First, there were the Muhillun, who continued to ignore the injunctions of the *haram*, or at least of Mecca's *haram*, and yet they were not incorporated into Mecca's framework as other tribes had been. Muhammad challenged Mecca's *haram* (not without controversy) two years after he moved to Medina. He dispatched a raiding party to intercept a Meccan caravan at Nakhla, between Ta'if and Mecca and the abode of the goddess al-'Uzza. The raid, during which blood was shed, took place during a sacred month and in a sacred area, and the Muslims were successful in capturing the caravan. The Quraish were gravely concerned about this apparent violation, as were the Muslims in Medina. As will be shown below, it was not until a Qur'anic verse (2:217) justified the attack that it became clear that Mecca's institutions could not withstand those institutions for which Muhammad preached.

As for the *ilaf,* it had been nearly a century since its introduction. It was certainly beneficial in expanding the contacts of Meccan merchants and in allowing them to build a network of international markets. But it was still tribally based, and not all of the tribes were under Mecca's influence. Undoubtedly, however, Mecca's commercial enterprises continued to flourish and capital continued to accumulate, especially after the Fijar War. Mecca's victory resulted in the realignment of internal forces and affected external relations. But there was no institution forthcoming to accommodate these changes, such as, for example, the institution of *hums,* which had been introduced after Abraha's debacle. The *ilaf* represented the interests of a different period, one considerably less complex than the turn of the seventh century A.D.

The same could be said of the practice of alliance formation, which had an even more serious shortcoming. *Hilf*s could be formed between tribes, clans, or individuals. Even though some boundaries were removed by forming alliances, not all were minimized; rather, new ones were created. In view of the far-reaching extent of Mecca's involvement with the rest of Arabia, *hilf* formation turned out to be an agonizingly slow way to advance the interests of the Meccans, especially their commercial interests.

Institutions related to the distribution of wealth were not spared, especially as the gap between the rich and the poor grew wider. The strain was especially acute regarding the food supply. Mecca had always been a food importer in spite of its heavy investment in land following the successful claim on Wadi Wajj. The problem of providing food continued after the acquisition of more land in Ta'if. The merchant-clan leader was obliged to give up part of his wealth to his poorer clansmen in the form of *sadaqa* (sanctioned by kinship ties). *Rifada,* on the other hand, was initially meant to provide food for the pilgrims. Thus, these food-distribution practices were either seasonal and could not provide for the needy who were in Mecca year round or kinship-based, which socially limited distribution. Merchants could not ignore the needs of the poor, as the imbalance in food distribution could result in social violence, as in the case of the Banu Laith. The merchant-clan leader was, therefore, faced by the contradictory demands of his capital and those of his clan inherent in the monopoly. At any rate, *sadaqa* and *rifada* had been developed or adapted when Mecca was less heterogeneous, less diversified, and had a smaller population. As components of a system to distribute wealth and to placate social violence, *sadaqa, rifada,* and *siqaya* were no longer viable in the highly differentiated structure of Mecca at the turn of the seventh century.

Thus, the situation in Mecca on the eve of Islam was characterized by a general decline of its tribally based institutional structure. This decline affected its social, economic, religious, and political life. Watt claims that the decline of the "muruwwa ideals," that is, tribal ideology, accounts for the rise of Islam.⁵ But this decline, as we have seen, was the symptom of a more significant transformation: the change in the nature and organization of society. This transformation required new ideals. Therefore, on the eve of Islam, Mecca's was a ripe environment in which change not only was required, but was eagerly sought by many members of society. These became the core of a new movement led by a prophet.

Muhammad in Mecca

Muhammad was born at a crucial period in Mecca's history. His birth is usually placed in the Islamic tradition in the Year of the Elephant. Abraha's unsuccessful attack, we have seen, was recorded on the inscription [Ry 506]. Of late, Western scholars have not been able to agree on the precise date of Abraha's expedition, leading some to wonder about even the birth date of Muhammad. But the placing of Muhammad's birth in the Year of the Elephant in the Islamic sources was not meant to locate Muhammad in a precise historical moment; rather, it was intended to tie two auspicious events together, two momentous events that changed the history of Mecca and the Quraish. More important, the two events were generated by one source, Allah, who in his divine grace delivered the Meccans from death at the hands of Abraha and who brought Muhammad to life to communicate His wish that the Quraish be saved. Qurʾanic commentaries on Sura 105, in fact, say that Muhammad was born two years after Abraha's defeat. Muhammad's birth, then, should be viewed within Mecca's changed circumstances to appreciate the conditions of his early socialization.

Muhammad was born to ʿAbdallah and Amina from the clans of Hashim and Zuhra, respectively. He grew up during a most critical period of Meccan history, a period when merchants were beginning to assert their authority over the surrounding areas. The wealth and power of the Banu Umayya and of Mecca as a whole grew. The Banu Hashim gradually lost some of the power they had earlier. Nevertheless, they were, as we have seen, an important segment of the ruling merchants. At the turn of the century, aside from Abu Lahab, al-ʿAbbas, another of Muhammad's uncles, seemed also to be a successful merchant. ʿAbdallah, in contrast, was poor. He died away from home before he could see his firstborn. Amina died when Muhammad was six years old. An orphan, Muhammad passed first to the care of his grandfather and then, when he was eight, to his uncle Abu Talib.[6]

At all levels, Muhammad's environment was permeated by the development of merchant capital. Until he was twenty-five, he did not own enough capital to invest in commerce and was thus in the employ of other merchants. One of those was Khadija, who was impressed by Muhammad's character and qualifications. She later proposed that they marry and he accepted. For the next fifteen years, Muhammad's material condition vastly improved, but he was still dissatisfied with conditions in Mecca. Freed from the responsibility of eking out a living, he took to the practice of *tahannuf* (ritual seclusion for prayer and contemplation) in Ghar Hira', a cave near Mecca.[7]

Muhammad started his career as a prophet at age forty. Suras of the Qur'an are full of his displeasure at the state of affairs in Mecca. Meccans were asked to moderate their social relations, especially those with the poor, the orphans, the widows, and all those who were weak and in need of aid. Wealth might have been the "pleasure of this world," but wealth based on the deprivation of a sizable sector of the society would be meaningless once the individual was called to account before God. Such deprivation was not economically sound, as has been pointed out. The widening gap between the rich and the poor not only created social tension, but required merchants to give up more of their wealth. They were asked to make their wealth more mobile by distributing it, not by accumulating excessively. Of Abu Lahab, Sura 111 says, "His wealth will be of no use to him and will [earn him] no profit [on the Day of Judgment]." Sura 102 notes, "Accumulation prepossessed you, until you reached the graveyards." Although at this time Muhammad did not specify the means of distribution, other than *sadaqa,* increasingly referred to as *zakat,* it is significant that he based the requirement on the individual's accountability before God, thus placing the necessity for distribution in the realm of religious responsibility as distinguished from that of traditional tribal responsibility.

Monotheism and Prophetic Authority

After a brief period during which Muhammad preached privately, he began publicly to attack the existing beliefs and practices of his fellow Meccans. In the face of their opposition, he began to elaborate the religious content of his early message. The most important question was that of authority. Clan leaders had built their authority on tribal traditions and on the power they nurtured as their capital strengthened. The strength of their capital had allowed them to mobilize more supporters to defend their interests. The development of their capital had diversified their clans, however, making their traditional moral authority weak and at times ineffectual. Moreover, the emergence of a single leader in Mecca was the outcome of a political process outside the bounds of tribal tradition.

This process of authority building was connected to competing economic interests. Simply put, tribal and clan authority were neither constant nor consistent. In their place, Muhammad introduced the authority of a supreme god, Allah. Allah created the universe and everything in it. He orders the universe and is responsible for life, death, and regeneration. All wealth belongs to Allah and He is bountiful toward His subjects. Allah is omnipotent, ever-present, and everlasting. He not only enjoins the act of distribution but also participates in it.

The Meccans were familiar with Allah, but they had developed a set of lesser gods to intercede with Him. These deities became important for the increased prestige of Mecca and the added wealth, power, and influence of the merchant-clan leaders. The authority of Allah, as introduced by Muhammad, was stronger and more enduring than that of the Meccan deities, all of which were immediately reduced to useless idols.

Rejection of these idols not only entailed the rejection of their divine attributes but also the rejection of the kind of authority that was developed around them in Mecca. Muhammad's authority as the messenger of the Divine Will would by far exceed that of any clan or tribal leader who based his authority on these lesser deities. Thus, not only the idols, but also the Meccans who benefited from them would lose influence. The Qur'an says that once a community has its prophet, that community will be rightly guided and will not be wronged. Most of the conflict between Muhammad and his Meccan opponents revolved around this point; they were unwilling to give up their authority to Muhammad.

In the context of the declining institutions in Mecca, Muhammad, therefore, adapted, introduced, and advocated the authority of a monotheistic God. Sura 112 says, "Proclaim, God is One. God is everlasting. He begets not, nor is He begotten. And there is no one who equals Him." This form of authority is a higher, more enduring and more inclusive form than that which is based on pagan and tribal traditions. Divine authority, communicated through the Qur'an, was to replace the existing form of authority, which was ephemeral, haphazard, and in a constant state of tension.

The relevance of religious beliefs and practices to economic and social development is of course evident in the case of Mecca. The more sacred the sacred center became, the wider Mecca's contacts became. And the more pilgrims and merchants who came to Mecca, the greater the exchange. But Mecca was not the only sacred center in Arabia.[8] The presence of other sacred centers might in itself have encouraged the development of commerce in those areas. It would also have encouraged the rise of competing centers. For the Meccans, the only way to solve this problem was by adopting as many deities as they deemed economically and politically feasible. But this led to the Meccans' acceptance of those deities as co-equal with their own. Thus, rather than elevating Meccan deities to a position of political dominance, which would elevate Mecca's position, this process helped only a little in the advancement of the political hegemony of Mecca's merchants.

To break this cycle, a more inclusive and universal god was sought. Allah, as a monotheistic Supreme Being was God of all creation. The worship of one god would lead to the formation of a single religious tradition. It would integrate more of society into a single unit in which other bonds—tribal, regional, or ethnic—would become less relevant. Hodgson characterizes this as populism.[9] In essence, a greater market was also created, to the benefit of the merchants. The relevance of monotheism to Mecca's merchants is best expressed by Hodgson's statement that "populism was especially appropriate to merchants when they were not the highest class."[10] Merchants were aspiring to consolidate their political leadership in Mecca and to expand it beyond their city as well, but they did not possess the institutional means to do so.

A significant aspect of the worship of one god is the contractual relationship between individuals and their Lord. This relationship encourages interpersonal justice and is expressed by the doctrine of the Day of Judgment, when the individual will be rewarded or punished according to his or her deeds.[11] An act that was looked on with great favor by the Qur'an was distribution of accumulated wealth (zakat), which "purified the soul." Salvation or damnation was then determined individually, not by the collectivity of the clan or the tribe. The emphasis on the individual inherent in this concept is recognized by Watt and Rodinson.[12] However, their evaluation emphasizes the concept within its social context, mainly as a recognition of the emergence of the individual as an independent social unit.

The growing importance of the individual was no doubt the result of the concentration of merchant capital in Mecca, which led to the diversification of society and the gradual shedding of clan responsibility and solidarity. Trade, by its very nature as an interaction or an exchange between a buyer and a seller, promoted the individual. The emergence of the individual, thus, had economic relevance, since it freed him or her from the economic restraints of clan responsibilities. This would facilitate direct participation in the economy, increase the possibilities of individual social and economic mobility, and channel wealth to further investments and away from unprofitable expenditure.

Muhammad in Medina

Despite the inherent advantages embodied in Muhammad's message, many merchant-clan leaders were not ready to relinquish their position in favor of his authority as a prophet. Because of this continued opposition, Muhammad was not able to widen his circle of followers to an effective level. His fortunes did not improve even after the boycott was lifted. The most difficult period of his career in Mecca began with the death of Abu Talib, his uncle and the senior member of the clan. His death was closely followed by the death of Khadija, Muhammad's wife, first follower, and confidante. Leadership of the Banu Hashim passed to Abu Lahab. Disregarding his traditional role as the protector of his clansmen, he immediately disavowed his "protection" of Muhammad, whereupon Muhammad was forced to abandon Mecca for the first time. He went to Ta'if, from which he was summarily ejected. He had to return to Mecca as an outsider and only after he had secured the *jiwar* of al-Mutʿim.[13]

Taking advantage of this status, Muhammad took his cause to other tribes during the pilgrimage season of the following three years, but he had no success. The tribesmen understood the significance of prophethood and were aware of the implications of supporting Muhammad. The B. ʿAmir ibn Saʿsaʿa, for example, demanded that authority (*al-Amr*) should pass to them once the Prophet died. Muhammad demurred, saying that authority rested with God and He alone could assign it. The Banu ʿAmir ibn Saʿsaʿa were not willing to take the risk and join Muhammad for no apparent political gains.[14] This exchange illustrates that Muhammad's concept of authority had evolved beyond current tribal understanding.

Success finally came after Muhammad met some pilgrims from Medina and discussed his message with them. A delegation more representative of the inhabitants of Medina came the following year and carried out secret negotiations with Muhammad, at a place called al-ʿAqaba, between Mina and Mecca. These negotiations finally led to a pact, or an exchange of oaths (*bai'at al-'Aqaba*), between them.[15] Three months later, Muhammad left Mecca and headed toward Medina, the Hijra, in the month of Rabi' Awwal (September), A.D. 622.

Muhammad did not emigrate to Medina without winning the support of a number of Meccan merchants who later played a significant role in Mecca's eventual reconciliation with Muhammad and the rest of the Muslims. His decision to emigrate to Medina changed the direction of his career altogether. When he arrived in Medina, he was already recognized as a prophet. It was on that basis that he was invited to the city in the first place. He was invited to put the house of Medina in order, as the Aws and the Khazraj, the two main Arab tribes, had just finished one of a long series of military confrontations. The Wars of Bu'ath had ended without any resolution, and an uneasy truce continued. The people of Medina realized that the solution to their conflicts lay outside traditional tribal bounds.[16]

Tribal social structure had failed to resolve social conflict in Medina. In fact, it had aggravated it. Muhammad immediately set out to produce an alternative social structure—the Umma—to support needed change.[17] At the center of the Umma was the Prophet. Muhammad's newly constructed house, with a courtyard for prayer, became the focal point where meetings, religious education, deliberations, and so on took place and from which pronouncements were issued. In many ways, Muhammad's house, later a *masjid* (mosque) functioned as the Ka'ba and Dar al-Nadwa combined. The area surrounding Medina was declared *haram*, a sacred area, and the usual restrictions guaranteeing life and property began to be rigorously applied.[18]

It was when the so-called Constitution of Medina was outlined that the Umma began to materialize and to take on a political meaning.[19] Although the provisions of the constitution changed, always reflecting Muhammad's growing power, two constant themes stand out as a significant departure from contemporary tribal structure. The first is the nature and content of the Umma; the second is the authority that led this Umma.

The word *umma,* as it appears in the Qur'an, refers to a community of beings, such as a group of people or a religious community, for example, the Christians and the Jews, communities with "revealed books."[20] Accordingly, an important characteristic of the Umma was its divinely ordained origin. God alone can make or unmake a community of believers. The Umma in Medina enjoyed the protection of God and would last as long as He willed. It was made up of individuals from different clans and tribes and, to give it a political dimension, it even included, in its early years, several religious affiliations, all of which pledged to support and defend it. Individuals within the Umma were responsible for their own actions, a significant departure from the usual custom; however, members of this Umma pledged to support one another against anyone outside it.

No one within the Umma was to seek alliances with the enemy, especially the Quraish. Yet, it was not a closed or exclusive social unit. It was flexible and inclusive and clan ties or tribal solidarity were no longer binding if they interfered with allegiance to the Umma.[21] As later events proved, especially the military confrontations between the Muslims and the Quraish, the Umma appeared more durable than clans or tribes, since clan ties did not deter Mecca's Muslims from fighting their pagan kin.

Muhammad was the recognized authority in the Umma. The Constitution makes it explicitly clear that the final authority in the Umma is God and the recipient of His divine command, His *rasul*, the messenger who will make sure that "judgment is given between them with justice, and [that] they are not wronged."[22] Accordingly, provisions in the Constitution related to Muhammad's position and authority were essentially an assertion of the kind of authority that he tried with little success to introduce to the Meccans.

Muhammad's move to Medina was thus the turning point in his career and in Islam's struggle for acceptance. Muhammad, basing himself on divine authority, was able to introduce a new form of authority and a new form of organization, which replaced the redundant authority of the tribal or clan head and the tribe or clan as a form of social organization.

The Material Dimension of the Umma

The economic underpinnings of the Umma took several forms. A constant theme was cooperation between members to provide avenues for further economic development. Certain types of transaction or contract were discouraged. Such was the case with *muhaqala* (the renting of land for gold) and *mukhadara* (the selling of green wheat before it was harvested in exchange for already harvested wheat). Also discouraged were the practices of *m'awama* (selling the crop several years in advance), *kira'* (the buying of a crop before it was ripe or harvested in exchange for another crop), and *muzabana* (the selling of grapes in exchange for raisins or wheat in exchange for prepared food). Finally, Muhammad discouraged merchants from meeting caravans before they reached the market to buy up their merchandise.[23] Such transactions were discouraged primarily to prevent monopoly and speculation and any practice that would be tantamount to *riba*.

There were, however, transactions that were encouraged as economically viable. Most important was *muzaraʿa*, a contract relationship similar to sharecropping whereby the produce was shared according to fixed ratios. Later, many Meccans, such as ʿAli ibn Abi Talib, Saʿd ibn Abi Waqqas, and ʿAbdallah ibn Masʿud, earned their livelihood through *muzaraʿa*.[24] ʿUmar, as head of state, collected two-thirds of the produce for the Central Treasury if he supplied the seeds and the tools; if the contractor supplied them, ʿUmar collected only half.[25]

Muhammad also encouraged the hiring of labor to help in the agricultural development of Medina. Some traditions even imply the extension of workdays to include evening hours.[26] Furthermore, Muhammad asked that those landlords who could not develop their land because they lacked time or expertise hire workers who might have both but own no land. At one point, he asked those landlords to give up the land for the benefit of those who could develop it.[27] With the regulation of the water supply that Muhammad devised, agricultural production was organized and land reclamation became possible; anyone who reclaimed fallow land owned it.[28] Years later, ʿUmar went so far as to confiscate land that was previously granted by Muhammad but was still undeveloped by its owner for the sake of immediate development by those who had the means to do so.[29] Finally, to facilitate commerce, Muhammad established a central market, instead of the small and localized markets in and around Medina. This market was modeled on the market of ʿUkaz in that it was tax-free.[30]

The reforms that Muhammad introduced in Medina not only set the city on a course of economic recovery and reduced social tension but also alleviated hardships. *Muzaraʿa* and land reclamation created many opportunities for employment. Furthermore, improved commerce gave *muhajirun* (Meccan immigrant) merchants an equally lucrative market. Talha ibn ʿAbdillah, for example, simply diverted his caravan to Medina when he was met by the news of the Hijra; Zubair ibn al-ʿAwwam did the same.[31] ʿAbd al-Rahman ibn ʿAwf continued to be the phenomenally successful merchant he was before. Nor did he lose his wealth in Mecca, for it was protected by none other than Umayya ibn Khalaf, an implacable enemy of Muhammad and one who went so far as to torture Bilal ibn Rabah to make him renounce Islam.[32]

Although conditions in Medina generally improved, some Muhajirun passed through difficult circumstances. They had just left their home.

Many of them were poor in the first place, and many others became poor after they left Mecca. Suhaib al-Rumi, for instance, was forced by the Meccans to leave his wealth behind. Other Muslim property in Mecca was confiscated several months later.[33]

The Muhajirun were offered another avenue for the distribution of wealth: the *mu'akha*, fraternization between the Muhajirun and the Medinan Ansar (supporters). Fraternization created a bond of kinship between a Muslim from Mecca and another from Medina. This relationship had a moral dimension in the affirmation of the spirit of the Umma by fostering kinship within it. Materially, fraternization allowed for the transfer of capital from the Ansar to the Muhajirun. This dimension was taken a step further when the Muhajirun were allowed to inherit from their Ansari brothers.[34]

Making brothers out of the Muhajirun and the Ansar is significant on another level. Not all Meccans were in need of financial help. In a sense, the Muslims remained as stratified economically as they were before. This was aggravated by the emigration of many without their wealth. Some were so poor that they had to eat dates of inferior quality placed in one corner of Muhammad's house.[35] In this instance, fraternization did not help. On closer examination, it appears that earlier stratification was maintained, since a poor Muhajir did not fraternize with a rich Ansar. Sa'd ibn al-Rabi', one of the richest people in Medina, was paired with 'Abd al-Rahman ibn 'Awf himself. Abu Hudhaifa, an early Meccan Muslim and a brother of Hind bint 'Utba, Abu Sufyan's wife, was paired with 'Abbad ibn Bishr, a close associate of Muhammad and an influential member of the Ansar. The *mawla* of Abu Hudhaifa, Salim ibn Ma'qil, was paired with the *mawla* of 'Abbad. Zaid ibn Haritha, a freedman of Muhammad, was paired off with a certain Asid ibn al-Hudair, who died so poor that 'Umar paid his debt over a period of time. The *halif* was paired off also with a *halif*, as evidenced by the fraternization of 'Ammar ibn Yasir and Hudaifa ibn al-Yaman.[36]

Thus, although fraternization allowed economic mobility, it did not allow social mobility. The former social status was reaffirmed and integrated into the new social structure. Fraternization, therefore, could be regarded in the larger sense as an attempt at class unity, initially between Mecca and Medina and later in the rest of the Hijaz. This rigid social structure was abandoned altogether in favor of wider social and economic mobility when fraternization, especially pertaining to inheritance, was formally annulled following the Muslim victory at Badr.

Thus, barely two years after his arrival in Medina, Muhammad was able to build a social structure, new in many respects and old in others. The Umma, as a social unit, with its own form of authority and organization, superseded the tribe and emerged, under the leadership of the Prophet, as a viable and effective challenge to the existing order.

The Winning of Mecca and Arabia

When Muhammad left Mecca he did not forget the Quraish. He immediately set out to isolate their commercial ventures, the source of their economic and political power. One provision of the Constitution prohibited trade with the Quraish. Using Meccan attacks on Muslim property as justification, Muhammad began a series of raids to harass Meccan caravans. These raids (*ghazwa* or *sariyya*) were conducted in an ever-widening field of operations and not all of them were of a military character. Some, indeed, seem to have been nothing but an opportunity to trade. Others were of a "diplomatic" nature, to win converts, form alliances, and show off Muslim strength.[37] Early on, these raids usually missed the mark, but a head-on conflict seemed inevitable.

The raid on Nakhla is of particular importance at this stage. A number of Muslims were dispatched to an area between Mecca and Ta'if. They came on a caravan laden with raisins and leather belonging to 'Imad al-Hadrami, among other Meccan merchants. The caravan sought shelter at Nakhla, since it was the *haram* of al-Uzza. In recognition of the *haram*, some Muslims shaved their heads, an act that seemed to allay the fears of the Meccans. But there was some confusion regarding whether the *haram* month of Rajab had started or whether it started the next day. This confusion seemed reason enough to attack the caravan and blood was shed.[38]

The raid, an unprecedented act, aroused much controversy. The Quraish rightfully saw it as a violation of their sacred institutions and a threat to their economic interests; the Muslims were equally concerned about the same sacred institution, as the confusion regarding Rajab persisted. Booty obtained at Nakhla was not distributed, but was deposited in Muhammad's house. Finally, the controversy was settled by the Qur'an, Sura 2:217, which says "[If] they ask you, should fighting be in the *haram* month, say fighting in it is grave, but blocking God's path and unbelief in Him and the Sacred House are graver." From then on, pagan institutions were no longer sacred. As the controversy abated, the booty was distributed, with one-fifth of it remaining with Muhammad to form the nucleus of the Central Treasury.[39] This division, ordained in the

Qur'an, added another form of distribution of wealth to the Umma and allowed it and its allies to grow. In addition to a new authority and a new social organization, Islam promised social and economic transformation by providing institutions for the distribution of wealth.

The Muslims and the Meccans fought each other again, at Badr in A.H. 2 (A.D. 624). The Muslims won a resounding victory against almost incredible odds. Abu Jahl and other Meccans were killed. Many were captured and ransomed later. The Muslims, on the other hand, success-fully defended their viability as a new force in the Hijaz and were able to win a moral and material victory.[40] But a year later, the Muslims were defeated at Uhud, near Medina; however, the Quraish were unable to de-feat Muhammad.[41]

The Quraish failed once more in the Battle of al-Khandaq (the Trench, A.H. 5 [A.D. 627]). The Meccan force, led by Abu Sufyan, made a stand at Medina, bringing ten thousand allies (*al-Ahzab*). This huge show of force was stopped with a trench, dug so that the Meccans could not storm Me-dina. Muhammad's diplomatic skill was also instrumental in breaking up the alliances within the Quraishi camp. After several days of frustrated attempts to cross the trench, Abu Sufyan, recognizing a change of for-tune, led his followers in retreat. Other Meccans—ʿAmr ibn al-ʿAs and Khalid ibn al-Walid—also recognized that "Muhammad does not lie [about his claim]."[42] When Muhammad learned of their departure, he commented, "Now we can raid them and they would not be able to raid us."[43]

Attacks against the interests of the Quraish continued, such as that led by Zaid ibn Haritha to al-ʿIs. Zaid and his 170 Muslim companions in-tercepted a Meccan caravan on its way back from Syria. The Muslims captured, in addition to several prisoners, the caravan's large silver con-signment, which was destined for Safwan ibn Umayya.[44] Other raids were sent against nomads who interfered with Muslim trade, such as that against the Judham, who had attacked a caravan belonging to Dihya al-Kalbi on his way back from Syria.[45]

As Muhammad grew stronger, the Meccans began to change their atti-tude toward him. Some recognized the validity of Muhammad's claims of prophethood after their frustration at the Trench. Others began to con-vert as a result of his lenient treatment of his Meccan captives. But the breakthrough in their relationship was the correspondence and the ex-change of gifts between Muhammad and Abu Sufyan after Mecca experi-enced a drought, no doubt aggravated by the Muslim encirclement of Meccan trade following Mecca's defeat at the Battle of the Trench. On this occasion, Muhammad sent barley and other food to Abu Sufyan to be distributed among the poor in Mecca. Abu Sufyan reciprocated by sending Muhammad fine-quality leather. It is reported also that Abu Sufyan came to Medina and paid Muhammad a visit.[46]

The final act of rapprochement was facilitated by the Truce of al-Hudaybiyya (A.H. 6 [A.D. 628]). Muhammad felt confident of his strength and he had a dream in which he performed, with his followers, the lesser pilgrimage, the ʿumra. Having already realized that the Quraish would be unable to mount an effective response, Muhammad also reasoned that "war had eaten up the [resources] of the Quraish."[47] After the preparations for the ʿumra were completed, Muhammad and ten thousand lightly armed followers, carrying only sheathed swords, proceeded toward Mecca intent on performing all the rites. A force of two hundred Meccan cavalry, led by Khalid ibn al-Walid, began to shadow the Muslims as they approached. When the Muslims reached al-Hudaybiyya, at the edge of the *haram* and thus at Mecca's boundary, they were stopped. The Meccans were determined to prevent them from entering Mecca, to prevent their weakness from being exposed. In fulfillment of the Prophet's vision and because of their confidence in their strength, the Muslims were equally determined to perform the rites of the lesser pilgrimage. Negotiations between the two sides were initiated after a delegation from the Khuzaʿa expressed the Meccans' concern. Eventually, the two parties signed a treaty that (1) called for a ten-year truce; (2) allowed the Muslims to return the following year to perform the lesser pilgrimage, during which time the Quraish would vacate Mecca; (3) stipulated that alliances could be formed without the interference of either side; (4) required that the Quraish who accepted Islam without the permission of their guardian were to be turned over to the Quraish, but did not require that the Quraish turn over the Muslims who renounced Islam.[48]

The treaty was not signed without controversy. ʿUmar ibn al-Khattab, like many other Muslims, was indignant at the insistence of Suhail ibn ʿAmr, the representative of the Quraish, that reference to Muhammad as a prophet should be struck from the treaty. Suhail argued that had he accepted Muhammad's prophethood the whole confrontation would not have taken place. Muhammad had built his authority not only on prophethood but also as a secular leader and thus agreed to the compromise. The treaty, therefore, was made between two contending social forces, elevating the one led by Muhammad ibn ʿAbdillah to a position equal to, if not stronger than, that held by the Quraish. The treaty became a testament to the decline of the Quraish.[49]

During the period of the truce, it was agreed, as noted earlier, that each side could form alliances and make contacts. At this point, the Khuzaʿa in Mecca, who had been allies of ʿAbd al-Muttalib, declared their desire to ally with Muhammad.[50] The Quraish could not oppose this alliance, which shows the degree of the split in Mecca. Muhammad and the Quraish also sought to establish good relations with the surrounding nomadic and settled areas. In none of these attempts did the Quraish better the Muslims.[51]

As the Quraish lost prestige outside of Arabia, their authority inside also diminished. According to the treaty, Muhammad was obliged to turn over those Meccans who converted without the permission of their guardian. One such person was Abu Jandal, son of Suhail ibn ʿAmr himself.[52] Apparently, this was not an isolated incident. Some of those turned over by Muhammad escaped from Mecca and congregated near the coast, between Mecca and Medina. Led by ʿUtba ibn Asid, known as Abu Basir, they began to harass Meccan caravans. Abu Jandal also escaped and joined Abu Basir. The Meccans were unable to exercise any authority over Abu Basir, Abu Jandal, or any other of the rebels. The situation became so critical that the Quraish, in recognition of the viability of Muhammad's authority and the futility of theirs, implored Muhammad to accept their conversion so that he could exert his authority over them.[53]

The seriousness of the defections in the Meccan ranks could be measured also by the prominence of some who had recently converted, such as ʿUthman ibn Talha, Abban ibn Saʿid ibn al-ʿAs, ʿAmr ibn al-ʿAs, and Khalid ibn al-Walid. ʿUthman ibn Talha received the keys of the Kaʿba after Mecca surrendered to Muhammad. Abban, in whose house ʿUthman stayed during the negotiation of al-Hudaybiyya, was immediately appointed commander of a raid to Najd and later became governor of Bahrain. ʿAmr was appointed tax collector for Oman and later became the conqueror of Egypt. Khalid ibn al-Walid played a decisive military role in the Muslim expansion inside Arabia and outside.[54] By accepting Muhammad at this time, these men retained their high positions by directing their efforts in the service of Islam. In all, the Treaty of al-Hudaybiyya represents a significant point in Muslim/Meccan relations and demonstrates the growth of one social order and the decline of another.[55]

In the month of Ramadan, A.H. 8 (A.D. 630), and nearly two years after al-Hudaybiyya, Muhammad returned to Mecca in triumph after some of the Quraish violated the terms of the truce by allowing an attack against the Khuzaʿa, Muhammad's allies. Muhammad declared the treaty null and void and called for a march against Mecca. Abu Sufyan came hurriedly to Medina hoping to negotiate a reinstatement of the treaty. Muhammad did not agree to the request, and yet when the Muslim forces entered Mecca the *jiwar* of Abu Sufyan was honored. It was declared that anyone who entered the "*dar*" (the house of Abu Sufyan) would be secure. This meant that anyone who complied with Abu Sufyan's recognition of Muhammad was secure; almost all of the inhabitants were included in this guarantee. Hardly any fighting took place, and both the integrity of the city and the position of Abu Sufyan were secured.[56] Mecca was finally brought within the framework of Islam. The Ka'ba was emptied of its idols and the worship of Allah was instituted. Mecca's *haram* was recognized, but this time its sacredness had a different origin: divine authority.

The conquest of Mecca was considered the conquest par excellence— the *fath*—which brought the stiffest opponents of Islam under the sway of Muhammad. Even though the Meccans accepted Muhammad's political authority over them, however, many did not accept Islam yet. They seemed to need further assurances of Muhammad's claims, especially since the Hawazin, a large nomadic confederation, in association with the Thaqif of the neighboring city of Ta'if, began preparations for an assault on Muhammad and his followers. Muhammad allowed the non-Muslim Meccan leaders—Hakim ibn Hizam, Safwan ibn Umayya, 'Abdallah ibn Abi Rabi'a, and Huwaitib ibn Abi Balta'a—to participate in the upcoming battle.[57] In addition to Abu Sufyan and other merchant-clan leaders, these men witnessed Muhammad's success against the Hawazin in the Battle of Hunain. The Hawazin were defeated and much booty was collected; the Thaqif were pursued to Ta'if and eventually surrendered.[58] Many received shares of the spoils, which they used to purchase land, as Abu Qatada al-Ansari and Abu Dharr and his brother had done.[59]

What is also significant regarding Hunain is that Muhammad financed the battle with Meccan capital, including capital owned by non-Muslim Meccans. He borrowed fifty thousand dirhams from Safwan ibn Umayya, who also delivered one hundred sets of mail armor and the accompanying weapons. Safwan also undertook the transportation of this equipment on his own camels to the battlefield. 'Abdallah ibn Abi Rabi'a and Huwaitib ibn Abi Balta'a each lent Muhammad forty thousand dirhams.[60] All of this money was repaid after Hunain, and these men also received a share of the spoils. In addition, those Meccan leaders who still wavered regarding outright recognition of Muhammad's prophethood and authority were rewarded once they were included in the ranks of the *mu'allafatu qulubuhum* (those whose hearts were reconciled) by giving them special rewards.[61]

Indeed, the conquest of Mecca caused most of the city's merchants to convert to Islam and "Islamicized" their capital by mobilizing it in the service of Islam. Even the non-Muslim merchants put their capital at Muhammad's disposal. This is significant, since Muhammad had the moral and material authority to confiscate their wealth had he wished. Instead, Meccan merchant capital as a whole was Islamicized and remained, as the Qur'an promised (Sura 2:280), in the possession of its owners. And as the Hijra had unified the merchants in Mecca and Medina, the conquest of Mecca unified the merchant class in the Hijaz. From that point on, Muhammad and his successors relied on Mecca's merchants for leadership in the expansion of Islam. The merchants had acquired the organizational and administrative skills that were necessary for this role and held this advantage by participating in highly organized and efficient commerce. Thus, one could say that, in addition to the investment of their capital in the service of Islam, it was their historical experience that allowed them to assume a highly visible role in setting up the new social order created by Muhammad and that allowed them to reap the most benefits from the expansion of Islam.

After the conquest of Mecca, the defeat of Hawazin, and the surrender of the Thaqif, all of the Hijaz came under Muhammad's authority. He came back to Medina to enjoy the apex of his career. He was able to muster a large enough force, mobilized by merchant capital and an ideological and institutional superstructure, to extend his influence over all of Arabia—as evidenced by the flow of *wufud*, delegates from cities and nomadic tribes (whether representing the whole or a fraction thereof) who came to pay homage to Muhammad.[62] He accepted their gesture and appointed officials (local or not) to oversee their religious instruction and to collect the *zakat*, part of which was sent to Medina to be distributed among the Muslims.[63] Thus, it was Islam that mobilized merchant capital to reach the surrounding regions, and it was institutions within Islam that carried the appropriated wealth back to Medina and the rest of the Hijaz.

One region that more readily accepted Muhammad's authority was Yemen. He received several delegations representing different localities and groups in the region, and he communicated with many others who did not come to Medina. Muhammad guaranteed them security ('ahd, or *aman*) for their life and property and usually confirmed their already-high status. Thus, Yemeni merchant leaders such as Dhu al-Kala', Hawshab dhu Zulaim, and the Qayels of Shabwa, Hamdan, and Hadramawt immediately became allies of the emerging state.[64]

In addition to his contacts with major Yemeni forces, Muhammad concluded a treaty with Najran, a rich commercial and productive center in southern Arabia. This treaty served as an excellent example of the kind of consolidation followed by the new state and of its value for the later political and economic success of Medina. Moreover, it served as a prototype for the numerous treaties that were concluded between the Muslims and the inhabitants of the conquered territories outside of Arabia. Following are the important provisions of the treaty:[65]

1. The inhabitants of Najran and its surrounding territory were placed under the protection (*jiwar*) of God and became the *dhimma* (protected people) of the Prophet. Their lives and wealth were guaranteed secure.
2. No bishop or priest could be removed from his position.
3. The inhabitants of Najran were not to pay the *'ushr* (tithe). They were to pay a tax in the amount of two thousand *hillas*, each *hilla* equal to an ounce of silver. One thousand *hillas* were due every Rajab, the other one thousand in Safar.
4. Whatever they paid of this tax in the form of shields, saddles, or any other movable commodity would be calculated according to the *hilla*.
5. The inhabitants of Najran had to provide hospitality for Muhammad's envoys for at least twenty days (the right of *nuzul*).
6. Najran had to lend the Muslims thirty shields, thirty mares, and thirty camels in case of any disturbance in Yemen. This loan was guaranteed and whatever was lost would be repaid.
7. The inhabitants of Najran were not to practice usury.

Later treaties reflect similar concerns and interests, mainly the guarantee of life and property in return for the payment of taxes.

The significance of the Najran treaty for the economic and political success of Medina should be readily apparent. Muhammad's willingness to leave local leaders in place helped cultivate new allies and contributed to the unification of merchant interests. This treaty and other pacts (Arabic *Kitab*) made with various localities in Yemen allowed Muhammad to send many of his officials to various locations in Yemen to collect taxes and carry out religious instruction. Among them was Mu'adh ibn Jabal, who became governor of San'a and was charged with the collection of the taxes from Yemen. He told Yemeni leaders that he would like to receive the tax in the form of cloth rather than any other commodity, because, as he explained, cloth was easier to tax (that is, it was more abundant) and it would be more beneficial to the recipients in Medina. That the state was already involved in merchant interests is revealed by the fact that ibn Jabal is said to be the first to use the tax for the purpose of trade. He went on to become so successful as a cloth merchant that he incurred ʿUmar's wrath.[66]

Muhammad cultivated similar support in other regions of Arabia. In Oman, he was able to win over Jaifar and ʿAbbad from the Banu Julanda. He was also able to win over the cities of Duma and Duba. His representative in this region was ʿAmir ibn al-ʿAs, who also supervised the collection of taxes.[67] Muhammad's governor in Bahrain was the local ruler, al-Mundhir ibn Sawi, who was charged with the collection of taxes. Al-Mundhir delivered the taxes to al-ʿAlʾ ibn ʿImad al-Hadrami, who was in charge of collecting the *sadaqa* from the Muslim tribe of ʿAbd al-Qais, a major tribe in the region.[68]

Central Arabia, with its center at al-Yamama, was the only major region that was not readily willing to follow Muhammad. Even though there were many who accepted Muhammad, Maslama (later Musailama, the false prophet) was able to lead a movement to oppose Muhammad and Medina. Maslama built his movement on an already-tried model, prophecy. When asked to submit, as other regions of Arabia had, the Banu Hanifa demanded a share in authority, saying, "From us a prophet and from you a prophet."[69] Muhammad was not able to influence central Arabia with the same results as he had elsewhere. There were also other nomadic confederations in other parts of Arabia that resisted submission.

In concluding this chapter, the following points should be made. As merchant capital concentrated in Mecca and as the material base of Meccan social formation changed, the tribal institutional structure could no longer support the rapidly changing conditions. Thus, the self-serving and cumulative institutions and institutional practices that formed part of the ideology of the Quraish also began to be transformed.

A significant change was the decline of the tribe or clan as a social unit. This was accompanied by a decline in the authority of tribal and clan leaders. Tribal institutions were no longer able to meet the needs of a growing dependent population. This not only made the gap between the rich and the poor more visible but also narrowed the social base of the wealthy, which exposed them to threats of social violence.

To remedy this situation, Muhammad offered monotheism, a unique and ever-lasting authority. He also introduced the Umma as a substitute social unit, a unit that turned out to be more durable, more flexible, and more expandable than the tribe. Solidarity in the Umma was expressed by allegiance to it, to the Prophet, and to Allah, and its founding became the base on which the state was erected.

In addition, Muhammad provided a system for the distribution of wealth that assured social and economic mobility for believers. This attracted new adherents to Islam and was a sound economic policy, as the success of Medina indicates. But distribution of wealth was also necessary on a different level. Through it, new members were recruited into the capital-owning class. This had the effect of widening the social base of both the merchants and the wealthy, thus making their position and wealth more secure, and of decreasing the dependent population, which freed the merchants from certain financial obligations, once the Fifth (the genesis of the Central Treasury) was instituted to meet those obligations.

After several years of preaching in Mecca, Muhammad left and set up operations in Medina, where he began to gather followers more rapidly. The Meccans opposed Muhammad specifically with regard to his authority. A good part of Muhammad's time in Medina was spent organizing a new social, economic, and political structure to challenge the Quraish and to isolate their commercial ventures. Muhammad was able, in the span of eight years, to isolate Mecca and to reduce the political and economic power of his primary opponent. He maneuvered the Meccans into a position in which their political and economic survival was only assured by accepting Muhammad's authority and their inclusion in the framework of Islam. Once Mecca's merchants accepted Islam, their capital was mobilized and a greater profit was their due. Also, because of their experience, merchants were relied on to finance, equip, organize, and lead the further expansion of Islam. Islam at once offered not only a set of rituals and beliefs but an ideological and institutional superstructure that allowed social, economic, and political progress for the Muslims, now led largely by Meccan merchants. Furthermore, with the institution of the Umma and Divine Authority, Islam not only gave Mecca's merchants political ascendancy but also legitimized and institutionalized their leadership.

5. Islamic Expansion and the Establishment of the Islamic State

An ancient system was coming to an end, not only in southern Arabia but also in the neighboring regions. The governing classes in those other empires were landowners, and the majority of the population was engaged in agricultural production. In pursuance of that production, governing institutions heavily favored landowners, burdening the population with debt bondage, corvée labor, exorbitant taxes, and immobility. Eventually, these factors became the undoing of the Arabian and neighboring states.

But as we have seen, a major difference characterized the political-economic process in Arabia: the position of merchants in the power structure. In the Roman world, for example, the merchant was often excluded from membership in the local town council. Merchants could be flogged by the aedelis, their presence in the municipal councils was considered unbecoming, and their profession was considered unworthy of the noble. An edict issued as late as A.D. 409 forbade "those who are decidedly noble by birth or resplendent with honor or notably rich in property to carry on trade."[1]

Such legislation and the attitudes born out of it must have retarded the growth of merchant capital in the Roman world. At the very least, merchants were socially marginalized; either they were foreigners (which might explain their exclusion from the town councils), or they came from the lower classes, which explains the nobility's disdain of their profession. These attitudes carried over to medieval Europe, and it was not until after the twelfth century that merchants began to improve their condition.

Their counterparts in Arabia, and most notably in Mecca, enjoyed the encouragement and support of the governing institutions. The governing class in Arabia was composed of landowners and the governing institutions favored them, but they and their capital were also engaged in commerce. Therefore, institutions and institutional practices that facilitated commerce were incorporated into the political system. Thus, the emancipation of merchants from this ancient system was much easier in Arabia than elsewhere, most specifically, Europe. Merchants, as we have seen, achieved greater power in Mecca, where they became masters of a state aided by Islamic institutional beliefs and practices. It is not surprising, then, to find that the accumulation of merchant capital was greatly advanced in the Islamic world. Its commercial practices, in fact, were adapted by European merchants after the Crusades.

In contradistinction to conditions in the ancient system, where most of the population was socially immobile, Islam freed the believers and promised upward mobility in social and economic position. It thus mobilized a significant social force to an unprecedented level, which allowed the Muslims to expand, first in Arabia, then outside, where they challenged and defeated the empires of the region.

The circumstances for this expansion could not have been more propitious. Both the Byzantines and the Sasanids were experiencing grave difficulties. Between A.D. 604 and 628, Sasanid armies attacked Mesopotamia, Syria, and Egypt, devastating, in the process, wide agricultural areas. And although the Persians held Egypt for only a decade, they occupied Syria until A.D. 628. These latest conflicts between the superpowers disrupted not only agriculture, but also the commercial network of the region. The Sasanids also became financially and physically exhausted by years of war and saw their agriculture devastated by the Byzantines, who received an annual indemnity at the conclusion of the war. Inhabitants of the central provinces suffered economic devastation as a result of floods and breaks in their irrigation system.[2] Yet, despite these economic difficulties, the producing classes continued to pay the high taxes of previous years.

Equally urgent was the political situation in both empires, which had to cope with succession crises and palace coups and another threatened flare-up of hostilities between them. As an indication of their preoccupation with problems at the center, these powers abandoned their respective client-states, thus leaving their southern flank exposed to attacks, and made it easier for the Muslims to penetrate.

In addition to these economic and political problems, there was the age-old religious persecution of the Monophysites of Syria, Egypt, and Iraq. This persecution highlighted the fact that there was little in common between the native inhabitants and those who ruled them. In the Sasanid realm, one finds, other than religious and linguistic differences, "the important, if predictable, class distinctions that separated soldiers from slaves, peasants from priests, merchants from gentry, and courtiers from kings."[3]

These distinctions were profoundly felt by these inhabitants to the extent that Michael the Syrian, the Patriarch of Antioch, after the Muslim conquest, said, "It was no small advantage to us to be delivered from the cruelty of the Romans [the Byzantines], their wickedness, their fury, their implacable zeal against us, and to find ourselves at peace."[4] According to Bishop John of Niku, a similar relief was felt by the Egyptians, and there was cooperation between the Copts and the Muslims, without which the conquest of Egypt would have been much more difficult than it was.[5] The widespread and deep-rooted dissatisfaction and resentment in Iraq, Syria, and Egypt were the principal reasons behind the Muslims' quick and successful conquest of these provinces.[6]

The Islamic expansion that began a little more than a decade after the Hijra remains controversial. Many theories have been put forward to explain this phenomenal process; however, nomadism appears as a general theme in the answers to questions of motive, organization, and authority. The expansion, furthermore, is usually seen as an independent phenomenon, rather than as a manifestation of a continuous historical process. Thus, hardly any emphasis is given to the significance of the institutions that Islam provided Arabian society in general and the merchants in particular, perhaps with the exception of *jihad*. Consequently, Muslim writers, like the early chroniclers, see the expansion mainly as *jihad* in its strictly religious application. They view the initiation and participation in the expansion as fulfillment of a religious duty. This explanation contributed to the modern attitude held by many that the expansion was motivated by the zeal and the fanaticism of the participants.

Most Western writers stress the material dimension of the expansion as a nomadic movement, either as a part of historical migrations, or as a result of the progressive dessication of Arabia, or as a result of "population explosion." These nomads, "driven by hunger and avarice," are considered to have initiated raiding parties for the purposes of plunder. Being a nomadic movement, therefore, the expansion lacked a central strategy, was haphazard, disorganized, and led by men motivated by personal motives.

Holding such a view, Gabrieli and Shaban connect the expansion to the *Ridda* War, which was fought in Arabia after Muhammad's death. Gabrieli claims that, at the conclusion of this war, "Arabia was seething with arms and armed men: the victors, no less than the vanquished, needed an outlet for their surplus energies, and felt a strong drive for action which would provide a diversion from fratricidal war. . . . Certainly one of the major incentives for the external conquest may have lain in this explosive internal situation, with its unchained passions, and in the desperate need for plunder and 'living space.'"[7] Using very much the same language, Shaban says that Arab forays into settled territories were a pre-Islamic practice that continued with the advent of Islam. These forays, Shaban continues, "were now an economic necessity," because trade, which had been at a "standstill" after a decade of war in Arabia, now lay in ruins as a result of the *Ridda* War. To compensate for this loss, the state unleashed these nomads to gain as much booty as they could.[8]

As variations on the leitmotif of nomadism, Gabrieli and Shaban provide nothing new. And if commerce declined, it declined only as far as the Quraish were concerned, even though there are indications to the contrary. This decline was forced on them by Muhammad; therefore, after the conquest of Mecca, Muhammad had no reason to continue his encirclement of the Quraish. In fact, he reversed his position and began to favor Quraishi merchants, some of whom, although non-Muslims, financed a substantial part of the Hunain expedition. Consequently, there already existed avenues for trade and for investment of merchant capital.

Donner ably disproves many of the above notions concerning the nature of, motive for, and organization of the expansion. He presents it, as the sources show, as an organized movement affected by the elite of the newly created state, directed by the caliph at the center, and well planned and well executed. Even this excellent study, however, retains some of the limitations of previous works, since the author sees the expansion mainly as the means by which the newly founded state, for its very survival, had to control Arab nomads who lived on the Syrian and Iraqi steppes. Otherwise, Donner argues, the balance of power between the nomads and the settled, now favoring the settled, thanks to Islam, would revert to the age-old conflict. Although Donner has challenged previous misconceptions, his discussion does not take into account the connection between the development of Mecca's economy and the conquests and the latter's relevance to merchants and merchant capital.[9]

I propose a different view of the expansion. I see it as affected by an emerging state largely controlled by, and serving the interests of, the merchants. The state even became a vehicle by which officials joined the merchant class. The Arab/Islamic expansion widened the available market, which merchants had been attempting to do since the introduction of the *ilaf*. This time, however, they acquired political control, thanks to the institution of the Umma. Within this perspective, the expansion may be viewed as the means by which merchants consolidated their political ascendancy. Control of state resources allowed them to distribute wealth to those who worked (*jihad*) in the interests of the Umma (the state). Consequently, the social and economic transformations promised by Islam widened the social base of the capital-owning class. This broader base secured and legitimized the merchants' position. The merchants, the most visible servants of the Umma, were successful because of their experience, their mercantile interests, and their acceptance of a favorable ideology and supportive institutions within Islam.

Viewing the expansion within the context of the demands of merchants and their capital will probably be rejected by both Muslim apologists and those who continue to rely on the nomadic paradigm. The first might object on the grounds that such an explanation is more materialist than spiritual. They will argue that religion, or spiritual rewards, was behind the expansion. This, of course, denies a considerable amount of evidence that clearly spells out the material concerns of the participants, whether the leaders or the rank and file. Seeing the expansion within the context of merchant capital does not deny the existence of those who were motivated by religious considerations—this is precisely the significance of *jihad* at this point, the convergence of ideology with the needs of the society. Thus, in mobilizing the troops to fight the Byzantines, Abu Bakr was careful to equate spiritual rewards with material rewards.[10]

Those who still support the nomadic explanation are likely to reject my thesis because it challenges the fundamental supposition on which they weave their own theories and explanations of later aspects of Islamic society. For example, it is consistent within a nomadic paradigm to represent the expansion as unorganized, haphazard, and without a central strategy. But the expansion and the kind of achievements it engendered cannot support such a view. These scholars also see Basra, Kufa, and Fustat (founded during the expansion) as merely garrison cities, camp towns, or ghettos built near the desert and with which these nomads were familiar. But if the expansion was affected by nomads, why would they inaugurate a process of urbanization unprecedented in the region and contrary to their life-style? Life-style changes, as illustrated by examples like that of Qusayy, presuppose a prior transformation. Such a transformation has been ignored in studying these cities. Furthermore, if the expansion was carried out for the purpose of booty and plunder, why did these "nomadic plunderers" enter into treaties or pacts with the conquered cities to guarantee life, property, and possessions?

Although it is generally recognized that Islam grew in a mercantile environment and that merchants played a leading role throughout, their role and the demands of their capital are neglected in the study of the expansion, the founding of cities, and the resultant social and economic transformations in the early period of Islamic history. After all, these new cities quickly became thriving markets with many avenues for investment and with an ideology favorable to the merchants. While this study does not deny the value of other theses, without the material dimension advocated here, our understanding of the expansion will remain flawed.

The discussion in this chapter will therefore show the relevance of the expansion to merchant interests. This will be done in part by highlighting various treaties with conquered areas and their significance to merchant capital and the policies that allowed them to consolidate control of the state. Admittedly, however, these treaties are problematic. The problem lies, as Noth has observed, in the fact that, while there is no evidence to suggest that there has been a systematic effort to falsify their content, the treaties as they appear in the sources cannot be taken as a literal copy of the signed originals.[11]

After a careful analysis of various treaty texts and the terms they contain, I am in agreement with Noth's classification of them into three categories: authentic, falsified, and completely fabricated. Those conditions that set a range of financial obligations in the form of tribute (whether lump sum or per capita), that guarantee security for life and property (whether termed *dhimma, man*, or *aman*), that set payment in kind to support the Muslim armies, and that provide for exchange of services and certain other nonproperty-connected arrangements appear to be authentic.[12] Falsification of treaty terms, Noth says, appears when the terms become too specific. For example, when a treaty requires the payment of foodstuffs, the term is considered authentic, but when a term is added that the foodstuffs should be of a specific kind and in a specific amount, the specification is most likely falsified. Those conditions that Noth deems fabricated include legal restrictions and punishments that had not yet developed in this early period (such as displaying the cross, ringing of church bells, dress codes, and general prescriptions on how Muslims and non-Muslims should interact) and financial obligations that appear more like tax than tribute.[13] With that in mind, it is significant for our discussion to remember that treaties were signed in the first place and that, although the terminology and the conditions were not uniform, the interests behind those treaties were uniform.

The Consolidation of Arabia: The *Ridda* War

With the death of Muhammad, various factions within Arabia stopped payment of the *zakat*. Abu Bakr was swiftly, although not without controversy, appointed as *khalifat rasul Allah,* successor or deputy of the Prophet. When he assumed office, Abu Bakr reasserted the authority of the Umma, as decreed by God and instituted by His Prophet, by declaring that those who submitted to Muhammad had given themselves to someone who had died. Those who submitted to God, however, were tied to a being who was alive and eternal. Rebellion against Medina was considered tantamount to rebellion against the Umma, that is, against the command of God. As such, the question of whether all of Arabia had adopted Islam by the time of Muhammad's death becomes immaterial. What mattered to the Muslims in Medina was that there were factions that questioned the authority of the Umma and prepared to break from it. Thus, to the Muslims in Medina, rebellion became associated with apostasy (*ridda*), which, therefore, had to be contained for political, economic, and religious reasons. The *Ridda* War followed and lasted nearly two years. The Muslims gained domination of Arabia and, in the process, consolidated that which Muhammad had initiated.[14]

As caliph, Abu Bakr was not satisfied by the mere acceptance of Islamic principles. Some, such as Talha of the Banu Asad, expressed only moral support of Medina. Abu Bakr demanded that they also pay the *zakat,* as they had when Muhammad was alive. Insistence on the payment of this basic tax was how Medina established its economic and political control of all of Arabia. Abu Bakr asserted the right of the state to rule and to appropriate part of the surplus wealth through the collection of *zakat*.

The office of the caliph as deputy to Muhammad was an ad hoc creation indeed, but the creation of a state structure had already been started through Muhammad's teachings and actions and those Muslims who surrounded the Prophet, namely, the Companions, who acted as scribes, stewards, military commanders, prayer leaders, advisers, and so on. All of these could be considered the nucleus of a developing bureaucracy. But this embryonic state form was threatened by the nonallegiance of the various factions in the peninsula.

Immediate danger came from Najd. Maslama, of the Banu Hanifa, threatened the nascent state politically and economically. His movement was also based on prophecy and thus was potentially on the same footing as that of Medina. Maslama was dubbed *al-Kadhdhab*, the liar, given the diminutive form of his name, Musailama, and his movement was declared false altogether. Economically, Najd, centered in al-Yamama, was well situated in the heart of the Arabian peninsula and commanded the routes that criss-crossed it. More important than its location, however, was its role as a production area and an important market.[15] Musailama, had he been allowed to succeed, would have cut off the Hijaz from eastern Arabian markets. He would also have been able to seal off Medina's access to this area all the way to the upper Euphrates had his alliance with the Banu Taghlib endured Medina's attack.[16] It is not surprising, therefore, that the situation demanded the ablest general available to Abu Bakr, Khalid ibn al-Walid.

Khalid's military ability is difficult to explain, since he had no formal military training and his field experience was rather limited. As head of the Quraishi cavalry, he is credited with the Muslim defeat at Uhud. He was present on the side of the Quraish at the Battle of the Trench but he hardly saw any fighting there. He also shadowed the Muslims as they approached al-Hudaybiyya, again without any military activity. After he joined Muhammad, Khalid led a Muslim contingent at the conquest of Mecca, but again saw very little fighting. Then he was charged with subduing tribes in the Tihama region, which he did with particular cruelty, even though the tribes did not resist. Perhaps Khalid's involvement with commerce, which required organizational ability and a knowledge of logistics and matters of security and tactics, prepared him well for his role as a military commander.[17] The same could be said of other merchants, such as ʿAmr ibn al-ʿAs, ʿAbd al-Rahman ibn ʿAwf, and Abu Sufyan, who at one time or another served either in the military or in the administration of the state.

Khalid was charged with subduing the *ridda* factions, settled and nomadic, in the northern half of the Arabian peninsula. He first defeated Talha ibn Khuwailid, who led the Banu Asad and the B. Fazara at Buzakha. Other factions, such as the Ghatfan and the Banu ʿAmir in Central Arabia, were similarly brought back to the fold. After nearly a year, Khalid and his followers confronted the Banu Hanifa in the bloodiest battle of the *Ridda* War, Hadiqat al-Mawt, the garden of death (Rabiʿ Awwal, A.H. 12 [A.D. 633]). Musailama was killed and the back of the Banu Hanifa was broken. A treaty of submission was signed and later confirmed by a delegation from al-Yamama to Medina.[18]

Meanwhile, Abu Bakr sent al-ʿAlaʾ ibn ʿImad al-Hadrami to Bahrain, where he discovered an attempt to revive the Lakhmid dynasty. A section of the Banu Bakr that had allied with the Sasanids wanted to rehabilitate the Lakhmids. They were ready to confront the Banu ʿAbd al-Qais, who refused to go along with the Lakhmid revival and openly declared their allegiance to Medina. The Banu ʿAbd al-Qais gave al-ʿAlaʾ the strength necessary to subdue his adversaries. Very soon, Bahrain and the cities and tribes in the area submitted and their inhabitants, Arabs and Persians, were given a guarantee of security in return for payment in cash and in kind.[19]

It was easy also to regain control of Oman. ʿAmr ibn al-ʿAs, Muhammad's tax collector, left Oman when he received the news of the Prophet's death. Although there were many who continued to pay allegiance to Medina, Laqit dhu al-Taj of the Banu Julanda refused to submit to Medina. Thus, when ʿIkrima ibn Abi Jahl arrived with his Meccan force, he immediately contacted the loyalists in Oman, in the persons of Jaifar and ʿAbbad, also from the Banu Julanda. When Laqit learned of the presence of Muslim troops, he massed his own in the market town of Duba. He would have won the ensuing battle, had it not been for Muslim reinforcements who arrived from Bahrain. After that, the Muslims won an easy victory and claimed the market as *faiʾ* (booty) one-fifth of which was sent to Medina.[20]

The situation in Yemen proved more complicated; nevertheless, it demanded the least attention. It appears that Abu Bakr relied on local forces to contain the situation and thus hoped to control the region without recourse to the military. The false prophet al-Aswad al-ʿAnasi, after gaining strength while Muhammad was alive, succumbed to a palace conspiracy in Rabiʿ in A.H. 11 (A.D. 632). During al-Aswad's meteoric rise, he gained control of such cities as Najran, Sanʿa, and ʿAden. In his final year, he became powerful enough to dismiss Muhammad's tax collectors as intruders and to demand that they give back the taxes they had collected.[21] But when Yemeni leaders such as Dhu Zulaim, Dhu al-Kalaʿ, and Dhu Murran withheld their support from al-Aswad, and when Najran broke away to reinstate its treaty with Medina, al-Aswad lost two significant areas of support and his movement began to disintegrate.[22] He lost not only the backing of the traditional leadership and the merchants, but also an important base of production. This weakness allowed Qais ibn Makshuh and the Persian garrison in Sanʿa to hatch the conspiracy that finally brought down al-Aswad and reaffirmed Medina's control of this important region.

The threat to the authority of Medina, however, was renewed in the person of Qais ibn Makshuh himself, as he felt slighted when Abu Bakr confirmed Fairuz, leader of the Persian garrison, as first in command. Qais incited the above-named Yemeni leaders to revolt, but apparently, they felt it was in their interests to remain within the Medinan framework, since they refused to back this rebellion. Qais, however, went ahead, even though the Yemeni leaders advised those under their sway against joining him. In response to Qais's revolt, Abu Bakr finally dispatched al-Muhajir ibn Umayya with an army raised largely from Ta'if and Mecca. Without the help and support of the Yemeni leaders, Qais remained weak and, although he was able to take San'a, he was not able to consolidate his control in the surrounding areas. By the time al-Muhajir arrived, Qais was already defeated. He and other *ridda* leaders were sent to Abu Bakr, who eventually set them free.[23]

With forces left behind to help Fairuz maintain control of San'a, al-Muhajir proceeded toward Hadramawt. Meanwhile, 'Ikrima, having subdued Oman, proceeded west, taking Muhra along the way, to meet up with al-Muhajir. Both forces easily defeated the *ridda* faction in Hadramawt. Al-Ash'ath ibn Qais, leader of the Kinda and a major force behind the *ridda*, was taken prisoner and sent to Abu Bakr. The caliph again set him free, in exchange for four thousand camels. Al-Ash'ath later married Abu Bakr's sister.[24]

After the Muslim victory in Hadramawt, the *Ridda* War was over. The subjugation of Arabia was accomplished in a relatively short period and was consolidated easily, helped, for the most part, by the presence of local forces whose interest lay in remaining with Medina. This appears clearly in the cooperation of the Yemeni leaders, the Banu 'Abd al-Qais, and a faction of the Banu Julanda. And it was not the kind of subjugation under which the defeated were excluded from the benefits of the state. *Ridda* factions, once defeated, were easily integrated into the Muslim army, allowing reinforcements to be dispatched to needed areas. Of the *ridda* leaders, only Musailama and al-Aswad were killed. Qais ibn Makshuh, Talha, and al-Ash'ath ibn Qais went on to play an important role on the eastern front of the Islamic expansion. Thus, as the *Ridda* War went on, Medina continuously integrated a deployed social force by promising to distribute wealth (as implied in the insistence on the collection of *zakat*). Medina's control of the Arabian peninsula was quicker, easier, and more thorough than that which had been achieved by the Himyarites and the Lakhmids.

It was as though the Arabian peninsula had shrunk all of a sudden so that its vast regions were now within easy striking distance of Medina. This seeming smallness was contrary to the experience of the southern Arabian states, which labored to expand their territory even the little they were able, as has been shown. The difficulty they had and their ultimate failure to expand their territory was primarily due to the nature of their social formation, based as it was on the production of an agricultural surplus.

This situation, we have seen, changed during the second Himyarite state, which pursued expansion more aggressively once its material base changed to one of commodity production, especially in the form of cloth. Hijazi merchants, represented by the newly emerging state in Medina, were able to pursue expansion systematically and even more aggressively than before, because of the ideological and institutional support provided them by Islam. The *Ridda* War became necessary to justify extending Medina's control to the rest of Arabia, and it provided the leaders of the state an already-deployed social force as the rank and file for later expansion. The state was interested in the subjugation not only of the nomads, but also of the settled areas of Najran, San'a, al-Qatif, al-Yamama, Duba, and other urban and productive centers in Arabia. Domination of the settled and the nomadic was the necessary precondition for the expansion of merchant control to other markets and trade routes outside of Arabia.

Syria

Muslim incursions—military, diplomatic, and commercial—inside Syria were initiated during Muhammad's lifetime. His efforts were not without their failures. With a precedent in the Prophet's actions, then, it should not be surprising to find Abu Bakr directing his attention toward Syria once the *Ridda* War was over. Indeed, Abu Bakr insisted on dispatching Usama ibn Zaid to the north to fulfill Muhammad's intentions, even though Medina was threatened by the *ridda*.[25]

The dust from the *Ridda* War had not even settled when troops from various regions of Arabia began to file into Medina in response to a general call proclaimed by Abu Bakr as he finished the rites of the pilgrimage in A.H. 12 (early A.D. 634). The troops assembled near Medina, where they remained for the whole month of Muharram, the first month of the new year. It was during Muharram that Abu Bakr could have laid the plans for the invasion of Syria. At the end of the month, he and other notables surveyed the assembled troops and aroused their enthusiasm. They were ready to start the Syrian campaign.[26]

The campaign was waged on three fronts, corresponding to the Byzantine *junds* (administrative military units) closest to Medina. Thus, armies were directed to the *junds* of Damascus, Jordan, and Palestine, led by Yazid ibn Abi Sufyan, Shurahbil ibn Hasna, and ʿAmr ibn al-ʿAs, respectively. They were later to be joined by the commander-general, Khalid ibn al-Walid.[27] The choice of commanders was not a haphazard selection of individuals but a conscious decision on the part of the caliph to impose his authority.[28]

Khalid arrived after his lightning-quick march across the Syrian desert to find the Muslims besieging Busra, near the grain-rich and strategically located Hawran district. It was known as "the port of Damascus," in fact. After brief resistance, Busra surrendered under the terms of a treaty stipulating the payment of one dinar and one *jarib* of wheat for each adult. The rest of the Hawran was taken afterwards.[29]

It was only after the surrender of Busra that any large-scale confrontation with Byzantine troops took place. The first of these was at Ajnadain in Jumada Awwal in A.H. 13 (July A.D. 634). It seems that the Muslim victory caused Heraclius to evacuate Hims and set up his headquarters farther north, in Antioch, the capital of the Syrian province. The retreat made it easier for a detachment of Muslims to secure a treaty with Hims. This treaty, reinstated several times, provided the inhabitants with a guarantee of security for their life and property in return for the payment of tribute in cash and in kind. Other provisions of the treaty were said to be similar to the provisions in the treaty with the inhabitants of Damascus and Baʿlabakk.[30]

Five months after Ajnadain, the Muslims met another Byzantine force, which they also defeated. This Muslim victory at Fihl (Dhu al-Hijja, A.H. 13 [February A.D. 635]) opened the road to Damascus. Twenty days later, another Byzantine force was defeated at Marj al-Suffar, to allow the Muslims to close in on Damascus. The Ghawta and its churches were taken by force. But the inhabitants of Damascus closed their gates and prepared for a siege that lasted nearly six months before the city finally surrendered under the terms of a treaty. The inhabitants were given the usual guarantee of security for their life and property in return for the payment of tribute in cash and in kind. In addition, city walls were not to be demolished and the Muslim troops were not to be quartered among the inhabitants.[31]

The most important battle between the Muslims and the Byzantines for the control of Syria was yet to be fought. In response to continued Muslim success, Heraclius finally advanced a huge army to meet the Muslim challenge. The Muslims retreated in alarm, abandoning both Hims and Damascus after they gave back the taxes that they had collected. They camped near al-Yarmuk, a tributary of the Jordan River. All of the Muslim troops in Syria gathered to participate in the upcoming encounter, and reinforcements were sent from Medina. Although the precise size of each army is unknown, it is clear that the battle of al-Yarmuk (A.H. 15 [A.D. 636]) was a decisive Muslim victory. The Byzantines, their backs to the river and dust blowing in their faces, were easily routed and many of them drowned. Heraclius and the Byzantines abandoned Syria after this crushing defeat, save for a few strongholds.[32]

After their success at Yarmuk, the Muslims came back to Damascus and Hims, which were easily retaken. They reinstated the former treaties. With a new caliph in Medina and a new commander-general for Syria, Abu ʿUbaida, the Muslims began a systematic drive to extend their control to other Syrian cities. Expecting no major Byzantine force to confront them, the Muslim army was redivided into its original three commands. Shurahbil won the cities of Tiberias and Baisan, among others in al-Urdunn, and signed treaties such as that with Damascus.[33] Under the orders of Abu ʿUbaida, Muʿawiya ibn Abi Sufyan went to the aid of Shurahbil and brought down Acr and Tyre. ʿAmr ibn al-ʿAs secured cities in Palestine such as Ludd, ʿAmwas, Sabastiya, and Nablus. But when ʿAmr besieged Jerusalem, he required further aid from Abu ʿUbaida. Finally, Caliph ʿUmar himself came out and accepted the city's surrender. A treaty was signed with its inhabitants that was similar to the treaties with other Syrian cities.[34]

Success in southern Syria was matched by success in the north. The *jund* of Damascus, the largest in Syria, included Tripoli, one of the most important ports on the eastern Mediterranean. Yazid ibn Abi Sufyan and his brother Muʿawiya were able to secure such coastal areas as ʿArqa, Jubail, Beirut, and Sidon. Tripoli was too fortified to be taken, so its conquest was delayed for several years.[35] Meanwhile, cities such as Baʿlabakk, Hama, Aleppo, and Antioch in Syria, and Raqqa and Edessa in the province of al-Jazira fell to Abu ʿUbaida and his lieutenant Iyad ibn Ghanam.

The sources provide more details on the treaty with Baʿlabakk. It provided the inhabitants—Greeks, Persians, and Arabs—security for their lives, property, churches, and houses, inside the city and outside. Their mills were to be secure. The Greeks could pasture their flocks within a fifteen-mile radius, but they were not to settle in an already-inhabited village. Two months after the treaty, they were allowed to go where they pleased. Those who became Muslim were promised the same duties and privileges of other Muslims. Merchants, in contrast, could travel to any area under Muslim control. Inhabitants who chose to stay in Ba'labakk were required to pay the *jizya* (poll-tax) and *kharaj* (produce or land tax).[36]

This treaty, along with that with Damascus, served as the model for the treaties with the inhabitants of the rest of Syria. The revenue from fixed tribute or a graded tax was channeled to Medina to augment the Central Treasury. Payment of the tax in Syria, as in Arabia, was considered a measure of submission. The Christians, the Jews, and eventually the Zoroastrians were considered People of the Book and thus received the status of *dhimmis*, protected communities. *Dhimmis*, although not politically dominant, participated in various administrative functions. They also participated freely in commerce. It is revealing that merchants were allowed to travel anywhere within the lands of Islam. This, in fact, was the general policy followed by 'Umar regarding non-Muslim merchants. Repeatedly, merchants are referred to as having a certain immunity as long as they paid their dues, tolls, and taxes. Merchants from lands that Muslims had no control over were also welcomed to trade in Muslim markets as long as they paid taxes equal to those that Muslims paid in those lands.[37] This seemingly fair exchange demonstrates that commerce not only was encouraged but also took place during the expansion and that it was an activity practiced by Muslim and non-Muslim merchants, as indicated by the requirement of *iqamat al-suq* (setting up of the market for the Muslims), as was required by Busra, Edessa, and Hims, among others.[38]

The treaty with Ba'labakk, therefore, reveals the concerns of merchant interests. The Arab/Muslim merchants, who largely effected these treaties, allowed non-Muslim merchants to participate in the vast market being created by the Islamic expansion. Thus, merchant capital in the region as a whole was mobilized. And with the kind of distribution of wealth that accompanied the expansion, greater wealth was circulated to the benefit of the merchants.

Merchant interests are clearly evident also in the case of Antioch and Edessa. Antioch, besides being the capital, was a great center for commerce, with a port linking it to other Mediterranean areas. It was a center of industry as well. Silk, olive oil, wine, and wheat, among other commodities, were shipped off from Antioch.[39] Owing to the significance of this city, 'Umar instructed Abu 'Ubaida to keep a contingent of Muslims from those "who are noble and have substantial means at their command."[40] The third caliph, ʿUthman, instructed his governor to settle a large Muslim population in Antioch and to grant them lands so that Muslim control would be more secure. Later, Muʿawiya transferred a large number of people to Antioch. Great wealth was gathered by the Muslims as a result of their control of Antioch. A fifth of the booty was sent to Medina, and individuals also sent part of their share to their families in Arabia.[41]

Edessa's inhabitants split over whether to pay a fixed tribute or a graded tax. One side wanted to pay a proportional tax to be levied according to one's means. The other argued for a fixed tax to be levied on a per capita basis. This side was made up largely of the wealthy, who had substantial assets that they did not want taxed. The wealthy side finally won and Iyad confirmed the treaty. With this treaty, he protected the economic interests of the leaders and the traditionally wealthy by opting for fixed rates and thus allowing their wealth to go untaxed.[42]

Muslim control of Syria had become so effective that even the plague of ʿAmwas (in A.H. 18 [A.D. 639]) could not shake their hold. The plague reportedly claimed the lives of twenty-five thousand troops. It certainly decimated the leadership of the army. Abu ʿUbaida, Shurahbil, and Yazid ibn Abi Sufyan all succumbed.

ʿUmar appointed Muʿawiya ibn Abi Sufyan, until then in the third rank, the commander and charged him with subjugating the last pockets of resistance, mainly Caesarea, ʿAsqalan, and Tripoli. Their ability to resume the expansion after the plague shows a certain resiliency on the part of the state and its institutions and an ability to mobilize the believers.

The Byzantines, meanwhile, even though they held some coastal cities, did not threaten the interior. Thus, Tripoli was still impregnable and Muʿawiya could not hope to take it. In the year following the plague, he was able to take Caesarea, however, which had been enduring a long siege. Later (in A.H. 23 [A.D. 643–644]), ʿAscalan was also taken after brief resistance and was given its former treaty. This time, Muslim troops were garrisoned in the city and given grants of land.[43]

According to some sources, when Muʿawiya took Caesarea, he found, among others, three hundred thousand Samaritans, two hundred thousand Jews, and three hundred markets. The prisoners of war numbered four thousand, and Muʿawiya sent them to Medina.[44] Obviously, these numbers should be regarded only as an indication of the wealth that passed into the control of the Muslims. The prisoners of war were settled in the same area from which the expansion was staged. Some of them were given to Muslim orphans to be employed as household servants. Others were assigned to public works.[45]

Thus, a large labor force was being gathered in the Hijaz as the expansion went on. Some workers were employed in the development of vast areas near Medina. ʿUmar employed many of them to develop the route between Mecca and Medina, where many wells were dug, orchards developed, and mosques built.[46] Other captives were artisans who continued to practice their skills. Any of these captives who joined Islam were given the status of a *mawla*, the same status found in Mecca earlier. Part of the income earned by the *mawalis* reverted to their former lord or master. The status of a *mawla* was no longer allowed to exist between two Arabs, on ʿUmar's insistence. The carry-over of the relationship is indicative of the dominant element in the emerging social structure and of the economic relationship between the *mawalis* and the Arabs.

With the exception of Tripoli, all of Syria, one of the richest Byzantine provinces, passed to Muslim rule no later than twelve years after the death of the Prophet. The Byzantines, deprived of the resources of a rich province, were unable to regroup. The only threat they could pose at this time was in the Mediterranean, where they continued to hold several strategic islands through which they could provision Tripoli. This mastery of the Mediterranean, however, was soon challenged when the Muslims followed up their success on land with seaborne expeditions.

Syria, with its commercial, agricultural, and manufacturing infrastructure, came under the control of an expanding merchant class that was quick to profit from its political ascendancy. Syrian merchants benefited also, since, even though they had been independent of Constantinople, they had been heavily taxed. It was only after the Islamic conquest that their taxes were lowered and better defined.[47]

The very areas through which Meccan and other Arab merchants needed safe-conduct now came under their political control. In controlling Syria and its resources, the Muslims also took over a vital network of trade routes that ultimately linked the land mass of Asia with various points on the Mediterranean. The appropriation of surplus wealth in Syria was facilitated by the cadastral survey that ʿUmar ordered and by the more uniform collection of taxes, in the form of *jizya* and *kharaj*.[48]

Iraq

Incursions into Iraq started earlier than the full-scale invasion of Syria, but were not initiated by the state. A number of raids were led by al-

Muthanna ibn Haritha al-Shaibani. These were merely tribal raids, as distinguished from the wars of expansion organized by Medina. It is instructive that al-Muthanna came to Medina while the *Ridda* War was being waged and sought the caliph's permission to continue his raids. Apparently Abu Bakr refused and instead dispatched Khalid, most likely from Bahrain. Abu Bakr instructed al-Muthanna to obey the new commander and to integrate his forces into Khalid's.[49]

The hurried manner in which Khalid was sent to Iraq (as opposed to the relatively meticulous start of the Syrian campaign) betrays Abu Bakr's desire to bring all troop movements under his control by incorporating the ongoing and independent actions of al-Muthanna within the activities of the state. Had Abu Bakr sanctioned an activity already in progress, like the tribal raids of al-Muthanna, it could have been argued that the caliph merely approved policies rather than initiated them. His refusal to grant al-Muthanna's request could hardly be attributed to any weakness in al-Muthanna, since he was known for his valor and leadership ability. In refusing to grant his request, therefore, Abu Bakr demonstrated that the state in Medina determined its own policies and that he was in charge of the armies.

Khalid remained in Iraq for several months before he was transferred to the Syrian front. During this time, he softened up the western defenses of the Sasanid empire by defeating several Sasanid/Arab contingents, by destroying most of the fortresses along the desert border, and by establishing several cities and oases, such as Anbar, Ulayyis, ʿAin al-Tamr, and Hira.[50] The tribute from Hira, totaling between eighty thousand and one hundred thousand dirhams a year, was the first tribute sent to Medina from outside the Arabian peninsula proper.[51]

But as matters were quickly developing on this front, Khalid was transferred to lead the Muslims against the Byzantines and to see them to victory at the Battle of al-Yarmuk. Soon after his departure, the Sasanids were forced to settle their succession disputes by appointing Yazdagird monarch. His first priority was the recovery of the western defenses. In response, the Muslims decided to withdraw to safety and await further reinforcements.

ʿUmar, as Abu Bakr's appointee to the caliphate (in A.H. 13 [A.D. 634]), sent Abu ʿUbaid al-Thaqafi with one thousand men to reinforce the Muslims and to take over command, once again, from al-Muthanna. Abu ʿUbaid was able to win several skirmishes against the Sasanids. Emboldened by his success, he decided, contrary to al-Muthanna's advice, to cross a pontoon bridge to meet a Sasanid army. With their backs to the river and with the bridge cut behind them, the Muslims suffered a serious defeat at the Battle of the Bridge (in A.H. 13). Abu 'Ubaid was killed and the shattered Muslim forces withdrew again. This disaster prompted 'Umar to proclaim a general mobilization. He sent letters to all of his officials in Arabia to recruit all those who could participate in any way in the war. Reversing the practice of Abu Bakr, he also allowed the *ridda* tribesmen to participate fully in the expansion.[52] Awaiting the result of his call for troops, he immediately sent 'Abdallah ibn Jarir al-Bajali with a force that was able to stabilize the situation after the Battle of Buwaib.

The troops that assembled in response to 'Umar's general mobilization were entrusted to the command of the Meccan Sa'd ibn Abi Waqqas. His army was "fortified" with many Companions of the Prophet, for the occasion was deemed auspicious yet tense, since the Muslims were to face a regrouped Sasanid army. Sa'd moved his army, which was reinforced along the way, and camped near the plains of Qadisiyya, not far from Hira. The two armies faced each other for four months. Finally, the battle started as a Sasanid contingent attacked a Muslim supply column.[53] The fierce battle lasted for three days, but in the end, the Sasanids were defeated, and the shattered army took flight throughout the Sawad (A.H. 16 [A.D. 637]). Many fled to al-Mada'in, Ctesiphon, the Sasanid imperial capital, and the apex of their administrative system.

The Battle of Qadisiyya was no less decisive than that of al-Yarmuk. The Muslims spread out in the Sawad in pursuit of the fleeing army and in the process easily brought the area under their control. Meanwhile, Sa'd advanced toward al-Mada'in. A siege ensued that lasted for two to three months, after which Yazdegird fled the city and headed toward Hulwan, on the eastern side of the Zagros. He left behind the Nakhirjan to evacuate the royal treasure. But after he left, much of the army and many inhabitants also fled, so that when the town surrendered, the treasure was captured almost intact.[54] In pursuit of Yazdegird, the Muslims were able to hand the Sasanids another defeat when they caught up with the rear guard at Jalula'. Yazdegird took flight again and Hulwan surrendered. Meanwhile, the conquest of Khuzistan and other provinces in the south was effected by another Muslim army, first led by 'Utba ibn Ghazwan, then by Abu Musa al-As'hari. This army's base of operations was near the ancient port of al-Ubulla, at the head of the Persian Gulf.[55]

By A.D. 641 (A.H. 20), Yazdegird at last was able to raise another huge army, which was directed toward Nihavand. The Sasanids hoped this time to block the Muslim advance and to recapture the Sawad. The seriousness of the situation compelled 'Umar to combine the Muslim fighters operating on the Sasanid front into one army. In fact, many other Muslim newcomers to Iraq were eager to participate in the battle. Al-Nuʿ man ibn al-Muqarrin was appointed commander of this combined force, which scored another decisive victory against their adversaries. This victory was hailed as the victory of victories.[56] The Sasanid state, losing its army for the final time, also lost its capital and the area that supplied nearly a third of its revenues. It quickly disintegrated. The Muslims pursued Yazdegird from province to province until he was finally killed in A.D. 651 (A.H. 31). By that time, nearly all of the Persian territories were under Muslim control.

The Muslims also concluded treaties with Persian cities that surrendered to them. These treaties closely resembled those with Syrian cities. Life and property were safeguarded in return for the payment of tribute, and all of those who fled were allowed to return, provided they paid the assigned taxes.

The treaty with Nihavand (Mah Dinar), which resembled that with Rayy, Qumis, and Jurjan, among others, provides an example. This treaty gave a guarantee of security for the lives, the wealth, and the land of the inhabitants. It also stipulated that the inhabitants not be required to change their faith and that no obstacles be placed before the performance of their rituals, and that they be protected as long as they paid the poll tax (which was to be paid proportionately, according to one's means). Finally, the treaty required that the inhabitants guide the travelers, that they keep the roads in good repair, and that they provide hospitality to passing Muslims (the right of *nuzul*) for at least a day and a night.[57]

As the expansion became more secure on the Persian front, ʿUmar ordered two of his officials to carry out a cadastral survey in the Sawad to determine appropriate taxation. Rather than divide up the population and the land among the conquerors, as the principle of *faiʾ* allowed, ʿUmar decided to leave the land and the inhabitants *waqf* (inalienable in perpetuity for the benefit of the state). The state undertook the distribution of wealth unto itself. In principle, the peasantry (*al-ʿuluj*) was regarded as free. Peasants were not to be enslaved, but they were to remain bound to the land and thus were relegated to the status of serfs.

Taxes in Iraq were also of two kinds, the graded poll tax and the proportional *kharaj* paid on the land. And as the treaty with Nihavand stipulated, the peasantry in the Sawad was also required to perform extra tasks, such as maintain roads, bridges, dams, and canals.[58] As elsewhere in the areas under the control of Medina, the peasants were to provide hospitality to the Muslims for a specific duration. They were also re-

quired to set up markets for the Muslims (*iqamat al-suq*). This requirement adds another dimension to the relationship between the Muslims
and the conquered territories, especially the merchants. Setting up the
market not only supplied the Muslims with provisions but also allowed
them to exchange whatever booty they acquired on the battlefield with
merchants, who continued their commerce as the expansion was in progress. Indeed, there is evidence that merchants financed later war efforts
and that they were the first to be rewarded for their contributions.

The agricultural area of Iraq, the Sawad, was similarly regarded by
ʿUmar as *waqf*. The state's domain also included fallow land (*mawat*),
the former royal domain, and land belonging to those who fled or per-
ished during the conquest. These lands became known as *sawafi*. It did
not include the land that belonged to cities with treaties. The state dis-
posed of large areas of fallow lands by granting them to Muslims for development. ʿUmar regarded the *sawafi* land as *faiʾ* and thus distributed
the income it generated among the soldiers who participated in the conquest of the Sawad. The *ʿushr* tax was collected from them.[59] Land grants
became a means by which the state consolidated its control of the newly
conquered territories and encouraged the transformation of the social
and economic position of the Muslims.

ʿUmar's regard of the Sawad and its inhabitants as state property further consolidated the Islamic state, since the collective peasantry and the
land was placed in the service of the Muslims in perpetuity. Without any
prohibition on private ownership, the state took on itself the responsibility of collecting and redistributing surplus wealth to the Muslims. This
formalized one of the basic relationships in a state structure and, in the
case of the caliphate, the Central Treasury organized and ensured the distribution of wealth and recipients were called on to defend and to expand
the state's frontiers.

A complex administrative structure emerged for the collection of taxes,
whether the tithe, the *kharaj*, the *jizya*, or the assessments on merchants.
The distribution of this wealth required a similarly complex organization.
In Iraq, this meant the creation of no fewer than two cities, which became
centers for this process. Basra was founded during the initial phase of the
conquest (A.H. 15 [A.D. 636]), Kufa, two years later. Both cities were established on orders from the caliph, and both were built near an already-
established urban center, the ports of al-Ubulla and Hira, respectively, to
demonstrate the newly created socioeconomic and political order and to
consolidate Medina's control of the newly conquered territories. Also,
both cities were founded away from already-developed land, which cre-

ated an enormous potential to develop new lands for cultivation and avoided the disruption of cultivation already in progress.[60]

Kufa was located three miles north of Hira, in whose markets the Muslims initially traded what wealth came into their possession. Kufa eventually expanded until it absorbed Hira altogether. It went on to play a sensitive role in early Islamic history and was not overshadowed in this region until the foundation of Baghdad. The army and its dependents were settled around a square where the mosque and the governor's residence were erected to signify the close association between the state and the religious institution. This wide square also provided plenty of space for the setting up of a market. Initially, merchants located on a first-come first-served basis. Later, these spaces developed into permanent shops. The hubbub of the market often prevented Sa'd ibn Abi Waqqas from conducting the business of the state. Several other markets were located around the city.[61]

The situation at Basra was similar. Basra's commerce surpassed al-Ubulla's by leaps and bounds. Basra remained a busy port where merchants prospered and where commerce played a crucial role. A great deal of attention was also paid to land reclamation, digging of wells and canals, and draining of the swampy area to the north.[62]

Because of the great increases in the fortunes of the merchants and the increase in their commercial activity, Basra and Kufa should not be described merely as camp towns, garrison cities, or ghettos, since these terms imply specialization of function or of ethnicity. Aside from the varied economic structure of these cities and their growth into thriving markets, their inhabitants were also diversified because Arabs and non-Arabs, Muslims and non-Muslims, came to reside in the city. And as Basra and Kufa became the capitals of their respective provinces, they were administrative centers where the state, representing the interests of the merchants, maintained a concrete expression of its political control. The urbanization that was effected by the Islamic expansion was unprecedented in the region, since not only Kufa and Basra were founded but also many other cities. Urbanization at this time was accomplished through the agency of the merchants, who had come at the command of an ideologically supported state structure that allowed them to exercise hegemony over the region of western Asia and, later, northern Africa. As far as merchants and merchant capital are concerned, the urbanization accomplished by the founding of these new cities provided a greater field of activity than obtained before Islam.

As recipients of waves of *rawadif* (newcomers), Basra and Kufa grew into the administrative centers that regulated the collection and the distribution of surplus wealth under the command of a governor appointed from Medina. Each of these cities developed a registry (Diwan al-Jund, Bureau of the Army) in which soldiers and their pay were recorded. Each soldier and his dependents received a specific amount of cash and in-kind payment as his annual 'ata' (stipend). This registry had its antecedents on the battlefield, since each army had an appointed official, known as *sahib al-aqbad wa al-maqasim,* in charge of receiving and dividing the spoils of war.[63] Another important registry at this time was Diwan al-Kharaj, where the collection of taxes was recorded.

As collection and distribution of surplus wealth were basic features of the state, Basra and Kufa, among others, became the centers from which this distribution took place. Therefore, with the presence of a large population, wide distribution of wealth, and a greater demand for goods, luxury or otherwise, Basra and Kufa became thriving markets that generated a great commercial exchange between Iraq and the Hijaz, on the one hand, and with other points in Arabia, on the other. And with the creation of Fustat in Egypt, Medina linked the economy of Iraq and the eastern provinces with the economies of Syria, Egypt, and, later, North Africa. With Medina at the center, the caliphate integrated into a single unit hitherto incompatible regions in which commercial exchange was facilitated to a degree unattained before. It was to consolidate this achievement that the Umayyad caliph 'Abd al-Malik fixed the rate of exchange between gold of the former Byzantine provinces and silver of the Sasanids. This exchange was based on the pre-Islamic weights of the Quraishi merchants.[64]

Egypt

With the conquest of 'Asqalan, the whole eastern front of the Mediterranean, except for Tripoli, was under Medina's control. This control, however, might be challenged by the Byzantines, especially if they continued to hold Tripoli and Alexandria. Egypt's strategic importance was matched by its economic value, as a surplus-producing region and as a familiar market for Mecca's merchants. The Egyptian campaign began shortly after the conference of al-Jabiya, where 'Umar laid down basic policies to be followed in the conquered territories. 'Amr ibn al-'As, who had served as tax collector in Oman and led the conquest of Palestine, was entrusted with the leadership of three thousand men who crossed the Sinai toward the end of A.H. 18 (A.D. 639). 'Amr's prior experience in

Egypt as a Meccan who traded in Alexandria no doubt added to his qualifications for leading the war on this new front.[65]

'Amr's first objective was Peliusium (al-Farma'), a fortress in the northeastern point of the delta.[66] It lay about a mile and a half from the sea and was connected to the harbor by a canal. 'Amr besieged the well-fortified fortress for nearly a month before he took it at the start of the new year. The Muslims then marched south to avoid crossing the delta on their way to Alexandria. Within three months of the capture of Peliusium, they reached Heliopolis and besieged the reinforced fortress of Babylon. The siege lasted for seven months, even after the arrival of Muslim reinforcements from Medina. Finally the fortress surrendered and a treaty was concluded between the two parties (in A.H. 19 [A.D. 641]). According to this treaty, life and property were secured, *kharaj* and *jizya* were to be collected, and the Egyptians were to build bridges and provide guides and hospitality. Another significant provision was a requirement for setting up a market for the Muslims, who could then obtain "food and fodder."[67] As the setting up of markets was also agreed to in other areas under Muslim control, commercial activity was thus part of the expansion; indeed, it was revitalized by the expansion.

After securing the bridges near Babylon, 'Amr crossed the Nile and marched downstream toward Alexandria, the Byzantine capital and the seat of the imperial patriarch and the viceroy of Egypt. By the time the Muslims reached Alexandria, they had reduced the number of fortresses on the western side of the delta. But Alexandria was heavily fortified and the Muslims could only besiege the city and isolate it from the rest of the province. During the siege, the Muslim army was provisioned by the markets set up by Coptic leaders. In the meantime, the Muslims were also able to subdue several points in the delta. After a siege of several months, Alexandria surrendered (in September A.D. 642 [A.H. 21]) under the terms of a treaty that was very similar to their other treaties. The major points of this treaty included security of life, property, and churches; payment of the poll tax and the *kharaj* in three installments; allowing those who wished to vacate Egypt to do so with their possessions; requiring that the Nubians who accepted the treaty provide horses and slaves, but guaranteeing that their territory would not be invaded if they did not "interfere in commerce whether going into Egypt or leaving it."[68]

The last provision of the treaty, pertaining to the Nubians, was reaffirmed when 'Abdallah ibn Sa'd became governor of Egypt. 'Abdallah, who had seen his predecessor fail to subdue the Nubians in Upper Egypt, concluded a treaty with them whereby they paid tribute in the form of slaves and the Muslims were allowed to market foodstuffs, such as lentils and wheat, in Nubia. But the provision is also significant because it reflected the conscious protection of merchant interests. As it implied, trade coming into Egypt or going outside was facilitated, since no obstacles could be placed in the way of merchants. Such a guarantee of unharassed movement was similar to what had been promised Baʿlabakk merchants when they were allowed to travel anywhere in areas under Muslim control. This fact should lead us to reconsider the implications of the term "*ibn al-Sabil*," translated as the wayfarer or traveler who commanded special attention in these treaties. At the time of the expansion, those travelers could not have been engaged in mere sightseeing, or in the holy act of travel for the sake of knowledge. They were, for the most part, merchants who were not molested during the expansion and who were encouraged to pursue their commerce by being given special privileges under these treaties.

After the surrender of Alexandria, ʿAmr secured the trade routes that came into Egypt from North Africa and the Libyan desert by attacking Cyranica, Tripolitania, and the oasis/trade centers in the interior of the Fezzan (A.H. 23 [A.D. 643–644]). The conquest of the rest of North Africa soon followed. This leg of ʿAmr's campaign was relatively easy, mainly because these areas depended on Alexandria as their primary market, either as the terminus for trade caravans or as a market for their products. Thus, once Alexandria surrendered and accepted Muslim rule, these localities had to follow suit to continue their economic relations with Alexandria.[69]

The Egyptian campaign is usually regarded as an illustration of the haphazard and spontaneous nature of the Arab/Islamic expansion. And ʿAmr is used to show how the commanders were self-serving and acting on their own initiative rather than following a centralized strategy.[70] The economic and strategic potential of Egypt, the conference of al-Jabiya, and the dispatch of ʿAmr himself immediately afterward are ignored in such explanations. Despite the negative way in which ʿAmr is usually portrayed, however, his actions turn out to be in complete accordance with the interests of the state in Medina. His accomplishments in Egypt could not have been realized without directives and active aid from the center.

ʿAmr's accomplishments in Egypt were crowned by the founding of Fustat, hardly a personal endeavor, to serve as the urban administrative center from which the distribution of wealth could be effected. Before the Muslim conquest, Egypt's surplus wealth was shipped abroad to Byzantium. For this purpose, Alexandria was the best location. It is natural, then, that Alexandria was the capital of the province and the place where the Byzantines concentrated their defenses. But with the Arab conquest, the surplus wealth of Egypt was redirected to Medina. For this purpose, Alexandria would be a very poor choice indeed. Therefore, a new capital had to be created to firm the new relationship and facilitate the flow of surplus wealth in the new direction. This center was Fustat.

Fustat was located at the southern tip of the delta, not far from the fortress of Babylon. The Nile supplied water to the inhabitants as well as to the fields. Fustat had a commanding position for the control of the delta and Upper Egypt. Furthermore, it was nearly on a straight line from the Gulf of Suez, so ʿAmr redug a defunct canal from the time of the pharaohs—the Khalij Amir al-Muʾminin—to connect Fustat with the Red Sea. Ships loaded with Egyptian wealth could sail easily to Medina, as easily as they had sailed from Alexandria to Constantinople. Consequently, just as Basra and Kufa had done, Fustat grew into the capital of a new province where the interests of the state and of the merchants were well served.[71]

The economic relationship between Medina and the provincial capitals is seen, among other examples, in the circumstances following the plague of ʿAmwas and ʿAm al-Ramada, Year of the Ashes. To alleviate the scarcity of food in Medina, Caliph ʿUmar called on his governors to send provisions. Abu ʿUbaida, we are told, sent four thousand loads of food from Syria before he finally succumbed to the plague. Abu Musa, governor of Basra, was similarly forthcoming. And after an initial delay concerning the Khalij, ʿAmr obliged the caliph's request and sent shiploads of wheat to Medina.[72]

Based on his initial delay, ʿAmr was accused of delaying the payment of Egyptian taxes to Medina. His sincerity was doubted further because of his later association with Muʿawiya. This perception is erroneous, however, as revealed in the exchange of letters between ʿAmr and the caliph. This correspondence began when ʿAmr informed the caliph that the canal that connected the Nile with the Red Sea had silted up; therefore, he was unable to comply readily with the caliph's request. ʿAmr went on to say that if the caliph desired that food prices in Medina should equal those in Egypt, he would dig up the canal.[73] The letter gives no indication which of the two prices was higher, but it is safe to assume that Medina's prices were higher, because of the famine, on the one hand, and because the *kharaj* was collected easily in Egypt due to a plentiful harvest. In this instance, if wheat, for example, was shipped to Medina at Egyptian prices, the Egyptians would lose on the transaction.

Accordingly, the beneficiaries of the Egyptian *kharaj* in Egypt protested the caliph's request by saying that it would cause them great harm and would mean that the "*kharaj* of Egypt will break." 'Amr dutifully relayed their concern to the caliph, who became angry enough to write back ordering his governor to proceed immediately with the dredging of the canal. He said, "May God break the *kharaj* of Egypt for the sake of building up Medina and its recovery." After that, we are told that 'Amr dug the canal and that ship after ship passed to Medina loaded with Egyptian wheat. We are told further that, when the prices between the two cities became equal, "the prosperity of Egypt only increased." [74]

'Amr, therefore, far from being self-serving, was protecting the interests of a larger constituency in his exchange with the caliph. And it is clear how the taxes of Egypt were channeled to Medina and how important Egypt was as a source of provisions for the Hijaz. When 'Umar decreed that each needy family should receive a camelload of provisions, including the camel, it was not only the poor who benefited. [75] The greatest benefit, however, accrued to the merchants. Since the state undertook the responsibility of distributing the wealth, it relieved the merchants of spending their resources, as they had been required to do before Islam. In addition, when the ships embarked to Medina, the caliph issued a *sakk* (a receipt, ration ticket) to the potential recipients in the amount due to them. This gave the merchants the opportunity to buy and sell the tickets at a profit even before the wheat had arrived. One of those merchants was Hakim ibn Hizam, already an important wheat merchant. Through his speculation with the tickets, he was able to realize an enormous profit. However, when this became known to 'Umar, he forced Hakim to donate his profits to be distributed as *sadaqa*. [76] Nevertheless, the economic benefits from Medina's control of Egypt are self-evident, the more so since Medina was at the center of a newly unified market and surplus-producing area, linking Egypt, Syria, and Iraq as the nucleus of a larger empire.

To conclude, the following points should be highlighted. The Islamic expansion started with the consolidation of Medina's control of Arabia. This control, justified by the "apostasy" of certain factions, was accomplished in a short period at the end of which Medina gained control of an already-deployed social force. The caliphate, relying on merchants to provide leaders and administrators, dispatched this force to fight the Byzantines and the Sasanids. As a result, the Muslims won control of the surrounding surplus-producing regions, with their trade routes, and placed them in the hands of the Muslim merchants. The Muslims were well received by the local merchants, who benefited due to less-burdensome and better-defined taxes as well as the freedom to trade in an expanded and safe market. The expansion at once consolidated the state and the political hegemony of the merchants and resulted in the distribution of wealth to the believers. Distribution of wealth enlarged the social base of the capital-owning class, thus further legitimizing merchant dominance of the state and securing their position in the new socioeconomic order.

Aside from land grants and other forms of distribution, such as the annual stipends, the state was consolidated by the massive urbanization process that was initiated right after the conquest. Not only did Muslims settle in already-built towns and cities, but new ones were created. Rather than camp cities or garrison towns, these urban centers were the concrete expression of the new socioeconomic and political order created by the Islamic expansion. They were the administrative centers from which the merchants exercised their political and ideological hegemony and the market towns in which commercial exchange took place and in which new avenues of economic investment were created.

A most conspicuous result of the expansion was the removal of several obstacles confronting the merchants. Muslim merchants became politically dominant in western Asia and northern Africa. This is a far cry from the position of the Meccan and other Arab merchants before Islam. Their hegemony was secured further by allowing other merchants to participate in the commercial dynamic in the lands under the control of the Muslims. Finally, the nature and motives of the expansion could be re-stated. The expansion, accomplished through *jihad,* was a movement for the purpose of gaining political control of the surrounding surplus-producing regions for the advantage of the merchants, who were the most visible component of the state, its leaders, organizers, administrators, and commanders. *Jihad,* therefore, not merely fulfilled a religious duty, but, from the very beginning, also offered material rewards. Those who died while exerting their efforts on behalf of the Umma, represented by the state, were assured of their reward in paradise.

Neither was it a haphazard movement initiated by nomads for the sake of plunder. Rather, it was well coordinated and served specific interests, as revealed by the numerous treaties and pacts that the Muslims signed with their conquered inhabitants. Thus, it was Islam that provided the merchants with ideological and institutional mechanisms by which they legitimized their political power, extended their markets, and created further avenues for the investment of their capital. It was Islam that mobilized merchant capital and it was Islam that brought the appropriated wealth back to Medina for the benefit of the Umma.

6. The Emergence of the New Segment

While an administrative structure was being developed to oversee the distribution of wealth, new members were being recruited into the ranks of the wealthy. Many Muslims acquired wealth for the first time, and the improvement in their economic fortunes was accompanied by an improvement in their social standing. Their social and economic transformation, then, was recent and came after their participation in the service of Islam. This part of the Arab/Islamic ruling elite should be distinguished from those Muslims who were wealthy and powerful before the coming of Islam. The ongoing distribution of wealth during the Islamic expansion resulted in the formation of two segments in the Muslim ruling elite: the New Segment, and the Traditional Segment. The distinctions between the two segments, their social and economic positions, their aspirations, and their interests, are real and must be examined for a clearer understanding of the events that unfolded during ʿUthman's caliphate.

By identifying these two segments we can also examine this controversial period more comprehensively than would be possible if we continued to rely on conventional explanations, based as they are on religious grounds, tribal antagonism, or the nomadic/settled paradigm. Such explanations do not take into account the substance behind the emergence of the interests and positions that were advocated and well articulated by each side. This chapter, then, examines the rise of the New Segment, its interests and its ideological bases, and discusses its struggle against the Traditional Segment, a struggle that eventually led to the murder of ʿUthman. I shall illustrate that, although there was a general distribution of wealth, the Traditional Segment received the lion's share. I shall also discuss ʿUthman's policies, for a better understanding of the issues behind the civil war. It will become apparent as the discussion unfolds that the two segments were social forces competing for the office of the caliph, each with its own legitimate aspirations and reasons for seeking control of political office.

Distribution of Wealth

Distribution of wealth and the opportunity to accumulate it were, in theory, equally guaranteed to all of the believers. But as it turned out, distribution favored the merchants, who made up the bulk of the Traditional Segment. Several factors tilted distribution in their favor. Their experience in finance offered them an edge over members of the New Segment, many of whom had had no opportunity to deal with capital before. Experience in dealing with capital helped the traditionally wealthy accumulate more capital than others by virtue of already-accumulated capital, which could be invested in the new business opportunities made available after the expansion. 'Amr ibn al-Huwairith al-Makhzumi, for example, realized greater profit than some of his contemporaries after the Battle of Nihawand. It is reported that al-Sa'ib ibn al-Aqra', *sahib al-aqbad wa al-aqsam*, did not distribute certain jewels that were part of the treasure of the Nakhirjan pending consultation with 'Umar. 'Umar later ordered him to sell the jewels on the market and deposit the money in the treasury (another report says he was to distribute it among the soldiers). Al-Sa'ib went back to Kufa, where "the merchants swarmed" over him. 'Amr bought some of the jewels after he had borrowed money from "the stipends of the subjects and the fighters," which might suggest that he either borrowed the money from individuals or from the treasury. He took the jewels and sold them in Hira, where he realized double his original investment. He invested his money in a public bath and agricultural land and remained one of the wealthiest in Kufa.[1]

In addition to and because of the advantage of their historical experience, the Traditional Segment had a visible and commanding role in the service of Islam, whether in administration or in leading the armies of the state. As officials, they had control of the resources and a ready access to the wealth of the treasury. Ready access to capital through the state, either by borrowing or by gifts, facilitated greater accumulation of wealth by officials who were largely merchants and traditionally wealthy. The state even became a vehicle by which to join the merchant class. The example of Mu'adh ibn Jabal has already been noted. Reports say that he was the first to use wealth from the Central Treasury for his own trade. Muhammad ignored the criticism levied against Mu'adh on the grounds that he had earlier lost most of his wealth.[2] ʿUtba ibn Abi Sufyan used his position as tax collector to conduct his own business.[3] In another example, Abu Musa al-Ashʿari, the second governor of Basra, was sending taxes paid in cash (*mal allah*) to the treasury in Medina. He suggested to ʿAbdallah and ʿUbaidallah, sons of ʿUmar, that they borrow from the tax, purchase some "wares of Iraq," and sell them in Medina, where "surely they would realize a profit." They then could repay the Central Treasury. The two followed his suggestion and they were able to realize as great a profit as predicted. When ʿUmar learned of their doings, he ordered his sons to place half of their profits in the Central Treasury on the grounds that not all Muslims had the same access to the treasury.[4] Many other officials and nonofficials took advantage of their access to the Central Treasury to invest in trade.[5] As a result, ʿUmar made it his policy to appropriate to the Central Treasury half of whatever his governors acquired during their tenure.[6]

Unlike members of the Traditional Segment, some members of the New Segment did not have business acumen, as they had no experience with capital. The following account illustrates this situation. During Khalid's siege of Hira, his soldiers were able to capture prisoners of war. One of the soldiers was a certain Khuraim from the B. Tamim who came into possession of an old woman "beyond his age." This woman, Bint Buqaila, happened to be from an influential and rich family. As was common then, Khuraim set her free in return for a ransom, which he set at one thousand dirhams. When some of his companions learned of this exchange, they asked him why he had set her free so cheaply when he could have asked and received many times that amount. Khuraim replied that he did not know any number higher than "ten hundreds."[7]

While Khuraim's ignorance of high finance might seem an extreme case, he should be regarded, nevertheless, as a fair representative of the tribesmen who participated in the expansion. The New Segment gained less than the Traditional Segment. Nevertheless, with the kind of distribution allowed by the conquest, Khuraim and those like him were entering the threshold of a new class. Other than the previously mentioned Abu Qatada and Abu Dharr and his brother, many individuals acquired property for the first time. Salama ibn al-Muhabbaq, for example, with his share of the booty bought land near the newly founded city of Basra. Investing in land, he remained rich for several generations and left a sizable legacy for his grandson al-Muthanna ibn Musa, who lived comfortably in Basra.[8] Distribution of wealth, however unequal, resulted in the economic transformation of a substantial segment of Muslim society.

It was not only in the economic sphere that the New Segment experienced a transformation, but also in its social standing. As members had owned no wealth before Islam, they were from an inferior social position, the *mustad*ᶜ*afun,* the *mawali,* the slaves, and other less-advantaged sectors of society. By embracing Islam, especially if they did so in the beginning, the social standing of the New Segment began to improve as the Umma became more powerful. They, in fact, became part of the elite of this new society. They were accorded special honor as Muhammad's companions, defenders of the new faith, teachers of the new religion, and so on. The New Segment, thus, can be characterized as made up of all of the Muslims who were not part of the traditional power structure in pre-Islamic times and yet acquired wealth and status after they became Muslim, especially early on.

It is clear that social and economic transformations took place during and as a result of the Islamic expansion. The expansion brought further consolidation of the economic and political power of the Arab merchants as they controlled the emerging state and recruited new members to the capital-owning class. Although this last expanded its social base and became even more secure, the expansion created, nevertheless, that sector that is distinguishable as the New Segment. But as the New Segment started out at a disadvantage, ʿUmar legitimized the transformation in its social and economic position when he institutionalized its gains. First, he established a new social hierarchy when he abolished the relationship of *wala*ʾ among Arabs, a step similar to that which Muhammad took when he disallowed the enslavement of other Arabs.[9] The relationship of *wala*ʾ remained, however, and was reserved for non-Arabs.

ʿUmar institutionalized the new social structure based on an Islamic hierarchy by creating what came to be known as Diwan Umar.[10] This hierarchy, with its material underpinnings in the form of stipends, rested on *al-sabiqa fi al-Islam* (precedence in Islam). The *sahaba,* companions of the Prophet, were further distinguished among those who have the precedence of *sabiqa.* The earlier one accepted Islam, the higher one's position and stipend; those who joined Islam before the Battle of Badr received higher stipends than those who joined after al-Hudaybiyya or after the conquest of Mecca. Muhammad's family members received special honor and were placed in a higher category than the rest. Muhammad's wives, for example, received an annual stipend of ten thousand dirhams; Hasan and Husain, Muhammad's grandsons, each received five thousand dirhams.[11]

A system for the distribution of stipends was also established in the provinces. This system was also based on the date of first participation in the Islamic expansion; those who fought in the early battles received higher stipends than those who joined later, when most of the battles had been won. There were three categories: those who participated in the earliest battles of the expansion (*ahl al-Ayyam*); those who participated in the decisive Battle of Qadisiyya (*ahl al-Qadisiyya*); and the latecomers (*rawadif*). The first category received an annual stipend that ranged over time from five thousand to three thousand dirhams, with extra for additional valor; the second received between three thousand and two thousand dirhams. The third category received stipends ranging between two hundred and fifteen hundred dirhams, based on the date they moved to the provincial capitals to be registered in their Diwan al-Jund. Women and children also received a share, women two hundred dirhams and children one hundred.[12] One can safely assume that latecomers did not claim any precedence in Islam either. This category was the most disadvantaged of the New Segment, as they had yet to experience the moral and material gains attained by earlier Muslims.

ʿUmar also recognized the New Segment by appointing many as officials of the state, such as ʿAmmar ibn Yasir, who was appointed governor of Kufa. ʿUmar's policies, therefore, legitimized the position of the New Segment by guaranteeing the payment of an annual income and by allowing them a share in the political structure, even though it was dominated by the Traditional Segment. ʿUmar's caliphate was based on a compromise that worked to the advantage of the largest number of Muslims, as nearly everyone received a share of the wealth, even the infants. It is for this reason that his caliphate served as a model for later generations and many advocated a return to its type, especially after the civil war that erupted between the two segments.

The *Shura* and the Seeds of the Fitna

ʿUmar's death was untimely, since he had indicated a wish to raise the lower stipends to a more substantial level. But he was assassinated by Abu Luʾluʾa, a *mawla* of al-Mughira ibn Shuʿba. It is reported that Abu Luʾluʾa worked in Medina as a carpenter, blacksmith, and engraver and had to pay his master, as required by his relationship of *walaʾ*, one hundred dirhams a month (some reports say sixty) as a *kharaj* on his income. Abu Luʾluʾa complained to ʿUmar that the amount was too high and requested that the caliph intercede on his behalf with al-Mughira. Some reports say that in considering the high demand for such professional skills,

ʿUmar did not agree with the complaint. Nevertheless, these reports say that he spoke with al-Mughira and asked him to lighten Abu Luʾluʾaʾs workload. But as al-Mughira was slow to respond, Abu Luʾluʾa vented his anger on the unguarded caliph by stabbing him during the morning prayer on 25 Dhul Hijja A.H. 23 (4 November A.D. 644).[13]

ʿUmar lived on for a few days, during which he appointed a council of *shura,* a consultation committee, made up of six men who were to choose the next caliph from among themselves. The six were ʿAbd al-Rahman ibn ʿAwf, ʿUthman ibn ʿAffan, ʿAli ibn Abi Talib, al-Zubair ibn al-ʿAwwam, Saʿd ibn Abi Waqqas, and Talha ibn ʿUbaidallah.[14] ʿUmar could have appointed a successor, as he had been appointed by Abu Bakr. It is reported that his choice had narrowed to two, ʿUthman and ʿAli, but he did not appoint either, since he feared that each would give members of his family high posts.[15] Thus, ʿUmar's appointment of the *shura* was recognition that the two most obvious candidates not only had conflicting interests but also would have abandoned the policy of compromise between the Traditional Segment and the New Segment.

If the nature of the new caliph was in doubt, there was no question about the office itself; an ad hoc creation at the accession of Abu Bakr, it became a permanent political institution at the death of ʿUmar. Conflict over the caliphate became a question of who should occupy the office and what interests it should represent.

The *shura,* comprising Meccans and Quraishites, had many shortcomings, the most obvious, its lack of wide representation, excluding even the Ansar. But there was no opposition to its makeup. The council reflected the power structure that existed in Mecca before Islam, thus the Traditional Segment was represented in the *shura* by five to one. We have seen that ʿAbd al-Rahman had no difficulty in securing his capital after his emigration to Medina, where he went on to become one of the richest of his time. Similarly, Talha and al-Zubair simply diverted their trade from Mecca to Medina after the Hijra. When ʿUmar died, Talha was attending to business in al-Sarah.[16] Apparently, his absence did not prevent ʿUmar from including him in the *shura.* Saʿd was the leader of Qadisiyya and the first governor of Kufa. His wealth was in the league of that of other members of the *shura.* As for ʿUthman, suffice it to say that he was an Umayyad, at the top of the traditional merchants.

In contrast to the traditionally wealthy, and now more powerful through Islam, ʿAli was the only member who was from the New Segment. Like the majority of his followers, ʿAli owed his position solely to Islam. He grew up in humble surroundings, first with his father, Abu

Talib, whose business went bankrupt, then with Muhammad. Abu Talib could not repay a loan to al-ʿAbbas, which stripped him of any material benefit from *siqaya* and *rifada*, which he was required to hand over to al-ʿAbbas. Abu Talib's inability to provide for his family forced Muhammad and al-ʿAbbas to adopt Abu Talib's children. Muhammad took ʿAli into his household to become his right-hand man. In a real sense, ʿAli was like a *mawla* of Muhammad, although the sources never speak of their relationship in those terms.

After he came to Medina, ʿAli began to engage in *muzaraʿa* (share-cropping), like many other Meccans. But with the increased distribution of wealth as a result of the spread of Islam, he began to acquire more, especially land. According to Saleh el-Ali,

> the greatest large estates owners are ʿAli, Zubair and their families, as well as Talha and ʿAbd al-Rahman b. ʿAwf. Ali b. Abi Talib owned Yanbuʿ. According to Ibn Shubba, he bought it from Kushud who, in turn got it as a grant from the Prophet; then ʿUmar granted him other estates in Yanbuʿ. According to ʿAmmar b. Yasir, the Prophet granted ʿAli Thil-Ashira in Yanbuʿ, but he reclaimed some land and dug several springs such as Ain Abi Naizar where he cultivated vegetables. It was valued at 200.000 in the time of Moʿawia; he dug in Yanbuʿ also al-Bughaibigha which was confiscated at the time of Yazid. . . . ʿAli also owned Wadi Turaʿa in Fadak, Wadi al-Ahmar, in Shiʿb Ziyad, Wadi al-Baida, Afa, and al-Qusaiba, all of which were in Harrat al-ridjla. He had also Sawiqa. His estates in Medina were al-Faqurain, Bir Qais, and al-Shajara.[17]

Thus it is clear that although ʿAli's wealth was in line with that of other members of the *shura*, his wealth was recently acquired and only through Islam.

Against this survey of the *shura* members, the competition for the caliphate was between Meccans who represented the two larger segments of the Muslims. Many urged ʿAbd al-Rahman to take the office, but he opted for the role of the caliph-maker rather than the caliph. He began a series of consultations with other members of the *shura* as soon as ʿUmar died. Talha was informed of the news and was asked to hurry back to Medina. In his absence, however, Saʿd assumed the responsibility of his vote. It quickly became clear that ʿUthman was the favorite, which prompted ʿAli to lobby with Saʿd for his two votes. In qualifying himself for the office, ʿAli repeatedly fell back on his close relations with Muhammad, on his early conversion, and on the fact that he was a member of the House of Prophethood.[18]

The discussion that went on in Medina once the choice was narrowed to ʿUthman and ʿAli is interesting. ʿAmmar ibn Yasir, a typical member of the New Segment, said to ʿAbd al-Rahman that if he sought the agreement of all the Muslims, then his choice should be ʿAli. ʿAbdallah ibn Abi al-Sarh from the B. Umayya countered that if ʿAbd al-Rahman wanted the agreement of all of the Quraish, then his choice should be ʿUthman.[19] The distinction made by ʿAmmar and ʿAbdallah reflects the competing interests for the position of caliph. By the Quraish, ʿAbdallah actually meant the Traditional Segment; by the Muslims, ʿAmmar meant the majority of the Muslims, all of whom had attained social and economic mobility as a result of Islam and its expansion.

In his concern to ascertain the policy direction of the potential caliphs, ʿAbd al-Rahman, the caliph-maker, put the same question to each of the two candidates: Would they base their policies on the Qurʾan, the precedence of Muhammad, and the policies of ʿUmar and Abu Bakr? ʿAli demurred, saying that he hoped to rule also according to his experience and ability. It was clear from his statement that he did not believe that the power of the caliph could be limited to those bases proposed by ʿAbd al-Rahman. He added his own knowledge and experience to them, which would orient the caliphate significantly toward the New Segment.

When ʿUthman was asked the question, he replied in the affirmative without any qualifications. As he was heavily favored by the *shura*, this was enough to tilt the decision in his favor, and ʿAbd al-Rahman promptly declared his allegiance (the *baiʿa*) to him. The rest of the *shura* followed suit. Apparently, ʿAli hesitated, and ʿAbd al-Rahman had to remind him of his duty. ʿAli gave his allegiance to ʿUthman and showed his displeasure at the selection when he added, "A trick, and what a trick!"[20] ʿUthman assumed office on the first of Muharram A.H. 24 (7 November A.D. 644) before Talha, the last member of the *shura*, could cast his vote.

When Talha finally arrived, the caliph had already been selected. Resentful at being excluded from the deliberations of the *shura*, Talha said that such a decision should not have excluded him and threatened to withhold his recognition of the new caliph. But as soon as he found out that "all of the Quraish" agreed with the selection, he came out in favor of ʿUthman also.[21] Thus, given a choice between ʿAli and ʿUthman, each qualified, but with a particular view of the caliphate, the electors chose ʿUthman. They saw him as a representative of their interests, the interests of the Traditional Segment.

Shaban characterizes ʿUthman as "a Makkan to the core. He had lived most of his life in Makka and, as a man of considerable wealth, had many trading connections there and well understood the interests of Quraish." [22] But Shaban fails to see the connection between those qualifications and the selection of ʿUthman as the next caliph when he calls his appointment "an unfortunate choice." [23] The promotion of ʿUthman to the caliphate was inspired by the interests of the electors, and it was specifically for his Meccan connections and as an Umayyad, distinguished merchant and leader, that he was chosen over ʿAli, who had already begun to articulate the aspirations of the New Segment for the highest political office.

ʿUthman used the mandate of the *shura* to consolidate his power. The New Segment, having a potential leader who had come so close to assuming the office of the caliphate, also used the *shura* to strengthen its position. As ʿUthman continued to consolidate the position of his constituency, the two segments grew farther apart. The conflict emerged gradually, starting with individual opposition and ending with a social movement that swept ʿUthman out of the caliphate, as we shall see presently.

ʿUthman's Caliphate

Although Medina was relatively tranquil when ʿUthman was chosen caliph, the situation in the provinces was not. It was becoming evident by A.H. 22 (A.D. 642) that expansion was needed, since, for example, too many Muslims had settled in Basra for the *kharaj* of the province. The distribution of wealth as set by ʿUmar could not be sustained and complaints were heard about the system's inadequacy, especially from the late arrivals. To alleviate the situation, ʿUmar proposed to transfer some of the *kharaj* of Kufa to the Basrans. But the Kufans objected. And when the Basrans tried to claim some of the *kharaj* from Isfahan, since they had helped the Kufans conquer it, the Kufans again objected, saying that the Basrans came as reinforcement only after the battle had been won. ʿUmar agreed with the Kufans; however, he transferred to the Basrans one hundred dirhams each for the earlycomers.[24]

ʿUmar's transfer could not solve the basic distribution problem, since only those who already received a higher stipend were rewarded with the additional income. The newcomers, on the other hand, were faced with the same dilemma: smaller stipends and lower social position. This worked to the disadvantage of the New Segment and ultimately led to its weakness, since the disparity in the amount of the annual stipends created the possibility of conflicting interests within the same segment.

Further Expansion

After ʿUthman took office, he inaugurated a new phase of the expansion, extending the conquest to areas in central Asia, north Africa, and the Mediterranean. He took advantage of the Basrans' unhappiness with their governor, Abu Musa, to dismiss him and to appoint in his place ʿAbdallah ibn ʿAmir from the B. Umayya. For the first time, Basra was given command of the eastern Arabian regions of Bahrain and Oman, which placed Basra in charge of all of the territories that surrounded the Gulf and added to the economic and strategic significance of this provincial capital. Many eastern Arabian tribesmen went to Basra to be included in the Diwan al-Jund. Ibn ʿAmir was welcomed by the Basrans and was able to finish the conquest of Sasanid territories, especially the rich Khurasan, and to push farther east toward Farghana.

ʿUthman dismissed ʿAmr ibn al-ʿAs in Egypt and appointed ʿAbdallah ibn Saʿd ibn al-Sarh, another Umayyad, who reorganized the financial system, increasing the revenue of the state severalfold. Similar inroads were made into the western front after Ibn al-Sarh took command of Egypt. Forces from Fustat were dispatched south to Nubia, where they were able to win some trade agreements. Other oases in the Libyan desert were secured. But most significantly, it was the expedition to Ifriqya that opened the gates for a takeover of the rest of north Africa. Ifriqya was finally pacified and the Byzantines were forced to evacuate after the establishment of Qairawan.

A qualitative difference in the expansion, which so far had been accomplished on land, was inaugurated during ʿUthman's caliphate. For the first time, seaborne expeditions in the Mediterranean were conducted in pursuit of the Byzantines. These sea operations were largely organized by Muʿawiya, who now governed the provinces of Syria and Jazira combined. Seaborne expeditions had not been possible as long as the Byzantines controlled Tripoli. The assault on Tripoli required long preparation, and ʿUmar had instructed Muʿawiya to rebuild towns and fortresses, to station garrisons in them, to distribute land to the soldiers, and to establish a system of light fires along the coast. Muʿawiya continued this program after ʿUthman took office and he rebuilt Antartus, Balda, Bulunyas, Jabala, and Maraqiya. Latakya was also rebuilt, repopulated, and a garrison stationed there. Muslims who settled on the coast and in the reconstructed cities and fortresses were again granted land to cultivate and thus consolidate Muslim control of the coastal areas. In fact, ʿUthman ordered Muʿawiya to distribute all the land and the houses that were evacuated during the conquest, to enlarge the mosques that were built before his caliphate, and to build more and larger ones. This attracted a great number of Muslims to the coast and, indeed, "the people moved to the coastal areas, coming from everywhere."[25] After a few years of resistance, Tripoli was isolated from the surrounding countryside, especially with the building of a fortress a few miles away. When a sea blockade was also instituted, Tripoli finally fell and the whole coast was free from the Byzantine presence. It was only then that Muʿawiya was allowed to embark on seaborne expeditions.

Much is made of ʿUmar's reluctance to allow Muʿawiya to "invade the sea." Some modern authors conclude that ʿUmar's refusal was inspired by the nature of the Arabs, who were considered "desert bedouins of inland areas." The sea was "an element with which they were neither ready nor willing to cope."[26] Rather than citing ignorance of the sea (which was not the case) and proferring misleading generalizations, the answer should be sought in the military/strategic situation along the coast, whether in Syria or in Egypt. The situation favored the Byzantines, as they were able to attack Alexandria (A.D. 645 [A.H. 24]) and to supply ʿAscalan, Caesarea, and Tripoli, helping them withstand the Muslim siege for as long as they did. It was natural, therefore, that ʿUmar would restrain Muʿawiya and instruct him to direct his attention to the improvement of the Muslims' position along the coast.

In addition to this strategic consideration, the seeming reluctance to take to the sea might be explained by a comparison between ʿUmar and ʿUthman. ʿUmar, a strict observer of Islamic principles and very sensitive about the enormous material gains of the Muslims, was at the same time wary of the traditional merchants and their power. His interests lay in the consolidation of the state and the establishment of a system for the distribution of wealth that would also reward the New Segment. ʿUthman, however, was inspired by traditional merchant interests, which lay in further expansion, to control not only more surplus-producing areas and markets but also more trade routes, as the venture in the Mediterranean suggests. Thus, now that the Muslims commanded the commercial network on land throughout western Asia and now that the Byzantines were driven off the Syrian coast, the Muslims could extend their control to the sea routes of the Mediterranean.

This change in the way the expansion was conducted was not only commercially advantageous but also strategically significant. The Muslims were in effect forcing the Byzantines to retreat toward Constantinople, at once securing the Syrian and Egyptian coasts and ensuring a trouble-free arena for Muslim shipping. The Byzantine retreat in the face of the Muslim advance was highlighted by repeated attempts to take Constantinople itself.

In giving Muʿawiya the go-ahead to initiate seaborne operations, ʿUthman stipulated that the soldiers should be a volunteer force and that they should be equipped and transported at the expense of the state. Muʿawiya wrote to the various locations along the coast ordering them to repair their ships and then to sail them to ʿAkka, the port selected as the gathering point of Muslim troops and the embarkation point of the fleet. Two hundred and twenty ships embarked before the noon prayer on a Friday in the spring of A.H. 28 (A.D. 648).[27] The destination of this fleet was Bahr al-Rum, the sea of the Byzantines, and, more specifically, Cyprus. The Muslims caught up with a fleet loaded with provisions and tribute destined for Constantinople and won an easy victory. Aside from the material wealth that they captured, they forced an agreement on Cyprus by which it had to pay a tribute of seven thousand dinars annually, desist from any harassment of Muslim ships, withhold aid to the Byzantines, and inform the Muslims of any hostile Byzantine movements. This treaty remained in effect until Cyprus revolted. It was reinstated again in A.H. 33 (A.D. 653). This time, around twelve thousand Muslims remained in Cyprus as a garrison.[28] The Muslims had also captured Rhodes in A.H. 31. It was eventually garrisoned by troops that received land grants.[29]

It is evident from the terms of the treaty with Cyprus that mercantile concerns were taken into consideration. This is especially true of the provisions that required the Cypriots to inform the Muslims of any hostile Byzantine movements and that forbade the harassment of Muslim ships. This probably indicates that the Muslims were already engaged in sea trade or were about to do so.

Although the greater rewards went to the merchants, the extension of the territorial hegemony of Medina was in the interests of the whole Umma. Thus, no opposition to this policy was voiced. In fact, the expansion was supported enthusiastically, since it benefited all. ʿUthman, however, began to apply certain fiscal measures that were associated with the conquest and that were identified later as generating opposition to the caliph. The most often-cited example was his gift to his kinsman and counselor in Medina, al-Hakam, of a fifth of the spoils of Ifriqya, in effect, the state's share. Another case was his gift of three hundred thousand dirhams to several Umayyads who were preparing themselves to join the conquest.[30] By thus manipulating the treasury for personal gifts, ʿUthman left himself wide open for criticism, since people felt ʿUmar would never have done such a thing. Therefore, although the expansion during 'Uthman's caliphate increased the wealth of the participants, the basic relations of distribution favoring the Traditional Segment remained the same, and may have intensified. Thus, further expansion did not solve the problems created by the unequal distribution of wealth. The whole distribution structure had to be changed, a demand to which 'Uthman's fiscal policies were in complete contradiction.

Centralization of Power

Centralization of the caliph's authority was a gradual process. It began during the tenure of 'Uthman's predecessors, especially 'Umar. We have seen that Abu Bakr's caliphate was an ad hoc creation. The extent of his involvement in state affairs may not have been foreseen, as suggested by the fact that he was still employed in the market-place and that, as caliph, he did not receive a salary. This did not mean, as we have seen, that Abu Bakr or any of his successors did not have power or did not exercise their authority over the armies. The caliph possessed power and authority by virtue of his election as a successor to and deputy of Muhammad charged with preserving the Umma. As the duties of the officials became more complex and required them to specialize in statecraft, 'Umar assigned a salary for the caliph and the various other officials, which allowed him to devote himself full time to the office.[31]

In addition to the salary, 'Umar changed the title of caliph from that of a deputy of Muhammad to that of *amir al-mu'minin*, commander of the faithful. Shaban misses the point altogether when he concludes that the change was simply to avoid "the cumbersome term, Khalifa of the Khalifa of the Prophet."[32] To Shaban, 'Umar gained no new powers and remained at best a "counsellor." 'Umar's actions and policies, as we have seen, as well as recent research disprove Shaban's assertion. As for 'Uthman, the mandate of the *shura* allowed him to continue the process of centralizing the authority of the caliph and consolidating the state. Mere centralization of authority was not the issue at this time or later; the issue was on what grounds this centralization should take place and what interests it should serve.

As mentioned earlier, 'Uthman initiated some administrative reorganization of the state. The state was divided into five major provinces with Medina at the center. Umayyad governors, moreover, were appointed to administer each of these provinces. Basra, now in command of Bahrain and Oman, was governed by 'Abdallah ibn 'Amir; Kufa was governed by al-Walid ibn 'Uqba, then by Sa'id ibn al-'As; Syria and Jazira were governed by Mu'awiya; Egypt was governed by 'Abdallah ibn Abi Sarh; and Yemen, by Ya'li ibn Umayya. Al-Hakam acted as a counselor to 'Uthman in Medina. The appointment of these Umayyads, with the attendant lucrative political and economic gains, was an outcome of 'Uthman's growing power. This, in turn, enhanced the position of the caliph even further, since these governors were answerable to the caliph on several grounds: as officials and protégés of 'Uthman; as members of the same clan; and as members of the Traditional Segment.

'Uthman opted for nepotism as a more effective method of rule; however, this did not turn out to be a simple case of nepotism, for his system proved to be an administrative convenience that accelerated centralization and, more important, helped concentrate political power in the hands of the Traditional Segment. Being members of the merchant class and experienced in administrative, fiscal, and organizational matters, these Umayyad governors served 'Uthman and the rest of the Umma by successfully enlarging the territorial hegemony of the state and by providing, in the process, more surplus-producing areas and trade routes. All of 'Uthman's governors were competent in executing their duties; therefore, 'Uthman's reliance on the Umayyads increased the power of the Traditional Segment, a power that it had not held at this level before Islam. 'Uthman's appointment of his relatives was not perceived immediately as nepotism or as providing for an Umayyad monopoly of the state structure. It was only later, when opposition intensified, that 'Uthman was criticized for these appointments and demands began to be heard for the removal of these officials.

Another facet of 'Uthman's centralization of authority lay in his conception of the role of the treasury. Unlike Abu Bakr and 'Umar, 'Uthman began to act as if the treasury were his personal funds. Although other rulers had held this view, he was the first caliph to do so. 'Uthman allowed members of the Traditional Segment greater access to the treasury. The case involving al-Walid ibn 'Uqba while governor of Kufa is illuminating. As was the usual practice, al-Walid borrowed a large amount of money from the treasury, to be repaid later. When payment was due, however, al-Walid refused to answer to the treasurer, 'Abdallah ibn Mas'ud. Disagreement between the two finally reached the caliph. 'Uthman wrote to Ibn Mas'ud and ordered him to desist from any further attempts to collect the loan and reminded him that he was merely "keeper of our treasury."[33] 'Uthman's largesse toward his relatives and members of the Traditional Segment became particularly objectionable to the New Segment and provided it with a source of discontent.

'Uthman also introduced a new taxation policy, which allowed the Traditional Segment to amass even greater wealth. Unlike his predecessors, he abolished the practice of taxing accumulated or "hidden" wealth (al-amwal al-batina).[34] Abolishing this tax was a clear testament to the alignment of his interests, since the most direct beneficiaries were members of the Traditional Segment.

Land Policies

'Uthman's centralization of political power was thus accompanied by parallel economic measures. Besides his ready access to the treasury, his interference in the governance of the land galvanized the opposition. We have seen that up to this point the state used the distribution of land as a means of consolidating its political hegemony, as the case on the Syrian coast illustrates, while following up on Islam's promise of distribution of wealth. Tracts of dead land were given to individuals who had enough resources to reclaim and develop them. Imperial estates (sawafi), in Iraq, Syria, and Egypt were initially considered to be spoils of war (faiʾ) and were thus reserved for the benefit of their respective conquerors, as was clearly the case in the Sawad. The rest belonged to the state and was reserved for the Muslims in posterity. 'Umar began to give land grants from the last category; 'Uthman increased these grants and, for the first time, claimed the right to the sawafi lands by dispensing grants from them. The recipients of these land grants came from both segments.[35]

But regardless of who the recipients of these land grants were, this policy did not favor the interests of the majority of the New Segment, who had acquired their wealth from this very land that had now become subject to individual appropriation. As soldiers, they received the annual stipend according to their grades and, as the original conquerors, enjoyed the income of the sawafi, which amounted to seven million dirhams at this time. Thus, 'Uthman's land policy not only meant greater power for the caliph but also the diminution of the economic strength of the New Segment.

Associated with 'Uthman's land policy is the rarely mentioned land exchange program. This program was started in A.H. 30 (A.D. 650) and perhaps coincided with the appointment of Saʿid ibn al-ʿAs as governor of Kufa to replace al-Walid. Because of mobility between the provinces, many who participated in the early conquest, sometimes in more than one province, returned either to Medina or to their original home. To use a prominent Muslim as an example, Zubair ibn al-ʿAwwam participated in the conquest of Egypt and thus received land in Fustat and Alexandria.

He also acquired property in Basra and other areas, but he lived in Medina. Apparently, many other Muslims followed this pattern. It was seemingly on behalf of these Muslims that ʿUthman argued that, by returning home, they did not forfeit their right to the *faiʾ*, which, after all, they had helped create. Therefore, he said, they should continue to receive the same privileges as if they had remained in the conquered territories.[36]

To make such a privilege manageable, ʿUthman suggested that those who left the provinces exchange their share of that land (that is, the income from it) for land near their residence. This program was popular and lands in all of the provinces were exchanged. Specific names are mentioned in the sources, such as al-Ashʿath, who exchanged land he owned in Hadramawt for land in Tiznabadh, a village near Kufa. Many who participated in Qadisiyya and the conquest of Madaʾin exchanged their land in Iraq for land near Khaybar owned by Talha. Talha, furthermore, was able to exchange land with the caliph himself. Talha's daily income from his property in Iraq was one thousand dinars. Marwan ibn al-Hakam exchanged a previous grant from ʿUthman for land in Ajama, near Basra, land that later became known as Nahr Marwan.[37]

Just as with political appointments, it was a while before the effects of this program were felt. Those who benefited the most from the land exchange were those who either already owned land or had enough capital to buy it. The greatest benefits, thus, went to the Traditional Segment, as exemplified by Talha and the various Umayyads. Although some members of the New Segment benefited also, the majority did not even possess the means by which to participate in this exchange. As such, they could not even reach the position of those who had *sabiqa* or were earlycomers in terms of social status, leadership positions, and benefits. Nevertheless, the encroachment of large landowners—the rich merchants of the Traditional Segment—was identified with ʿUthman's land policy. The clearest illustration of the resentment caused by this policy is seen in an incident in the court of Saʿid, who declared that "the Sawad [became] the garden of Quraish."[38] Members of the New Segment were outraged at the declaration, and al-Ashtar ibn Malik was particularly indignant and had to be restrained from attacking one of the speakers. Opposition, which had been slowly brewing, grew rapidly and more openly from this point on.

Before proceeding to an analysis of the opposition, it is important to restate a few points raised in the discussion of ʿUthman's policies. Having been chosen by the *shura*, ʿUthman used the mandate to transform the caliphate from an instrument of compromise, as it had been under ʿUmar, to one that favored the Traditional Segment. He accomplished this by appointing competent Umayyad administrators for the key provinces of the caliphate, thereby giving the Traditional Segment, led by the Umayyads, a monopoly over the state structure. In relying on this segment, ʿUthman gradually changed the qualification for holding such offices to past experience rather than one's precedence in Islam. This change deprived many of the New Segment of their chance to be included in the power structure.

Centralization of authority in the hands of the Traditional Segment was paralleled by certain economic measures, which further strengthened the wealth of that segment. ʿUthman assumed personal control of the treasury as well as instituting discriminatory land policies. Land was sought after by the merchants as another means of investing their capital and of holding a monopoly over the product as well as over the market. As a result, the Traditional Segment grew richer and more powerful and the New Segment became weaker, divided, and resentful. It is no wonder, then, that ʿUthman was accused of deviating from ʿUmar's policies and of introducing "innovations."

Growth of the Opposition

Opposition to ʿUthman grew during the last six years of his caliphate. This very crucial period of early Islamic history, a period that left an indelible mark on Islam and Muslim society, is the subject of much discussion and has been variously interpreted by modern scholars. Some follow the early chroniclers in suggesting that religious motives were behind the rebellion. They cite criticism of ʿUthman's compilation of one recension of the Qurʾan, of his introduction of certain rituals, and of the moral laxity that became more common as huge wealth was accumulated by the few. In such interpretations, a group known as *qurraʾ* played an important role. *Qurraʾ* was taken to mean Qurʾan reciters, thus they were dubbed the "pious party."

Others saw the rebellion as one of nomads trying to shake off the weight of a central authority or as tribespeople rebelling against Meccan and Quraishi control. The so-called pious party played its part here as well. These tribally based interpretations also hypothesize a dichotomy between northern and southern Arabs, the Qais and Yemen.

Such simplified explanations do not suffice to uncover the complex political and economic issues of this period. These explanations have been challenged recently by Shaban and Hinds. Shaban clears up some of the confusion about the *qurraʾ* by tracing the word to "*qarya*," village, but this does not necessarily mean that they were villagers (as opposed to city dwellers), as he seems to imply. It probably refers to landed interests, especially as some owned whole villages, as has been indicated earlier. Shaban sees the rise of opposition as a reaction to ʿUthman's "assumption of more authority than he was supposed to possess." [39] In his drive to assert his authority, the caliph followed a number of policies, and the casus belli was when he "added insult to injury by finally breaking down the distinction between ridda and pre-ridda Muslims," [40] citing al-Ashʿath as an example. Consequently, a deputation of tribesmen came to Medina to seek redress of their grievances and killed the caliph when negotiations proved fruitless.

Hinds' contributions, on the other hand, reveal much of the complexities of ʿUthman's caliphate. He says that ʿUthman's caliphate was characterized by the declining influence of an elite that had been promoted by ʿUmar and by the increasing power of tribal aristocracy of the pre-Islamic type. [41] The conflict that erupted was led by men who were "seeking to preserve positions and interests which they had either lost or were in the process of losing. Basically, they were provincial early comers with small followings who were trying to retain privileges acquired in the disorder that followed the conquests and who were sensitive to the threat posed to their position both by more substantial leaders . . . and by the central government itself." [42] Hinds disregards Shaban's explanation of the *qurraʾ* and continues to see them as a pious party. He is in agreement with Shaban regarding the rise of the *ridda* leaders, but he refers to them as "substantial" or as "old-style" leaders, since he cites none other than al-Ashʿath as an illustration of his point. Nevertheless, Hinds provides us with a better understanding of the conflict, except that as a conflict between elites, Islamic and tribal, there was little analysis of the nature of the political and economic interests of each of the sides of the conflict, beyond, again, disagreement with the caliph's policies.

The controversy raised around al-Ashʿath and the *ridda* stems from Abu Bakr's initial exclusion of the *ridda* tribesmen from the conquest (during the brief period of al-Ayyam) and from ʿUmar's supposed policy to exclude *ridda* leaders from command posts. ʿUmar, however, allowed *ridda* tribesmen to participate fully in the conquest as early as Qadisiyya. Thus, very early on, especially with the institution of Diwan al-Jund, the distinction between *ridda* and non-*ridda* became immaterial. In the Diwan, the annual stipends were determined according to when one joined the conquest, not whether one was *ridda* or non-*ridda*. When exclusion from command posts is discussed, reference is made to al-Ashʿath, Talha ibn Khuwailid, and ʿAmr ibn Maʿdi Karib. Their having led a *ridda* attempt is the reason usually given for their exclusion. The sources note, however, that these men participated valiantly in the conquest while holding various command posts. All three were present at Qadisiyya and subsequent major battles. At Qadisiyya, ʿAmr and Talha were in charge of a force in the vanguard that gathered information and employed diversionary tactics against the enemy. Both were also present at Nihawand and both were consulted in planning the battle, and it was Talha's opinion that carried the day and led to the success of the Muslims.[43] Al-Ashʿath's position was respected from the very beginning. On his arrival at Medina, he married none other than the caliph's sister. He must have been a man of considerable wealth, since he contributed four thousand camels to the war effort as a price for his freedom and later was also able to partake of ʿUthman's land exchange program. Finally, al-Ashʿath is mentioned in the chain of command at Nihawand.[44]

Exclusion from command posts, then, means that they were not appointed *first*-in-command. This was not unusual, however. We have already seen that Abu Bakr and ʿUmar chose their first-in-command from the Quraish. The exclusion of al-Ashʿath, Talha ibn Khuwailid, and ʿAmr ibn Maʿdi Karib should be seen as in line with excluding al-Muthanna ibn Haritha from the position of first-in-command of the Iraqi front. ʿUthman's elevation of al-Ashʿath's already high rank, therefore, was consistent with his policy of favoring the Traditional Segment.

Therefore, it is unjustified to speak of al-Ashʿath as having reemerged, whether as a *ridda* leader or as a "substantial" one, when he was prominent all along. Also, any role played by the fading stigma of once having been a member of a *ridda* faction in the opposition to ʿUthman could not have been significant, because of the new hierarchy established by ʿUmar. Furthermore, in all of the complaints of the opposition, hardly any reference can be found to the *ridda*. Complaints and the demands for redress were clearly concerned with the political and economic interests of the New Segment, with specific reference to land, stipends, and appointments to political office.

It has been my aim thus far to bring to light the formation of the two distinct segments of the Arab/Islamic ruling class, each with its own historical experience and its own conception of the caliphate. Distinguishing the Traditional Segment from the New Segment should help to reveal the social, economic, and political interests of the two, how they came into conflict, and how each side legitimized its action in the defense of these interests.

Opposition to ʿUthman came from two sides and sprang from completely different motives. One area of opposition was mounted by such men as Talha, ʿAbd al-Rahman ibn ʿAwf, Zubair, and by Aʾishah, the prophet's wife. These were Quraishites and represented the interests of the Traditional Segment. Although they benefited from ʿUthman's caliphate, their opposition stemmed from their objection to the growing Umayyad monopoly of the state structure. Talha, it may be recalled, had expressed a desire for the position of caliph when he declared that he was qualified for it. In fact, after ʿUthman was murdered, Talha, with the cooperation of Zubair and Aʾishah, led a movement to challenge ʿAli's caliphate. Aside from an Umayyad monopoly, Aʾishah may have also resented ʿUthman's ill-treatment of Muhammad's companions. The same motives could be ascribed to ʿAbd al-Rahman ibn ʿAwf, who disliked the actions of the caliph so much that he willed that ʿUthman should not be present at his funeral.[45]

ʿUthman was unable to strike at this group as he did against the New Segment, as will be seen below. He could not attack them, perhaps because they could mobilize greater resources than his other opponents, because they were members of the *shura,* and because they were close to Muhammad. Yet although they criticized ʿUthman, they never organized a concerted action against him. This may indicate more that their disagreement with the caliph was in the nature of an "internal squabble," a disagreement regarding appointments rather than about the nature of the caliphate. This seems even more likely, since this type of opposition ceased once the caliphate reverted to ʿAli. Opposition became redirected against the new caliph and was now based on avenging the death of ʿUthman. Once ʿAli, who represented the interests of the New Segment, came to power these Quraishites realigned their interests with the rest of the Traditional Segment in opposition to the new caliph.

The other type of opposition was, naturally, the New Segment. In the initial stages, however, this was more criticism verbalized by individuals rather than groups. One of ʿUthman's earliest critics was Abu Dharr al-Ghifari, a companion of Muhammad and perhaps the fourth or fifth person to join Islam. The Ghifar were located north of Mecca on the trade route to Syria. They were poor and were known for their attacks on Meccan caravans. Because of this activity, especially by Abu Dharr, Muhammad was greatly surprised when Abu Dharr expressed a desire to join Islam. But once he became a Muslim, his social and economic position continuously improved. As a companion of the Prophet, he began to acquire property in Medina. His annual stipend as set by ʿUmar was four thousand dirhams. He also joined in the conquest of Syria, Cyprus, and Egypt, where he was granted more land. Thus, Abu Dharr could hardly have been poor, as he is popularly portrayed.[46]

Abu Dharr resided in Damascus, where he began to criticize the growing tendency to amass enormous fortunes and threatened "those who hoard gold and silver" with hellfire if they did not distribute this wealth to the poor and those in need. Very likely, the more Muslims who experienced social and economic change, the more secure the position of Abu Dharr and others like him became. Abu Dharr, thus, advocated the continuation of the distribution of wealth to make available social and economic advances to more Muslims. He preached this with such vigor that the poor in Damascus began to rally behind him. They even began to view distribution as a right. This criticism embarrassed Mu'awiya, who expressed his discomfort in a letter to 'Uthman.[47]

Mu'awiya attempted to silence Abu Dharr in many ways and went as far as forbidding anyone to speak to him. But Abu Dharr was relentless, no doubt protected by his status as a companion of the Prophet. Not being able to silence him, Mu'awiya finally packed him off to 'Uthman. When Abu Dharr reached Medina, many people flocked to him. Disgruntled men offered to make him a leader "to accomplish that which he set out to do." But he was not strong enough to lead such a movement against the caliph as he was finally banished to al-Rabadha, where he died in A.H. 32 (A.D. 652). Yet even as he lay dead, his *da'wa* (case against 'Uthman) did not end, for several other opponents were at graveside.[48]

Another opponent was 'Abdallah ibn Mas'ud, from the B. Hudhail, allies of the Banu Zuhra of the Quraish. As a youth, he was a shepherd of the Umayyad 'Uqba ibn Abi Mu'it, none other than the father of al-Walid, one-time governor of Kufa. 'Abdallah joined Islam early on, even before 'Umar did. He migrated to Abyssinia and finally to Medina, where he became the personal attendant of Muhammad. He was appointed treasurer of Kufa by 'Umar. 'Abdallah came to possess lands in the Sawad, which he leased out for a third and at times for a fourth of the produce. The proximity of 'Abdallah ibn Mas'ud to al-Walid ibn 'Uqba (in pre-Islamic times, 'Abdallah's employer) is indicative of the social and economic transformations in Arab/Islamic society and the kind of interaction between the two segments.[49]

'Abdallah's opposition to 'Uthman began when he resigned to protest 'Uthman's forgiveness of al-Walid's loan. Another source of his opposition seems to have been 'Uthman's decision to make the recitation of the Qur'an uniform according to the reading of Zaid ibn Thabit, a younger and, it seems, less expert reader than ʿAbdallah. After his resignation, ʿAbdallah remained in Kufa and began to agitate against the policies of the caliph, accusing him of introducing policies so different from his predecessors' as to be *bidʿah* (an innovation). Al-Walid wrote to ʿUthman of ʿAbdallah's speeches and the caliph ordered him to appear in Medina. When he arrived, ʿUthman is said to have insulted him by saying that "an evil beast had arrived." ʿAbdallah replied, "I am not like that. Rather, I am a companion of the Prophet." [50] ʿUthman ordered him out of the mosque, and his ribs were broken during his removal. Many Muslims were outraged at this, and ʿAʾishah and ʿAli protested such treatment of a companion of Muhammad.

Another case that illustrates ʿUthman's use of force against opposition from the New Segment is that of ʿAmmar ibn Yasir. In pre-Islamic times, ʿAmmar was a *mawla* of the Banu Makhzum. He was one of the *mustadʿafun,* the socially weak who had no clan backing. His parents were tortured by the pagan Meccans, and his mother, Sumayya, is said to be the first martyr in Islam. Yasir also died under torture. ʿAmmar himself was tortured because of his acceptance of Islam. He, like Abu Dharr and ʿAbdallah, was an early convert, a companion of Muhammad. When ʿUmar appointed him governor of Kufa, the caliph recited Qurʾanic verse 5:28: "We want to grant [the favors] to those who had been made weak on earth [*mustadʿafun*], to make them the leaders and the inheritors [of earth]." ʿAmmar was appointed despite his poor knowledge of politics. [51]

The change in ʿAmmar's position serves as a further illustration of the social and economic transformation of the New Segment. A former *mawla,* he finally received his freedom from Abu Hudhaifa ibn al-Mughira. In addition to being poor, he was persecuted because he had no social backing. But with Islam, he became part of the leadership and a high official in the state. Muhammad granted him land on which he built a house. He was also granted the village of Istabnia by none other than ʿUthman. His stipend was set at six thousand dirhams. [52] Like the rest of the New Segment, ʿAmmar, thus, could rely only on his early acceptance of Islam to maintain his social and economic position. This manifested itself clearly in his solid stand behind ʿAli during the negotiations of the *shura* and is echoed in his advice to ʿAbd al-Rahman ibn ʿAwf to seek the agreement of all the Muslims by selecting ʿAli.

It was ʿUthman's conception of the treasury as his personal property that forced ʿAmmar into open conflict. ʿUthman appropriated some jewelry from the Central Treasury and gave it as gifts to his family. Many protested this action, but ʿUthman said resolutely that he would take what he needed from the treasury regardless of objections. ʿAmmar declared himself to be the first to object to such a policy. At this, ʿUthman ordered him seized, and he was whipped until he fell unconscious.[53] Many were angry at his treatment, including the Banu Makhzum. ʿAmmar went on to be a most vehement opponent of ʿUthman and an ardent supporter of ʿAli until he died in Siffin.

The relationship of ʿUthman to these three critics shows the caliph, representing a specific established social force, reacting to an emerging social force that competed for political power. As far as Islamic *sabiqa,* the three opponents were in the vanguard. They relied primarily on their standing in Islam for their social, economic, and political influence. But ʿUthman totally disregarded their standing when he banished Abu Dharr and beat ʿAbdallah and ʿAmmar. Such disregard betrays an attempt on the part of the state to suppress Islamic *sabiqa* as a basis for sharing the political structure. Naturally, this suppression meant an attack on the aspirations of the New Segment and broken promises made to the believers. One could even say that ʿUthman's actions negated what standing had been achieved on the basis of Islamic *sabiqa.*

Open Revolt

Because of the nature of this conflict, the opposition could not remain purely individual. As more people began to feel the effects of ʿUthman's policies, the more widespread became the opposition. A group from Kufa, described as *qurraʾ* (and none of them from the Quraish!), wrote a letter to the caliph protesting his policies. The most notable issue addressed was ʿUthman's exclusive appointment of Umayyads to the governing posts. Their letter said, "We fear that your actions will cause the corruption of the Umma because you appointed your relatives to govern the Muslims. [You should] know that you have supporters who are unjust and opponents who are oppressed, and when the unjust support you and the oppressed oppose you, there will be separation and disagreement in the community."[54]

With this letter, opposition to ʿUthman was no longer individually initiated. Individual criticism had proved fruitless, since it was easily suppressed. These men also knew too well the power that ʿUthman could bring to bear, since they opted to send the letter without their signatures. ʿUthman tried in vain to have the messenger reveal the names of the men by throwing him in jail. The one person who sent an independent, signed letter, Kaʿb ibn ʿAbda al-Nahdi, was whipped and transferred to Rayy.[55]

Although ʿUthman later had a change of heart and allowed Kaʿb to return to Kufa, he did not do anything regarding the Umayyad monopoly of the state structure.

It was only a matter of time before conflict erupted. It was at the court of Saʿid that the opposition revealed its displeasure at the advantages that the Traditional Segment had acquired at its expense. Their advantages were so great, in fact, that Saʿid could declare before his audience that the Sawad had become a garden for the Quraish. ʿUthman's land exchange policy thus amounted to tremendous benefits for the Quraish and the rest of the Traditional Segment. Earlycomers who began to feel the loss of their privileges grew more resentful as ʿUthman went ahead with economic measures that further reduced their stipends. In response to the continued arrival of *rawadif*, ʿUthman ordered Saʿid to pay their stipends, low as they were, from the stipends of the earlycomers. The news of this policy inflamed the New Segment in Kufa like "fire that catches on dry grass." [56]

No sooner was Saʿid able to restore the calm at his court than open revolt began. The opposition began to hold its own councils, where it "cursed ʿUthman and Saʿid." Many others began to join the opposition and Saʿid began to lose control of Kufa. In a letter to the caliph, he singled out al-Ashtar as the ringleader and the main threat to Saʿid's control. Failing to pacify the opposition, he wrote again for instructions. This time, ʿUthman ordered him to send the opposition leaders, including al-Ashtar, to Muʿawiya in the hope that he might succeed with them. [57]

Muʿawiya welcomed them and put them up in a monastery near Damascus. He continued to give them their stipends. During negotiations with them, several points were raised. The opposition readily identified the Quraish as the beneficiaries of ʿUthman's "unjust" policies. Therefore, they argued, it became incumbent on them to reject injustice and to pursue the truth by questioning ʿUthman. Muʿawiya was undaunted by the attack on the Quraish. He said that the Quraish had not become powerful during the Jahiliyya or later except by the will of God. He added, "God founded this caliphate with the Quraish, and it suits only them." [58]

More discussion between Muʿawiya and his guests revolved around the Quraish. In defending the position of the Quraish, Muʿawiya said, "You [opposition leaders] have attained nobility [*sharaf*] through Islam and you defeated other nations and came to govern their territories. But if the Quraish had not been [around to lead you], you would revert to the servile status that you had before." [59] Muʿawiya touched on the essence of the conflict between the New Segment and the Traditional Segment. Recognizing the nobility that the opposition had gained through Islam, he reminded them that it was thanks to the Quraish that they were able to reach the point they had. Positions of leadership were justifiably only for the Quraish, since leadership "suits only them."

The opposition then turned to political appointments and urged that some governors be removed and suggested that Mu'awiya step down for other "worthy Muslims." Mu'awiya responded that he had a mandate from three successive caliphs who recognized his ability. He added that there was no one alive who could discharge the duties of his office better than he. Moreover, Mu'awiya was not ready to step down, since he had not done anything that required him to do so.[60]

In these negotiations, not only the issues were significant but also the kind of legitimization that was utilized by both sides to defend their respective positions. The New Segment could only rely on its early acceptance of Islam. This was considered enough to justify positions of authority and thus share in the power structure. The Traditional Segment, on the other hand, was so powerful in its own right that it was the Quraish, as the leaders, who allowed the Muslims to reap the advantages of the expansion. In addition, members of the Traditional Segment, like Mu'awiya, were well qualified for their role. Because they were appointed for their abilities, the Umayyad monopoly of the state structure, by implication, should not be questioned. But since the New Segment felt equally qualified, based on Islamic *sabiqa*, for the very same positions, one is led to believe that 'Uthman's attacks on men like Abu Dharr, 'Abdallah ibn Mas'ud, and 'Ammar ibn Yasir were really attacks on an equally legitimate but conflicting basis for power. Thus, 'Uthman threatened not only the material interests of the New Segment by his economic policies, but also its moral basis by his ill-treatment of prominent *sahaba*, companions of Muhammad. Failing to dissuade the opposition leaders from sedition, Mu'awiya waited for further instructions from the caliph. He became concerned when some Syrians began to discuss their grievances with the Kufans. Finally, 'Uthman allowed Mu'awiya to send them back to Kufa.

Meanwhile, and as conditions in the provinces grew worse, 'Uthman summoned his key governors to Medina to discuss the situation firsthand. The governors who attended this council, held toward the end of A.H. 34 (A.D. 655), were Mu'awiya, Sa'id ibn al-'As, 'Abdallah ibn Sa'd ibn Abi al-Sarh, and 'Abdallah ibn 'Amir. Several courses of action were suggested: that the caliph engage the Muslims in further expansion and keep them at the frontiers; that each governor be empowered in his province to "deal with the opposition"; that the caliph eliminate the leaders of the opposition; that he increase the distribution of wealth; and, finally, that he vacate Medina and reside at Damascus, where Mu'awiya promised him ample protection. 'Uthman, it seems, sent back his governors with orders to withhold the stipends from the opposition until they obeyed the caliph, to keep the soldiers at the frontiers, and to tighten their grip on the opposition in their respective provinces.[61]

But while the Umayyad executive council was being held in Medina, the provinces had already declared revolt. After Sa'id left Kufa, the opposition came out publicly for the first time calling for the overthrow of 'Uthman. This demand was articulated by another principal leader, Yazid ibn Qais. He and other members of the opposition wrote to their companions in Damascus and Hims and called them back. Al-Ashtar and the rest of his associates immediately set out for Kufa.

We see again the points of conflict between the New Segment and the Traditional Segment in al-Ashtar's proclamations aimed at whipping up opposition against 'Uthman. Al-Ashtar declared that the caliph had ordered Sa'id to reduce the stipends of valor to two thousand dirhams (whereas some received up to five thousand) and to reduce the stipend of women from two hundred to one hundred dirhams. He added that this was the same Sa'id who declared that the Sawad was the garden of the Quraish. Al-Ashtar rallied many around him and they began to call for the removal of Sa'id and the overthrow of 'Uthman.[62]

Al-Ashtar quickly gained control of Kufa because Sa'id had earlier dispersed the army leaving the coordination to al-Qa'qa' ibn 'Amr. But as it turned out, al-Qa'qa' was not sympathetic to Sa'id and, when the revolt was proclaimed, he joined it, at least as far as supporting the removal of Sa'id. Devoid of any commander sympathetic to Sa'id, Kufa thus fell easily to al-Ashtar, who immediately caused Sa'id's house to be demolished. He then dispatched armed units to control the important areas of the Kufan province: a detachment of five hundred men to 'Ain al-Tamr to be the *maslaha* (an advanced post) between Kufa and Damascus; a force of one thousand to protect the road in the Jibal, toward Hulwan; another force to al-Mada'in and Jukha; another force, camped near Kaskar, to guard against Basra; and, finally, yet another force to police the area between Kufa and al-Mada'in. All of the commanders were instructed specifically not to levy any taxes, to calm the people, and to take firm hold of the outlying areas.[63]

In the meantime, al-Ashtar left Kufa and camped at a forward post at a place called al-Jara'a, between Kufa and Hira. He then sent Malik ibn

Kaʿb, one of the people deported to Muʿawiya, with five hundred horsemen to intercept Saʿid, who was already coming back from Medina. Malik stopped Saʿid, vowing that he would not allow him "to drink another drop from the Euphrates." [64] Saʿid was forced to return to ʿUthman. But rather than maintain the momentum of their revolt, the revolutionaries decided to negotiate with the caliph for a new governor. They demanded the appointment of Abu Musa, and ʿUthman was forced to comply.

Although the Kufan takeover indicates the strength of the opposition to ʿUthman, choosing Abu Musa as their governor betrays a lack of clearsightedness. No doubt Abu Musa knew the situation in Kufa and in Basra well. But although he was not an Umayyad, he was a member of the traditional merchants. He lacked only a traditional base of support within Mecca or the Hijaz; therefore, he did not have connections with Mecca's leading merchants or enough followers to support his decisions. This made his position within the ruling circles extremely shaky, as his dismissal from his posts, especially at Basra, should indicate. Lacking such support, Abu Musa preferred that others initiate policies, which he then followed. His dilemma can be seen in his rejection as governor of Basra and the demand for his reinstatement in Kufa, for here again the revolutionaries were not his base of support but he was their preference over Saʿid. Ultimately, then, Abu Musa was forced by virtue of his position to vacillate between the New Segment and the Traditional Segment. This was made very clear in his reluctant support of ʿAli (the leader of the movement that gave him the governorship) and especially in the *tahkim* (arbitration), when he abandoned ʿAli altogether, as will be shown below.

During the period of the Kufan uprising, Egypt was also taken over by an opposition group headed by Muhammad ibn Abi Bakr and Muhammad ibn Abi Hudhaifa. The development of the opposition in Egypt is poorly documented, so we know little about it. But it was a movement born out of the same conditions that obtained in Kufa. The Egyptian opposition attempted to negate ʿUthman's land exchange program. It asked that the revenues from Egypt be given out as stipends only to those who remained in the province. Furthermore, there is evidence to show that opposition leaders communicated between the provinces, especially after the beginning of A.H. 35 (A.D. 655), when better coordination became necessary. [65]

Open dissension in the Egyptian ranks surfaced for the first time during the preparations for the seaborne campaign of Dhat al-Sawari. Ibn Abi Bakr and Ibn Hudhaifa exhorted the troops with the declaration that their enemy lay behind them in Medina.[66] Both came to Egypt with ʿAbdallah ibn Saʿd and it seems that neither held any important post in the administration of the province. Ibn Hudhaifa grew up as an orphan in ʿUthman's household. It is reported that he had asked ʿUthman to bestow upon him the governorship, but the caliph refused. And while Muhammad was the son of Abu Bakr, the first caliph, he was not from the circle of rich merchants. Sources indicate that personal motives were behind the agitation against ʿUthman; Ibn Hudhaifa had been beaten for his drinking, for example. Nevertheless, the two leaders articulated the same complaints as their brethren in Kufa and elsewhere, namely, that ʿUthman appointed his relatives to high posts, including some who were specifically banished by the Prophet, excluded other qualified Muslims from the government, and ignored previous policies and began to introduce his own.

Coming at a time when the Muslims were preparing for the most important sea campaign yet, one would think that the preparations would be postponed. But apparently the rift was not so serious. Ibn Saʿd merely refused to let Ibn Abi Bakr and Ibn Hudhaifa board his ship. Instead, they boarded another ship, where they continued to agitate against ʿUthman. Although the campaign of Dhat al-Sawari was successful and the Byzantine fleet was crushed, the Muslims came back bearing the effects of these verbal attacks against the caliph. Al-Baladhuri reports that the soldiers came back with a different attitude toward ʿUthman.[67] Thus, the seeds of rebellion were also sown in Egypt and the continued proclamations against ʿUthman rallied the discontented, who seemed to wait for the opportune moment to declare the revolt openly.

They did not have to wait long, because, as soon as the Muslims returned from the campaign, Ibn Saʿd was called to Medina to attend the Umayyad executive council meeting. This ill-timed recall, coming at a time when the opposition was becoming more vocal, gave Ibn Hudhaifa the chance to take over Fustat, just as al-Ashtar had done in Kufa. The revolutionaries refused to let Ibn Saʿd return to the seat of his governorship, but, contrary to the course of events in Kufa, Ibn Hudhaifa and his supporters faced stiff resistance, especially from a loyalist force (estimated at ten thousand) headed by Muʿawiya ibn Hudaij and Busr ibn Abi Artaʾah. This group gathered at Khirbitha, in the Delta, and successfully beat off several attempts to bring them down.[68] Ibn Hudhaifa was not able to consolidate real control of the province before he was killed by Muʿawiya's soldiers.

With Egypt and Kufa in rebellion at the time of the Umayyad executive meeting, representatives of the revolutionaries, including some from Basra, met in Mecca at the end of the pilgrimage. The Kufans apparently were still unhappy with ʿUthman's policies, despite the appointment of Abu Musa as their governor. After discussing ʿUthman's policies and voicing their complaints, those who were meeting resolved that they should go back to their respective provinces to agitate further against ʿUthman and to mobilize those who sympathized with their cause. They also agreed to meet the next year in Medina to present their case before the caliph himself.[69]

When the pilgrimage season of A.H. 35 (A.D. 656) came around, the revolutionaries set out as planned toward Medina. An equal number, ranging between five hundred and one thousand men, from the provinces of Egypt, Kufa, and Basra, converged on Medina to negotiate with the caliph. Once in Medina, however, they tried to enlist the support of Talha, Zubair, and ʿAli, the three most highly placed critics of ʿUthman. None of the three would pledge his outright support for the revolutionaries; although they criticized ʿUthman for the same policies, they were unwilling to negotiate with him on behalf of the revolutionaries, either because they wanted to avoid finding themselves in the position in which Abu Musa found himself or because they disagreed with the kind of action that the revolutionaries had initiated. Because they failed to gain the outright support of these prominent Muslims, the case of the revolutionaries was weakened and that of ʿUthman was strengthened when the negotiations began.

The issues that separated the revolutionaries from the caliph have already been described. It is not surprising, then, that the same issues were raised again in Medina. ʿUthman, however, was unmoved. In replying to the Egyptian demand to abolish the land exchange program he said, "I granted land to [many] people. The Muhajirun and the Ansar also participated in the conquest of these lands. Whoever remained in the conquered areas, his rights are guaranteed, and whoever returned to his family, returning did not abrogate the share that God had given him. So I looked into [the matter] of their God-given share and I sold it to men who have property in Arabia. Therefore, I only transferred their shares to them on their orders. It is in their hands, not in mine."[70] ʿUthman thus continued to reject the demands of the opposition.

It was not a situation in which he could back down on his land policy or any other. Regardless of the claims of the opposition, ʿUthman felt justified in his policies and refused to see any error in his actions as caliph. Moreover, these policies were not merely the whims of an individual, but represented the interests of a significant segment of Muslim society, since, as ʿUthman said, the land was in the hands of many other Muslims, not in his own. ʿUthman was protecting the rights of his constituency and facilitating their access to these rights.

The two contending social forces thus had equally legitimate demands. But those demands were in conflict and neither of the sides was willing to budge. Finally, the opposition began to ask for ʿUthman's abdication; ʿUthman saw no reason to comply. This impasse led to the takeover of Medina, after which a siege of ʿUthman's house followed. This siege lasted forty days and ended when some of the revolutionaries stormed the house and murdered the helpless caliph.

In conclusion, Muslim society came to be distinguished by two segments after the benefits accruing from the expansions were distributed: the New Segment and the Traditional Segment. The first based its social and economic transformation on Islamic *sabiqa;* the second based itself primarily on historical experience and service to Islam. ʿUthman's economic policies and his creation of an Umayyad monopoly of the state structure widened the rift between the two segments. The opposition was galvanized by these policies, and only after the revolt began to brew did other issues such as nepotism and the single recension of the Qurʾan come up. The demands of each segment were equally legitimate so an impasse occurred. There was no solution except for one party to eliminate the other. These events set the stage for a new caliphate and for the first civil war in Islam.

Explaining the revolt against ʿUthman by resorting to artificial distinctions—*ridda* versus non-*ridda* or Qais versus Yemen—cannot explain all of the complex issues behind either the policies of the caliph or the opposition to them. It is equally inadequate to see this conflict as opposition to the Quraish per se, or as nomadic opposition to the settled, or as opposition to centralization of authority. It is by identifying the concrete issues of stipends, land distribution, and political appointments that the conflict between the two segments becomes more comprehensible.

7. The Civil War and the Struggle for Power

The murder of ʿUthman tore the Muslim community apart. The event itself and those that took place during the following six years constitute a most crucial period in Islamic history, for they occasioned, among other things, the rise of Islamic sects, the beginning of Islamic doctrine, and the formulation of positions regarding the nature of political office.

The civil war is indeed a complex one and cannot be adequately understood by reference only to the tribal origin of the participants, since the tribes were not clearly aligned on the two sides. Attempts to explain the period by the supposed dichotomy between northern Arabs and southern Arabs (Qais versus Yemen) also fail for the same reason. Rather, as has been demonstrated, the civil war started as a result of irreconcilable difference between the two segments of Muslim society, two segments that were not differentiated according to their tribal or geographic origin but according to their social and economic background and the degree of the transformation of their wealth and power after the Islamic expansion.

The New Segment came to power for the first time when ʿAli was chosen caliph three days after ʿUthman was killed. ʿAli fit the qualifications propounded by the New Segment. As far as his Islamic *sabiqa,* he was the most senior of the surviving companions of Muhammad. In addition, he was a member of the House of Prophethood, being the cousin and son-in-law of the Prophet and having been reared in his household.

But, inexperienced and weakened by factionalism, the New Segment was challenged from the beginning. Muʿawiya, leading the Traditional Segment, developed a well-coordinated strategy and waged a struggle to capture ʿAli's office. Muʿawiya's primary objective was to undermine ʿAli's authority (and that of the New Segment) and to destroy his base of support. Muʿawiya accomplished this, as the following discussion will show, first by demanding that, before declaring his recognition of ʿAli as caliph, those who killed ʿUthman must be brought to justice, and second, by calling for *tahkim* (arbitration) after the inconclusive Battle of Siffin, which split ʿAli's coalition apart. Successful in undermining ʿAli's authority and in destroying his base of support, Muʿawiya went on to assert his own authority. This was the third stage, the "inner conquest" of the provinces of the caliphate, which reestablished the authority of the Traditional Segment and brought them back in to control the state.

The Election of ʿAli

It is very clear that ʿAli came to the caliphate against the wishes of the Traditional Segment, since he was opposed outright by some and was only half-heartedly accepted by others. Many prominent Umayyads fled to Mecca. It is not clear whether their lives were in danger, but their flight might suggest so, especially men like al-Hakam, who was implicated in many of ʿUthman's unpopular policies. Another reason might have been to avoid recognizing the new caliph.[1]

The murder of ʿUthman must have dampened the aspirations of ʿAli, Talha, and Zubair, who, among many others, refused to negotiate with the revolutionaries. But the revolutionaries did not want to return to their respective provinces before the deadlock was broken and a new caliph was chosen.

It was the Egyptian force that provided the opportunity to break the deadlock. After three days of unsuccessful negotiations, they declared that the Medinans were "the people of the *shura* who decide on the caliphate."[2] If a council of electors (*shura*) was formed to include the Medinans in the negotiations (rather than exclusively Quraishites) it would increase the chances for ʿAli's nomination, since they were mostly Ansar, Muhajirun, and some of Muhammad's close associates who were from the New Segment. But there is no indication that the revolutionaries were addressing a specific body of electors like those appointed by ʿUmar.

After this declaration of solidarity, ʿAli was approached again with a plea to accept their nomination. He accepted only to save the deteriorating situation. He insisted, furthermore, on his own terms, which were that he would govern as he knew best and as he saw fit.[3] In this regard, ʿAli was not much different from ʿUthman. They were different, however, in terms of their historical experience, which, in the absence of clear-cut and well-established prerogatives of power, determined their understanding of the caliphate and of its powers. ʿAli was conditioned by the experiences of the New Segment. It is natural then that he demanded of his electors the right to implement the policies he saw fit, that is, policies that would strengthen the control of the New Segment.

The revolutionaries deliberated that night and decided to accept ʿAli's terms. They recognized correctly that if Talha and Zubair agreed to ʿAli's nomination, the election would succeed. Next day, leaders of the revolutionaries met with ʿAli while others went and forcibly brought Talha and Zubair before the assembly. The *baiʿa* to ʿAli was declared and he was proclaimed caliph. Immediately, Talha was ordered to give his allegiance. After some hesitation, he complied, saying that he gave it against his will. Zubair similarly gave his unwilling consent. Saʿd ibn Abi Waqqas and ʿAbdallah ibn ʿUmar, among others, refused to give their allegiance altogether. When al-Ashtar, who is said to be the first revolutionary to declare his allegiance to ʿAli, pressed them on the matter, ʿAli ordered him to stop, apparently because they posed no danger, as they claimed neutrality. It may also be that they were unable to mount the kind of opposition that Talha and Zubair could mount, which made their refusal to give their oath of allegiance less of a threat to the new caliph. In addition, there were many others who refused to give their allegiance and who began to steal away to Muʿawiya.[4]

The most serious challenge to ʿAli and the New Segment was yet to come. It began to materialize with the new caliph's first action, the dismissal of ʿUthman's governors and the appointment of his own. As an example of the delicate relationship between the caliph and the revolutionaries who brought him to power, al-Ashtar insisted that Abu Musa be left in his post at Kufa; therefore, ʿAli was forced to compromise in this instance. For other appointments, however, ʿAli chose members of the New Segment, especially his relatives, who could give him the same loyalty as the Umayyads had given ʿUthman. Qutham ibn al-ʿAbbas, ʿAli's cousin, was appointed governor of Mecca, and ʿUbaidallah ibn al-ʿAbbas was named governor of Yemen.[5] Just as with ʿUthman and his relatives, ʿAli's appointment of his relatives was not simply a case of nepotism but an attempt at centralization. By centralizing the authority of the caliph, there was no difference between ʿUthman and ʿAli except in who should effect centralization and who should benefit.

ʿAli also appointed Medinans who were very supportive of the new caliph: ʿUthman ibn Hunaif was appointed governor of Basra, and Sahl ibn Hanif of Syria. Sahl, however, was turned back by a Syrian force at Tabuk. Ibn Abi Hudhaifa seems to have remained in his position in

Fustat, although there is no report to indicate his confirmation. Two other appointments were made a few months after ʿAli took office: Abu Ayyub al-Ansari was appointed governor of Medina after ʿAli left for Iraq, and ʿAbdallah ibn al-ʿAbbas, a third cousin, was appointed governor of Basra after ʿAli's victory in the Battle of the Camel.[6]

Several weaknesses can be pointed out early in ʿAli's caliphate. They beset the New Segment until the end. The first was the fact that ʿAli became a caliph on the heels of ʿUthman's murder, which made his caliphate questionable to the extent that some Muslims had to be coerced into accepting it and others refused to give their allegiance altogether. The outright refusal of some to recognize the new caliph, whether they were neutral, like Ibn ʿUmar, or not, like al-Hakam and other Umayyads, opened up the possibility of revolt. This situation was exacerbated by the hesitant support of many who could easily shift their allegiance if the situation so dictated.

Another serious weakness was ʿAli's delicate position vis-à-vis the revolutionaries, or, at least, their leaders. Although the demands ʿAli made on nomination imply that he would govern in any way he saw fit, he could not have been an authoritarian ruler, for he had to accommodate some of the revolutionaries' demands, as evident in the reinstatement of Abu Musa. This initial compromise set a precedent and led to a more dangerous one when Abu Musa was forced on ʿAli as arbiter in the *tahkim,* as we shall see below. The danger of such a delicate relationship is revealed by a statement attributed to the revolutionaries threatening ʿAli with death if he treated them as ʿUthman had done.[7] ʿAli revealed his weakness when he exclaimed, as Talha pressed him to prosecute ʿUthman's killers, "What do we do with a group that controls us and we do not control them?"[8] ʿAli's inability to fulfill this sensitive demand eventually exposed him to accusations of complicity with the murderers.

The fact that the revolutionaries were even in ʿAli's camp was damaging, because Muʿawiya based his challenge of the caliph on their presence at his side. He insisted that if ʿAli did not want to be associated with ʿUthman's murder, he should deliver the killers to Muʿawiya so that he could punish them and thus fulfill his duty toward his dead relative. Muʿawiya was basing his right to punish them on social custom and, more important, on the Qurʾan (Sura 17:33). It is important to note that, although Talha demanded only that the killers be put on trial, Muʿawiya asked that they be turned over to him so that he could punish them personally. Muʿawiya was in fact challenging ʿAli's authority by presuming a right that was reserved for the state. ʿAli's dilemma is clear. If he complied with Muʿawiya's demand, he would be required to turn against his own forces. Compliance would also delegitimize his assumption of the caliphate. But if he chose to ignore Muʿawiya's demand, he would be associated with those who murdered ʿUthman. Confronted with this no-win situation, ʿAli understood from the very beginning that Muʿawiya's demand was a way to compete for the office of the caliphate.[9]

In addition, ʿAli's authority, questionable as it was, was exercised over a coalition of interest groups that joined in their opposition to ʿUthman. This coalition was made up of the disadvantaged members of the merchant class, such as Abu Musa and al-Ashʿath, of early Muslims who were Meccans and Medinans, of those who participated in the early conquests, and of latecomers to the provinces whose stipends and other material benefits were far below those of others. Consequently, although these groups were in agreement in their opposition to ʿUthman, they were in disagreement regarding other issues such as stipends, land distribution, and social status.

To add to these complications, the New Segment was unable to consolidate its control of the provinces, since ʿAli's governors were not able to secure their respective areas. Ibn Abi Hudhaifa could not defeat the loyalist group that withdrew from Fustat to Khirbitha. ʿUthman ibn Hunaif secured Basra for no more than three months, after which he was swept off by Talha and Zubair. Even after the appointment of ʿAbdallah ibn al-ʿAbbas, ʿAli's control was continuously challenged. Sahl ibn Hanif was compelled to turn back at Tabuk and never entered Syria. Abu Musa supported ʿAli half-heartedly, and Muʿawiya opposed him outright in Syria. ʿAli firmly controlled only Medina and some other parts of Arabia.

This administrative weakness could stem from the weakness of the center. It could also be the result of the different historical experience of the New Segment. As a new social force, its ability to govern was limited because it had no previous experience in this position. Those who had the ability to govern were few and not as readily identifiable as they were in the Traditional Segment. As such, ʿAli was forced to concentrate governing positions in the Banu Hashim, although none of them had held the position of a governor from Muhammad's time through ʿUthman's caliphate. Certainly, none of them had held this position before Islam. The appointment of his relatives was not a case of nepotism, as I have pointed out, but an administrative expedient and a visible change of the guard necessitated by the changing power base brought by the New Segment. Adding to these difficulties, Muʿawiya applied constant pressure to destabilize ʿAli's control.

The Revolt of Talha and Zubair

The first public challenge to ʿAli came from Talha and Zubair. Three months into the new caliphate and only after Muʿawiya refused to recognize the new caliph, Talha and Zubair began to foment a revolt of their own. It became evident that their interests were not satisfied by the new caliph when he failed or was unwilling to bring ʿUthman's murderers to justice. This meant that the transformation in the caliphate was there to stay and, therefore, implied that the New Segment would monopolize the state, as the Traditional Segment had done before. Disappointed by their exclusion from the governing process, especially when ʿAli refused to give them high posts, both withdrew to Mecca, allegedly to perform the lesser pilgrimage.[10]

ʿAli was suspicious, but he could not refuse to let them go. Once in Mecca, they were joined by ʿAʾishah, the Prophet's wife, and all declared a revolt against ʿAli. Although vehement opponents of ʿUthman during his last years and critical of his policies to the last day, they justified their revolt on the grounds that ʿAli had failed to punish ʿUthman's murderers and said that their intention was to bring those killers to justice.

The timing of their revolt is instructive and confirms that ʿAli was challenged from the beginning by the Traditional Segment. This challenge, however, was muted in expectation of Muʿawiya's response. When Talha and Zubair realized that Muʿawiya was determined not to recognize ʿAli, they became open and more vocal in their challenge to the caliph. The death of ʿUthman, thus, served as a convenient rallying cry for the Traditional Segment, regardless of who would lead it against ʿAli. And to preempt Muʿawiya's leadership of the Traditional Segment (which would place them in the same position they had had when ʿUthman was alive), they came out publicly against ʿAli and challenged his caliphate on the same basis on which Muʿawiya based his refusal to recognize ʿAli: revenge for the death of ʿUthman.

When Talha and Zubair reached Mecca, they were joined by the Umayyads who had fled from Medina, as well as by Yaʿli ibn Umayya, who left Yemen with its treasury after ʿUthman was killed. Marwan ibn al-Hakam, ʿAbdallah ibn ʿAmir and Yaʿli tried to convince them that they ought to join Muʿawiya in Damascus.[11] These Umayyads naturally argued that Muʿawiya was more qualified for the leadership role in which Talha and Zubair cast themselves. But as Talha and Zubair's revolt was to preempt Muʿawiya's leadership, the two did not accept such a proposition and decided instead to head for Basra.

Talha and Zubair corresponded with leaders in Basra to drum up support for their cause. They contacted such men as al-Ahnaf ibn Qais, Kaʿb ibn Sur, and al-Mundhir ibn Rabiʿah. Each of these men was described as being an obeyed chief. Talha and Zubair addressed al-Mundhir as one whose father had been a leader in the *jahiliyya* and a chief in Islam. Al-Ahnaf was described as chief of Mudar, and Kaʿb as an elder of Basra and chief of the Yemeni tribes. This is indicative of the kind of support Talha and Zubair were hoping to mobilize—heads of the Traditional Segment. All the while Talha and Zubair insisted that they wanted to avenge the death of ʿUthman, the caliph who had represented their interests. The Basrans, however, refused to follow Talha and Zubair and also suggested that they should leave the task to Muʿawiya.[12]

The suggestions of the leadership in Basra, as well as those of the Umayyads, were ignored and the two went ahead with their plan. At this point, to protect their interests, Marwan and ʿAbdallah ibn ʿAmir, among other Umayyads, joined the march to Basra. ʿAbdallah, eager to return to the seat of his governorship (where he had many investments), supplied a large sum of money in addition to one thousand camels to equip the campaign. Yaʿli also put the Yemeni treasury at their disposal.[13]

Counting on their own wealth as well as on the money supplied by the Umayyads, Talha and Zubair equipped about a thousand supporters and headed for Basra, where they quickly took over and put ʿAli's governor in prison. But, isolating itself from the mainstream of its support and ignoring the suggestion of the leadership in Basra, this revolt by a splinter group of the Traditional Segment proved to be only an irritant to ʿAli. Nevertheless, it diverted him from his main task and complicated his already-troubled caliphate.

Because Basra was lost to Talha and Zubair, ʿAli was forced to leave Medina to confront them and to prevent them from taking over other provinces. When ʿAli decided to move his base to Iraq, he met considerable resistance from the Ansar. They insisted that he remain in Medina and direct his operations from there, just as Abu Bakr and ʿUmar had done before him. But ʿAli could not stay in Medina, since, as he put it "manpower and capital are in Iraq."[14] He decided to transfer his base to Kufa.

This could be seen as a strategic move whereby ʿAli would place a wedge between a possible alliance between Muʿawiya and the group in Basra. Its significance lay also in the fact that Muslim society, and certainly the merchants, could center themselves in the new provinces as a sign of the entrenchment of their interests in those regions. This is the more so, since local interests, certainly those of the merchants, were incorporated into the new economic system. It must be that the "manpower and capital" in the new provinces began to outweigh those found in Arabia. Consequently, for any mobilization to be successful, it had to take place in the provinces. It is hardly surprising, then, to find that the Ansar were reluctant to join ʿAli on this campaign, since their city would never recover the preeminence it had enjoyed when it was the capital, the center of the political and economic dynamic created by the Islamic expansion. Arabia was reduced to a mere spectator in the ensuing conflict.

ʿAli bade farewell to Medina and moved to Dhu Qar, where he pitched his base camp awaiting further reinforcements. True to his interests, Abu Musa hedged on his support for ʿAli and was unwilling to rally the Kufans to the aid of their caliph. Abu Musa's tactics placed ʿAli in an urgent position. He dispatched al-Ashtar and ʿAbdallah ibn al-ʿAbbas to rally the Kufans, but they were unsuccessful. He then sent ʿAmmar ibn Yasir, a former governor of Kufa, and his own son Hasan, who were able to muster, according to some sources, nine thousand fighters.[15] It was not until Jumada II, A.H. 36 (December A.D. 656), four months after ʿAli became caliph, that the two armies met in the vicinity of Basra and fought what became known as the Battle of the Camel. It was an easy victory for ʿAli; Talha and Zubair were killed and ʿAʾishah, around whose camel most of the fighting took place, was reprimanded and packed off to Medina.

It was a bittersweet victory because—and this is the most striking feature of the battle—Muslims fought each other for the first time on such a scale, with tribes represented on both sides of the conflict. The casualties suffered in the fighting could only dampen the victory and increase the tension in ʿAli's camp. ʿAli's bitterness at this episode is revealed in his vilifying address to the Basrans after he moved into the city. In keeping with his position to widen the distribution of wealth, ʿAli distributed among his followers what he found in the treasury and promised them the same once they reached Damascus. To secure his hold on Basra, he appointed his cousin ʿAbdallah ibn al-ʿAbbas as governor.[16]

Having defeated his first opponents, ʿAli felt strong enough to pursue diplomatic channels once more to secure Muʿawiya's allegiance. This time he sent a prominent Muslim, Jarir ibn ʿAbdillah, leader of the Bajila, the most numerous tribe at Qadisiyya. ʿAli then set out for Kufa, which became his final base of operations.

Muʿawiya's Strategy

We have seen that the man ʿAli intended to govern Syria was turned back by a Syrian force. No sooner had Muʿawiya received the news of ʿUthman's death than he began to mobilize his supporters in Syria. It is reported that he was able to rouse the Syrians by displaying ʿUthman's bloodstained shirt. At this time, he was surrounded by men like Busr ibn Abi Artaʾa, who came from Egypt and remained with Muʿawiya thereafter. Another important figure was al-Dahhak ibn Qais al-Fihri, a prominent Quraishite who remained faithful to Muʿawiya throughout and became a top military commander. Other names, such as Yazid ibn Asad, Hamza ibn Malik, Habis ibn Saʿd, and Mukhariq ibn ʿAbdallah, are mentioned as Muʿawiya's confidants and close associates. They are described as the heads of Qahtan and Yemen.[17]

Describing them as heads of their respective groups indicates their high social and economic position and illustrates the kind of support on which Muʿawiya depended. Among other important supporters of Muʿawiya, mention should also be made of Dhu al-Kalaʿ al-Himyari and Hawshab dhu Zulaim. These two men were most influential in the Yemeni merchant class well before the Islamic expansion. Dhu al-Kalaʿ and Dhu Zulaim continued to support Medina in the midst of the turmoil of the *Ridda* War by withholding their support from al-Aswad and Qais ibn Makshuh and thus made it possible for Medina to maintain its control over Yemen. Dhu al-Kalaʿ, mobilizing his own wealth, led the Yemeni armies that came to Medina after Abu Bakr called for recruits to participate in the expansion.[18] It should be clear that Muʿawiya's trusted confidants and commanders were either from the Quraish, like Busr and other Umayyads, or from Mecca, like al-Dahhak, or from the Traditional Segment of the merchant class, like Dhu al-Kalaʿ.

In contrast to ʿAli, on the one hand, and to Talha and Zubair, on the other, Muʿawiya was able to win the confidence and the support of the Syrians without much difficulty. Within three months of the death of ʿUthman, Muʿawiya was hailed as an amir, as a leader of a movement to bring ʿUthman's murderers to justice. His demand that he be allowed to exercise this duty was sanctioned, as we have seen, by social custom as well as by the Qurʾan. It was because of this show of support that Muʿawiya dismissed ʿAli's first emissary.

Jarir, ʿAli's second emissary, finally arrived to find that Muʿawiya was continuing to expand his base of support by enlisting more prominent

Muslims from the Traditional Segment and those who were dissatisfied with ʿAli's caliphate. In direct response to Jarir's mission, Muʿawiya recruited ʿAmr ibn al-ʿAs. We have seen that ʿAmr had played an important role in expanding the territorial hegemony of the state under ʿUthman by his campaigns in Palestine and, more significantly, in Egypt, where he founded Fustat. ʿAmr was later dismissed from his post by ʿUthman when he complained about the administrative arrangements introduced by the caliph. ʿAmr joined Muʿawiya in his effort to regain the caliphate from ʿAli.

ʿAmr was then residing in Palestine and quickly joined Muʿawiya when the latter asked for him. Sources insist that in the negotiations between the two, Muʿawiya agreed to appoint ʿAmr governor of Egypt and to give him its taxes as a salary for as long as he kept the post.[19] This, of course, did not mean that the whole tax was earmarked for ʿAmr, but rather, that he was responsible for carrying out the usual fiscal duties in the province, such as payments to the military and officials, repairs, and other expenditures. ʿAmr's share still must have amounted to a considerable sum, which led many to accuse him and Muʿawiya of seeking "the pleasures of this world not the hereafter" and to use the arrangement to malign the two. Regardless, ʿAmr was a devoted member of the Traditional Segment and would have opposed ʿAli anyway. Muʿawiya's promise, furthermore, should indicate his conception of the Central Treasury, which became even more centralized than under ʿUthman. He even took personal possession of the *sawafi* lands, the very lands that produced the original dispute between ʿUthman and the New Segment.

Muʿawiya was also careful to recruit Shurahbil ibn al-Simt al-Kindi. Shurahbil was in Hims, where he commanded great support. In fact, he was described as "head" of the people of Syria. Another report says that "all of Syria was with Shurahbil."[20] He was a well-known soldier who had commanded the left flank at al-Qadisiyya. Later, ʿUmar appointed him governor of al-Madaʾin, but Shurahbil seemed dissatisfied with the post and left for Kufa. He was unhappy there because, with the presence of al-Ashʿath, he could not be the "senior" of his clan. His father, al-Simt, who conquered Hims under the command of Abu ʿUbaida, complained to ʿUmar of their separation. Shurahbil was finally transferred to Hims, where he stayed in its administration for twenty years, as long as Muʿawiya stayed in the administration of Damascus. This, no doubt, allowed Shurahbil to cultivate a wide network of support. Describing him as head of Syria is, no doubt, an exaggeration, but he did seem to command considerable respect. Therefore, Muʿawiya instructed his trusted men and confidants to prevail on Shurahbil and convince him of the rightness of Muʿawiya's cause.[21]

Shurahbil was won over and the significance of his backing is revealed clearly when we find that Muʿawiya immediately asked him to mobilize the Syrians. Furthermore, Muʿawiya did not publicly seek the caliphate until Shurahbil expressed his support for such an undertaking by saying that Muʿawiya ought to be declared caliph so that he could legitimately pursue his duty.[22]

Having secured Shurahbil's endorsement, Muʿawiya dismissed Jarir, who had been languishing at Damascus for four months, and sent him back to ʿAli with the same answer: no recognition until Muʿawiya could fulfill his rightful duty toward his dead relative. Obviously, this was contrary to ʿAli's stand that Muʿawiya should recognize him first, then pursue his duty through state channels.

Muʿawiya's delay of Jarir was inspired, no doubt, by his desire to place his challenge to ʿAli on firm ground. The amir was in no hurry to respond to the caliph, since maintaining the status quo meant the prolongation of the time it took ʿAli to legitimize his caliphate fully. As it favored Muʿawiya, the delay created tension in ʿAli's camp, where some, such as al-Ashtar, were impatient for a reply. No sooner had Jarir reached Kufa than discord broke out openly, especially when al-Ashtar accused Jarir of wavering to Muʿawiya's side. And when al-Ashtar complained that he should have been the emissary, Jarir snapped that he would have been killed by such followers of Muʿawiya as ʿAmr, Hawshab Dhu Zulaim, and Dhu al-Kalaʿ.[23] Apparently then, having witnessed Muʿawiya cultivate his network of support, Jarir was sufficiently impressed by their strength. Disgusted with the affair, Jarir left ʿAli altogether and withdrew to Qarqisya before he finally threw his lot in with Muʿawiya.[24] For his part, Muʿawiya continuously recruited men from among ʿAli's supporters. They began to join Muʿawiya especially when it became apparent that ʿAli could not consolidate his caliphate.

We have seen that the two major segments of Arab society at this time were two social forces whose interests were threatened by the other and that the conflict was expressed in two opposing views of the office of the caliph and its powers. This conflict, furthermore, was within an Islamic framework, as both sides justified their respective positions by recourse to the Qurʾan, the precedents of Muhammad, and his successors. These two groups of Muslims, then, did not dispute religious issues or claim that one side was more pious than the other. Rather, their dispute was clearly over political office; the principal combatants understood it to be that way from the very beginning. Mu'awiya's leadership of the Traditional Segment was undisputed and it was evident that, should he win, he would become the caliph. Therefore, even before any military confrontation took place between them, the contenders, aware of the issue behind the conflict, disqualified each other from the caliphate.

The New Segment held that Mu'awiya was a *taliq*, freed by the Prophet when he conquered Mecca. Being a *taliq* may have implied that he was of inferior social status, such as that inherent in the status of a freedman or a *mawla*. A *taliq* would also have no Islamic *sabiqa*, since it meant that he accepted Islam only at the last minute. Furthermore, Mu'awiya did not have any kinship ties to the Prophet, as 'Ali did. Thus, having no Islamic *sabiqa* and no kinship ties to the Prophet, and being of an inferior social status, Mu'awiya, in the eyes of the New Segment, was unfit to be caliph. Therefore, he was asked to refrain from any further sedition and to recognize the rightful caliph, as other Muslims had done.[25]

Mu'awiya's side responded by saying that he had accepted Islam at an early stage but, as a worthy son, he had kept it secret lest he seem disrespectful of his father. His relationship to Muhammad was also played up through his kinship to Umm Habiba, Muhammad's wife. As she was known to be "mother of the believers," Mu'awiya became "uncle of the believers." Furthermore, it was pointed out that Mu'awiya was one of the scribes of Muhammad and that he took down Qur'anic revelations as they were dictated by the Prophet.[26] It is evident, thus, that the two sides held to an equally legitimate position. Accordingly, any discussion between them seemed to be fruitless, making war the inevitable next step to breaking the deadlock.

Siffin

As Jarir delivered his message, the two sides began to prepare for war. Before Mu'awiya marched to Siffin, he secured Syria by concluding a treaty with the Byzantines and by appointing commanders to take charge of Qinnasrin, Hims, and Damascus. Furthermore, in the Jund of Palestine he stationed three men—Habbab ibn Asmar, Samir ibn Ka'b, and Hail ibn Samha—to protect Mu'awiya's rear and to engage and harass the Egyptians who supported 'Ali.[27] The vanguard, commanded by Abu al-A'war al-Sullami, then proceeded northeast without any difficulty. Unhurried, Mu'awiya reached the plains of Siffin, a few miles west of Raqqa and near the border of the province of al-Jazira, well in advance of 'Ali's army and thus gained a strategic advantage by controlling the available water in the area.

The preparations for Siffin were not so easy for ʿAli. It has been pointed out that after Jarir arrived at Kufa, ʿAli's supporters split. The news of Muʿawiya's determination to pursue a confrontation only added to the tension, to the extent that some refused to go with ʿAli on his march. He finally sent these to Rayy.[28] But for ʿAli and the core of his group—men like al-Ashtar, Shabat ibn Ribʿi, Saʿsaʿa ibn Suhan, ʿAdiyy ibn Hatim, and ʿAmmar ibn Yasir—there was no alternative but to meet Muʿawiya's challenge.

ʿAli charged Ziyad ibn al-Nadar and Shuraih ibn Hani with leading the vanguard. They were instructed to march along the western side of the Euphrates. From Nukhaila, just outside of Kufa, where he received further reinforcements, ʿAli and his army marched upriver on the eastern bank. Contrary to the ease with which Muʿawiya's army reached Siffin, ʿAli's army faced a difficult task, since it had to cross the river a number of times and, on occasion, to make its way through marshes.[29] To complicate matters even further, no sooner had ʿAli reached Qarqisya than his vanguard joined him from the rear. Shuraih and Ziyad, hearing that Abu al-Aʿwar was nearby, decided to recross the river at a lower point after the inhabitants of Qarqisya refused to give them access to the eastern bank. Although ʿAli agreed with their decision to avoid a direct confrontation without the benefit of the main army, he expressed his concern at this retreat by exclaiming, "My vanguard joins me in the rear!?"[30]

The vanguard and the main army then moved along the same side of the river until they reached Raqqa, which they found to be filled with "ʿUthmaniyya" who had fled from Kufa. As they were loyal to ʿUthman, they did not cooperate with ʿAli and closed the gates of the city after they had gathered in their boats. They initially refused to allow their boats to be used as a bridge, but they consented when al-Ashtar threatened to storm the city. The army then crossed the Euphrates, and al-Ashtar, with a force of three thousand soldiers, was the last to cross.[31]

The two armies finally met at Siffin in Dhul-Hijja of A.H. 36 (February A.D. 657). Muʿawiya's army had gained control of the only watering place in the area and he was determined to withhold water from ʿAli's soldiers, who nearly panicked at the prospect. Negotiations were carried out immediately. ʿAli's representative, Saʿsaʿa, said that the issue between the two sides should not be access to the water but that for which they came in the first place. Muʿawiya was adamant in his position. Viewing his control of the water as part of his war with ʿAli, he said that "he who wins something, it is his." Addressing his supporters, Mu'awiya asked, "Tell me, what made 'Ali ibn Abi Talib more deserving of the caliphate than I?"[32]

After deliberating with his advisers, Mu'awiya refused to grant his opponents any share of the water. Consequently, a contingent of 'Ali's army fought the Syrian force that secured the water and drove them away. In keeping with his word, however, 'Ali allowed the Syrians access to the water, and the two sides seemed to mingle freely while procuring their supply.[33]

Negotiations, interrupted by small-scale skirmishes, characterized the confrontation at Siffin during the month of Dhul-Hijja. The two sides arranged for a truce during the month of Muharram A.H. 37 (March A.D. 657), allowing for further negotiations in hopes of avoiding a full-scale confrontation. Many letters were written between the two sides in which each side repeated the same leitmotif. The New Segment once more said that Mu'awiya could not aspire to the caliphate because he was a *taliq,* because he had no Islamic *sabiqa* or any kinship to the Prophet. Since 'Ali was the recognized caliph, Mu'awiya should also recognize him.[34]

The New Segment regarded Mu'awiya as a rebel against the rightful caliph; the Traditional Segment responded that, to gain the legitimacy he was seeking, 'Ali should give up 'Uthman's killers. If he did not, they held, he would be accused of complicity in the murder. The New Segment answered that Mu'awiya should recognize 'Ali first, then pursue his claim. In essence, the New Segment said that the Traditional Segment should accept the entire transformation brought about by the death of 'Uthman. The Traditional Segment, on the other hand, continued to question this transformation by insisting on punishing the perpetrators of the crime against their caliph. 'Ali, of course, could not do so, for it would mean that he had turned against his own forces and, more important, had undermined his own authority.

As there was nothing new in the position of either side, the impasse continued. It is clear that any continuation of the status quo was to Mu'awiya's advantage, since 'Ali was still required to legitimize his position and to make his caliphate fully acceptable. Therefore, Mu'awiya welcomed any opportunity to postpone armed conflict, appearing all the while as willing to negotiate and to spare the Muslims further bloodshed.

Therefore, aside from letters, more delegates were exchanged between the two sides. Hoping to break the impasse, Shabat ibn Rib'i, one of the four emissaries sent by 'Ali, suggested to the caliph that it would be prudent if he conceded Muʿawiya's position in Syria as a "sweetener" for his recognition. But such an offer could not solve ʿAli's quandary. In fact, he had rejected such a suggestion earlier when it was made by al-Mughira ibn Shuʿba.[35] This round of negotiations also brought no results, since each side held to its previous position.

Muʿawiya's next delegation, perhaps sensing the weakness of ʿAli's position, demanded that ʿAli should resign his office to let a *shura* elect a new caliph. This new demand could only widen the impasse. The Syrian delegation then pressed ʿAli to declare at least that ʿUthman was killed without any justification. But ʿAli said that he could not commit himself to that position or, for that matter, to the opposite position, that ʿUthman was justifiably killed.[36] He refused to declare either way, since neither position would gain him anything. In fact, both would hurt him, since he would either confirm what Muʿawiya had been saying all along or expose himself publicly on the side of those who murdered ʿUthman. The negotiations, therefore, were dropped once again, and the Syrians declared categorically that they were free of the responsibility of shedding the blood of anyone who did not claim that ʿUthman was unjustifiably killed.[37]

Muharram, the truce month, was drawing to a close. Continuation of the impasse gravely endangered ʿAli's position, since as yet he was unable to legitimize his caliphate in the eyes of all of the Muslims. Indeed, rumblings began to be heard in his camp complaining of the standoff. Complaints also implied dissatisfaction with ʿAli, who, unable to legitimize his caliphate, had not secured their interests. The increased pressure on ʿAli is revealed in his wavering at this time regarding ʿUthman's killers. It is said that he withdrew into his tent to ponder a decision regarding their fate. But a crowd gathered in front of his tent and began to shout, "All of us killed ʿUthman."[38] Thus, ʿAli was maneuvered into a position from which he could not meet Muʿawiya's demand even if he wanted to. Distressed by the continued delay and frustrated by the fruitless negotiations, ʿAli had no choice but to order his troops to stand in battle formation.

The *Tahkim*

The month of Safar brought with it small skirmishes. Limited advantage was gained back and forth, which produced, generally, another stalemate on the battlefield. Fighting picked up, however, by the end of the first week, especially on Thursday, when fighting was so fierce, it was likened to that of the main engagement at Qadisiyya. But again there was no clear winner and fighting resumed on Friday. By midday, Mu'awiya instructed some of his soldiers to hoist a copy of the Qur'an, or fragments of it, on their lances, it being understood that this gesture was a call for arbitration (*tahkim*). Regardless of the usual understanding, which holds that Mu'awiya's move was made to avert defeat, arbitration was nothing more than a renewal of the status quo, which, as we have seen, hurt 'Ali's position and worked to Mu'awiya's advantage. Mu'awiya well understood that the *tahkim* would deliver the coup de grace to 'Ali and, indeed, 'Ali's forces began to disintegrate as soon as the call for arbitration was raised.[39]

Fighting continued, however, while 'Ali's side deliberated its answer. 'Ali and the core of his group wanted to continue the battle. Men like al-Ashtar, Sa'sa'a ibn Suhan, 'Adiyy ibn Hatim, and 'Amr ibn al-Hamiq, among others, sided with 'Ali in his rejection of the *tahkim*. But a growing number, among whom were al-Ash'ath ibn Qais, Sufyan ibn Thawr, and 'Abd al-Rahman ibn Harith, favored it.[40]

It was a difficult decision for 'Ali. He did not want to accept the *tahkim*, since it would, at best, put him in the same position as before the fighting commenced. The majority of his followers, however, accepted *tahkim*, because it appealed to the Qur'anic principles shared by both camps. Because those followers urged 'Ali to accept the *tahkim*, he did not want to appear as one who contradicted the Qur'an. This would undermine his position altogether. Also, fighting during the two previous days had contributed greatly toward feelings of peace on both sides. Although 'Ali felt strongly about continuing the battle, he had to accept the *tahkim*, especially when al-Ash'ath threatened to withdraw his forces from the battlefield.[41] After two months of intermittent clashes, with many casualties on both sides, it was natural that the battle-weary soldiers would welcome any chance for a truce. What better truce could they have than one that rested on principles shared by all the combatants? This feeling, however, did not seem to be as decisive as the actions of al-Ash'ath ibn Qais.

Al-Ash'ath's controversial actions should clarify further the balance of social forces at Siffin. It appears that the New Segment was as determined to fight for its interests as was the Traditional Segment. The moral and military positions of each of the segments were equally strong, producing a standoff. But, at each step in this drawn-out stalemate, 'Ali's position weakened. His growing weakness allowed the contradictions within the New Segment to emerge. Therefore, when the *tahkim* was proposed, a realignment of forces within the New Segment took place. The first group, which wanted to disassociate itself from ʿAli, was the closest to the other side and the one whose interests would not be served by continued fighting. Indeed, when al-Ashʿath's background is studied more carefully, he emerges, as has been shown, as a member of the Traditional Segment. His position thus resembled to some extent that of Abu Musa, except that the latter stayed out of the fighting altogether.

Like Abu Musa, al-Ashʿath was hesitant in his support for ʿAli and from the beginning showed signs that he was more inclined to follow Muʿawiya.[42] At this stage of the conflict, especially since ʿAli had failed to confirm his legitimacy as caliph, it became in al-Ashʿath's interests and, those he represented, to break away from ʿAli.

ʿAli's position after the *tahkim* deteriorated further when the question of his representative to the arbitration was raised. His choice, naturally, was his relative ʿAbdallah ibn al-ʿAbbas, who would very closely articulate his views. This choice was met with considerable resistance on the grounds that Ibn al-ʿAbbas was too close to ʿAli to be able to represent the interests of all of the groups, especially that led by al-Ashʿath. ʿAli then proposed al-Ashtar, to al-Ashʿath's immediate claim that no one but al-Ashtar had called for this war. As his second choice was considered to be too involved in the war to act as a negotiator, ʿAli was forced to back down again. Thus, matters had reached the point where ʿAli's position did not reflect the "majority opinion" and increasingly even became the minority in his own coalition.[43]

Al-Ashʿath and his followers argued that they wanted someone who would be strictly neutral, and they proposed Abu Musa. Because he did not support ʿAli wholeheartedly and was neutral during this whole confrontation he was considered advantageous to them. In reality, however, Abu Musa's neutrality at this juncture was disguised opposition to ʿAli. It seems that al-Ashʿath and his group came to appreciate Abu Musa's position only after the fighting took its toll of the New Segment. Accordingly, no one, they insisted, could better represent them than Abu Musa.[44] In reality then, he did not represent ʿAli's position, but the position of a faction of the coalition, a position that was close to that of ʿAli's opponents right from the start. Despite ʿAli's objections, Abu Musa was thrust on him and the decision was made that he would become the representative to the arbitration. In contrast, ʿAmr ibn al-ʿAs, Abu Musa's counterpart, was the most natural choice that Muʿawiya could make on this occasion.

The call for *tahkim* had already produced positive results for the Traditional Segment. Muʿawiya was to reap even more benefits when the points of the arbitration were discussed. First, by insisting that the title "Amir al-Mu'minin" should not be adjoined to the name of ʿAli, Muʿawiya not only delivered a crushing blow to ʿAli's claim to legitimacy, but also elevated himself to the position of an equal contender.[45] The Prophet's agreement to delete his title in the document of Sulh al-Hudaybiyya has been pointed to as a precedent to explain ʿAli's willingness to do the same, but the analogy is not pertinent. Muʿawiya was the stronger of the two, just as Muhammad had been, and he, not ʿAli, could afford the concession.

Second, and equally damaging, was the provision that required the two representatives to examine the Qur'an for a possible solution to the conflict. If they failed, they were instructed to seek the solution in the Sunna of the Prophet. However, one version of the document, which Hinds deems more authentic than the others, differs on which Sunna they were to follow. Instead of the Sunna of Muhammad, this version says that they should consult the just Sunna, and the Sunna that unites rather than disunites.[46] If we consider for a moment that ʿAli's position had deteriorated with regard to the general Islamic body as well as to his own coalition, the significance of this statement should be understood as a last measure to block his aspirations. Appealing for unity and consensus hardly left room for a minority opinion, such as ʿAli was maneuvered into at each step in this confrontation.

Having stripped ʿAli of his title and having insisted on a consensus-producing Sunna, the final document was designed to arbitrate the issue of ʿUthman's murder.[47] This was another step in Muʿawiya's march to victory. Consequently, it was not a discussion of whether Muʿawiya was rebelling against the caliph or not, but of whether the action of the New Segment against ʿUthman was lawful or not. As such, the very act that brought the New Segment to power was put on trial and, therefore, the legality of ʿAli's caliphate became suspect. Whatever gains the New Segment had made in its short tenure were seriously threatened by this provision.

When the contents of the document were made known in ʿAli's camp, some protested by crying out, "No judgment [in divine matters] except to God." A section of ʿAli's coalition, mainly members of tribal groups from eastern and northeastern Arabia, withdrew from his camp. They became known later as the Khawarij. The Khawarij found many objectionable points in the document. They disagreed vehemently with ʿAli when he gave up his title. In addition, when the arbiters were charged with examining the legality of ʿUthman's death, the Khawarij accused ʿAli of introducing doubt regarding his caliphate, since implicit in the question was the whole transfer of power to the New Segment. These Khawarij withdrew from ʿAli's side, but did not join Muʿawiya and rejected the *tahkim* as it was designed. They called on ʿAli to reject the *tahkim* if he were to win back their support.[48]

ʿAli was faced with a whole new dilemma, since he could not go back on his word and on the oaths that he had given when he agreed to arbitrate. As the Khawarij split from his camp, the burden of bringing them back into line fell on him, and, consequently, armed conflict between them erupted. As ʿAli was preoccupied with the secession of the Khawarij, Muʿawiya was left to consolidate his gains.

The Khawarij were essentially the most disenfranchised of the New Segment. Being from eastern and northeastern tribes, they were the closest to Iraq but had been the latest to arrive. They were the latecomers, the *rawadif*, who were also participating for the first time in the Islamic expansion. They had barely started to receive benefits from the expansion when ʿUthman began to create a merchant state that would have squeezed them out of power and wealth. Furthermore, they were not in the same economic position as the early participants, who had already developed and secured their landed interests in the new provinces. This disadvantage was heightened when the arbitration document, instead of guaranteeing their new position, put their power into question. The Khawarij declared that they would accede only to the strictest application of Islam through the speech of Allah, the Qurʾan, for it was through the strictest interpretation that their actions could be justified and their social and economic transformation achieved. In addition, their inclusion in the power structure could be assured only by appealing to the Qurʾan.

The Khawarij were differentiated from the rest by their lack of a power base, in either a moral (Islamic *sabiqa*) or a material sense. We have seen that a part of ʿAli's coalition was made up of early-comers who had already secured an economic base through their landed interests and thus were not so seriously threatened by Muʿawiya's victory. These were the ones who accepted the *tahkim*. Another part of ʿAli's coalition was what later became known as the Shiʿa. They continued to articulate the aspirations of the New Segment and thus maintained the belief that Islamic precedence should be the basis for acquiring political office. For them, ʿAli's kinship to the Prophet was a strong enough basis for their struggle against the caliphate; this eventually set them apart from the rest of the Muslims.

It was by necessity, therefore, that the Khawarij appealed to Islamic principles found in the Qurʾan, not because they were the "pious party," for which they have been mistaken.[49] As the caliphate was increasingly being disputed between ʿAli and Muʿawiya, each with his own background and qualifications, the Khawarij were excluded from the power structure, since they lacked the qualities of both the Traditional Segment and the privileged members of the New Segment—land, stipends, and social status. It should not be so difficult to realize, then, that this group began to express its demands and aspirations within a strictly religious context when it held that there should be no rule but the rule of Allah. To be included in the power structure, members opted, therefore, for the position that the office of the caliphate could be occupied by any Muslim of unimpeachable character. Such character would be assured only by the continuation of the social and economic transformation brought by Islam.

By insisting on a continuation of the Islamic revolution and advocating a "populist" vision of the caliphate, the Khawarij were forced by the central government to remain a radical minority on the fringes of the Islamic state. Consequently, after the *tahkim* document was announced, they elected a caliph of their own, giving us the earliest application of three different caliphates: the capital-based caliphate of the Traditional Segment, centered around Muʿawiya; the Islamic *sabiqa*–based caliphate (increasingly restricted to members of the House of the Prophet) of the New Segment, centered around ʿAli; and the more "populist"-based caliphate of the Khawarij, centered around ʿAbdallah ibn Wahb al-Rasibi.

ʿAli's forces were thus in total disarray by the time ʿAmr ibn al-ʿAs and Abu Musa met at Adhruh in Ramadan A.H. 37 (February A.D. 658). ʿAli was the loser from the very beginning. This could be seen in the fact that Abu Musa did not represent him and that the Khawarij had already rejected whatever the two groups would agree on. In keeping with his interests, Abu Musa proposed the removal of both ʿAli and Muʿawiya from the caliphate so that it could be given to ʿAbdallah ibn ʿUmar. Abu Musa hoped indeed to revive a caliphate of ʿUmar's type, not "harking back to the disorganized days of ʿUmar," [50] as Hinds claims, but to revive the kind of compromise that he worked out between the two segments. From the few details of the talks preserved, it is apparent that ʿAmr rejected such a proposition and demanded that the caliphate be given to Muʿawiya. The talks needed to go no farther. ʿAli was already removed from the caliphate by his own representative but Muʿawiya remained. This position reflected the supposedly final decision of the arbiters, arrived at when Abu Musa was "duped" by ʿAmr's "gambit."

The factionalism in ʿAli's coalition, nonetheless, had already made the decision of the arbiters unbinding. After the decision was made, ʿAli remained a caliph, Muʿawiya was declared a caliph once more, and the

Khawarij elected ʿAbdallah ibn Wahb al-Rasibi as their own.[51] But while Muʿawiya succeeded to a certain extent, ʿAli failed at each step to consolidate his position, and now he was forced to turn against the Khawarij, leaving the field wide open for his primary opponent to reap the advantages.

The Internal Conquest: The Return of the Traditional Segment

Having achieved a degree of success, Muʿawiya embarked on a final course of military action to reinforce his claim to the caliphate. He directed small strike forces against selected provinces and nomadic groups in the Syrian desert to secure the allegiance of settled communities and nomadic groups that had stayed out of the conflict. He also wanted to demonstrate the strength of the Traditional Segment, especially by its attempt to lead the pilgrimage. His most important objective, however, was to destabilize ʿAli's hold over Egypt, Arabia, and Iraq, which would isolate his control in Kufa. Only then could Muʿawiya deal the final blow to ʿAli and reestablish the rule of the Traditional Segment.

Muʿawiya's first concern was Egypt, because of its strategic location in the dispute with ʿAli and its financial contribution to the Central Treasury. Although Fustat was held by Ibn Hudhaifa for the New Segment, a loyalist group of ten thousand held out in Khirbitha and repelled several attempts to bring it down. Thus, to start with, ʿAli's control over Egypt was tenuous at best. Ibn Hudhaifa could not consolidate his control even though he withheld the pay of the loyalists, among whom were Muʿawiya ibn Hudaij, Busr ibn Abi Artaʾa, Maslama ibn Mukhallid, and Kharija Ibn Hudhaifa. This group had been in touch with Muʿawiya earlier and, indeed, Busr ibn Abi Artaʾa joined Muʿawiya in Damascus, where he stayed to play a significant military role, as we shall see below. Furthermore, the three contingents that Muʿawiya left behind in Palestine had succeeded in disengaging Egypt from the main conflict. They were finally able to lure Ibn Hudhaifa to the vicinity of Ludd, where they killed him (in Dhul-Hijja of A.H. 36 [June A.D. 657]), while Muʿawiya and ʿAli were at Siffin.[52]

During the confrontation at Siffin, Egypt was left without a governor. Apparently, either the loyalists did not attempt to take Fustat or they were unsuccessful in doing so. Nevertheless, it was important to sever any links with ʿAli and to immobilize any possible Egyptian reinforcements. ʿAli finally sent the Medinan Qais ibn Saʿd to Fustat. He reached it in

Rabiᶜ Awwal 37 (September A.D. 657). Contrary to the expectations of many in ᶜAli's camp, Qais followed a lenient policy toward Muᶜawiya ibn Hudaij and his followers and resumed the payment of their stipends. He also avoided any military engagement with them. This policy supported the rumors that began to circulate saying that Qais favored Muᶜawiya. ᶜAli, thus, was forced to remove him from the post three months later, especially after he refused to attack Khirbitha on ᶜAli's orders. His replacement, al-Ashtar, did not fare any better; he died on the way, most likely at the hands of Muᶜawiya's followers.[53]

ᶜAli's third governor, Muhammad ibn Abi Bakr, reached Fustat around the middle of Ramadan (A.H. 37 [February A.D. 658]). On his arrival, Muhammad tried to engage the loyalist group, but he was unsuccessful. Soon afterward, however, the decision of the arbiters was publicized and Muhammad ibn Abi Bakr had to face the toughest challenge yet from Muᶜawiya's supporters, now headed by ᶜAmr ibn al-ᶜAs.

When ᶜAmr finished with the affairs of the *tahkim*, he was equipped with a force of six thousand men and immediately sent to Egypt. ᶜAmr's expertise in this region, combined with the strength of the loyalist group, enabled him successfully to fight ibn Abi Bakr, who was left to fend for himself without any help from Kufa. Ibn Abi Bakr was killed and ᶜAmr moved into Fustat to proclaim Muᶜawiya caliph in Rabiᶜ Awwal A.H. 38 (August A.D. 658).[54]

Having secured Egypt, Muᶜawiya turned his attention to Basra, where he sent ᶜAbdallah ibn ᶜAmr al-Hadrami to mobilize his supporters and to foment trouble against Ziyad ibn Abihi, deputy of ᶜAbdallah ibn al-ᶜAbbas. Al-Hadrami, however, was no match for Ziyad, who skillfully kept ᶜAli's control alive and thwarted Muᶜawiya's bid. Basra, for the time being, remained in ᶜAli's camp, even though many began to support Muᶜawiya outright.[55]

Failure to take Basra might have influenced Muᶜawiya to send his armies to isolated areas instead of to large cities to avert another defeat and possibly undermine his prestige. Thus, beginning in A.H. 39 (29 May A.D. 659), Muᶜawiya dispatched al-Nuᶜman ibn Bashir to ᶜAin al-Tamr. After a brief engagement with ᶜAli's supporters, al-Nuᶜman withdrew. Significantly, ᶜAli was unable to muster any troops to reinforce those in ᶜAin al-Tamr, a sign that even in Kufa ᶜAli's control had reached a low point.[56]

Sufyan ibn ᶜAwf was sent with six thousand men to Hit and to Anbar, on the Euphrates above Kufa, where a garrison of five hundred men loyal to ʿAli was stationed. Sufyan fought with ʿAli's supporters and was able to carry off some booty. Help arrived too late and the attackers returned safely.[57]

The expedition that Muʿawiya sent to Taimaʾ in northern Arabia is significant because he ordered his commander, ʿAbdallah ibn Masʿud al-Fazari, to collect the *sadaqa* from the nomads along the way. Muʿawiya, thus, was asserting his claim to the caliphate by insisting on his right to appropriate the taxes from these nomads. ʿAli sent a counter force headed by al-Musayyab ibn Najaba al-Fazari, who engaged ʿAbdallah and drove him and some of his followers into a fortified post. But, being from the same tribe, al-Musayyab allowed ʿAbdallah to escape with his followers. The *sadaqa* tax, however, was retaken by the nomads.[58]

Other nomads in the Syrian desert, especially those who still recognized ʿAli, were attacked by Al-Dahhak ibn Qais al-Fihri. In this expedition, al-Dahhak attacked Waqisa, then al-Thaʿlabiyya, where he fought with ʿAli's garrison, then proceeded to Qutqutana, not very far from Hira and Kufa, where the Lakhmids had kept their jail, before he returned to Damascus.[59] That he got so close to Kufa indicates that ʿAli's position was growing weaker while Muʿawiya's position was getting stronger.

As leading the pilgrimage was an apparent symbol of political control, the pilgrimage season of A.H. 39 (April A.D. 660) became another occasion for Muʿawiya to challenge ʿAli. Muʿawiya sent Yazid ibn Shajara ar-Rahawi to lead the pilgrimage to Mecca and to receive the pilgrims' oath of allegiance in Muʿawiya's name. ʿAli's governor, Qutham ibn al-ʿAbbas, could not mobilize any resistance to Yazid and prepared to evacuate the city. But it became apparent that the Syrian force did not intend to fight Qutham, which allowed for a compromise in which Shaiba ibn ʿUthman (from the Banu ʿAbd al-Dar) led the prayers during the pilgrimage. However, when Yazid reached Wadi al-Qura on his return to Syria, he was intercepted by a force headed by Maʿqil ibn Qais and several of Muʿawiya's followers were captured.[60]

Another force was dispatched to the area of Siffin and Dara, where supporters of ʿAli from the Banu Taghlib were attacked and eight of them captured. This led to an exchange of prisoners at the request of ʿAli, and the Taghlibis were set free for those who were captured in Wadi al-Qura.[61] Other members of the Banu Taghlib, however, had already joined Muʿawiya. As an indication that the struggle and the realignment of forces during the course of the Fitna could be expressed in concrete economic interests, these Taghlibis explained their allegiance to Muʿawiya in the following words, "We did not opt for Muʿawiya. Rather, we opted for dates, wheat, and olive oil." [62]

Another important skirmish between the two sides took place in Dawmat al-Jandal, the site of a *mawsim,* a fair that equaled that in ʿUkaz. Reminiscent of cities in southern Arabia during periods of political turmoil, Dawmat al-Jandal did not support either Muʿawiya or ʿAli. So, after the *tahkim* decision was announced and while Muʿawiya was attacking other areas, Muslim ibn ʿUqba was sent to Dawmat al-Jandal to convince the inhabitants to pay allegiance to Muʿawiya. While Muslim was trying to win the support of the city, ʿAli sent Malik ibn Kaʿb to counter his attempts. Malik and Muslim engaged in a battle and Muslim had to withdraw with his force. Malik, however, was unable to win Dawmat al-Jandal to ʿAli either. [63]

Muʿawiya also sent Zuhair ibn Makhul to al-Samawa, in the Syrian desert, to collect *sadaqa* taxes from the nomads of the Kalb and Bakr ibn Waʾil. ʿAli, too, sent his force, but it was defeated by Zuhair. [64]

In the following year (A.H. 40 [A.D. 660]) Muʿawiya sent Busr ibn Abi Artaʾa to different points in Arabia. ʿAli's governor in Medina, Abu Ayyub al-Ansari, fled the city when Busr approached. After threats of violence and after burning some houses as an example of what he could do, the inhabitants gave their oath of allegiance to Muʿawiya without further resistance. Busr remained a month in Medina, during which he hunted down anyone who was implicated in ʿUthman's murder. Indeed, the city that gave rise to ʿAli fell into Muʿawiya's hands. Busr then proceeded to Mecca, where he had no difficulty in securing its allegiance, especially after Qutham could not counter Busr with any resistance of his own. From Mecca, he went to Taʾif, where al-Mughira ibn Shuʿba assured him of the city's allegiance. Passing through Najran, whose allegiance he also received, Busr proceeded toward Sanʿa. Muʿawiya's supporters, who had been in communication with Damascus, were stirred into action by the news of this movement. Once exposed, however, ʿUbaidallah ibn al-ʿAbbas imprisoned several of their leaders. But when Busr reached the city, ʿUbaidallah could not offer any defense and was forced to flee to Kufa. It is reported that Busr killed two of his sons among the many of ʿAli's followers whom he put to death during his campaign. From there, Busr proceeded to Hadramawt, where he similarly affirmed Muʿawiya's control. [65] Arabia was thus reconquered by its own sons and the Traditional Segment was triumphant once again.

Muʿawiya's continuous attacks severely weakened ʿAli, who had, moreover, to fight the Khawarij. Muʿawiya secured the allegiance of cities and of tribal groups to a point at which ʿAli was isolated in Kufa where he increasingly failed to muster enough troops to defend his caliphate. Unable to stand in the face of Muʿawiya's continued success, ʿAli also gradually began to lose some of his officials, who abandoned him and threw their lot in with Muʿawiya.[66] At this point in the conflict, ʿAli could fight no more and a truce with Muʿawiya was arranged that provided that neither side should attack the territories of the other.[67]

Several months later, on 17 Ramadan A.H. 40 (24 January A.D. 661), ʿAli was assassinated by a Khariji in Kufa, thus ending a tumultuous period of five years, during which ʿAli tried in every way to maintain the rule of the New Segment. It is significant that Hasan, ʿAli's eldest son, was chosen to the caliphate by some of the Kufans because, for the first time, the caliphate passed from father to son. Muʿawiya also nominated his own son, Yazid, for the caliphate. Both actions were indicative of the political necessity each segment saw of securing its hold on the state. Thus, dynastic succession, at this time, symbolized the continuous hold on the state.

Hasan, however, was aware of the weakness of his forces. He found them to be unreliable and divided.[68] He knew, therefore, that he could not match Muʿawiya, who was confirmed once again in his caliphate while in Jerusalem. Finally, Muʿawiya was ready for the final step in his strategy and proceeded toward Kufa in early A.H. 41 (May A.D. 661). When his troops approached al-Madaʾin, Hasan's forces fled after they plundered their own camp, stabbing Hasan in the thigh during the melee. At that, Hasan was compelled to ask for safety from Muʿawiya in return for his abdication. After agreement on conditions, Muʿawiya moved into Kufa, where he received the allegiance of its inhabitants and thus was proclaimed caliph by *al-Jamaʿah,* the majority of the Muslims, beginning on 25 Rabiʿ Awwal A.H. 41 (29 July A.D. 661).

With Kufa in hand, Basra fell next to Busr, who prepared the way for ʿAbdallah ibn ʿAmir to regain his governorship. Muʿawiya's caliphate, thus, was finally recognized over all the provinces of the caliphate, ushering in a period during which the Traditional Segment—the Arab merchant class—maintained its hegemony over an ever-expanding state.

In conclusion, then, the two segments fought each other for political control of the caliphate, not because of their tribal origin or because one side was nomadic and the other was settled. It was a conflict motivated by political reasons and it was fought in a religious context, since it was Islam that allowed them to attain political and economic power, regardless of whether they were from the Traditional Segment or from the New Segment. As such, both segments justified their claims and aspirations and both sides felt equally legitimate in the pursuit of their claims, especially since ʿAli was not proclaimed caliph by all of the Muslims. Encouraged by this lack of unanimous support for the caliphate of ʿAli, the Traditional Segment challenged him on the grounds that it wanted to avenge the death of ʿUthman. As its primary motive was political control, the desire to avenge the death of ʿUthman proved to be an effective way to rally support.

The Traditional Segment had several advantages that allowed it to win the conflict. Unlike the inexperienced New Segment, the Traditional Segment had ample experience in government and could draw on vast resources to mobilize an effective challenge to its adversaries. More important, the factionalism of the New Segment, as opposed to the solid block of the Traditional Segment, allowed Muʿawiya to bring out the contradictions within it with a well-orchestrated strategy. As Muʿawiya prolonged the status quo, whether by drawn-out negotiations, a military stand-off, or the *tahkim*, ʿAli's coalition began to fall apart, and neither his prestige as the legitimate caliph and the son-in-law and cousin of the Prophet nor his Islamic *sabiqa* could save the situation. He was increasingly isolated in Kufa and could not muster any troops to defend his position in the face of Muʿawiya's repeated attacks. By the time ʿAli was assassinated, Muʿawiya had been proclaimed caliph several times and the New Segment, now split into Khawarij, Shiʿa, and others, could not withstand his claim to the caliphate. The Traditional Segment finally reasserted itself when Muʿawiya was hailed caliph for the final time in Kufa, the very city in which ʿAli had hoped to consolidate his caliphate.

Epilogue

The Umayyad Caliphate

Muʿawiya established the Umayyad caliphate to articulate the interests of the Traditional Segment. As in pre-Islamic Mecca, the merchants were best represented by the Umayyads, whose continuity in power was the visible and practical symbol of the continuity of the control of the Traditional Segment of both the state structure and the distribution of wealth. Consequently, the Umayyad dynasty guaranteed the hegemony of the Arab merchants and their capital just as the Banu Umayya did in Mecca after the Fijar War. The position of the merchants, therefore, changed significantly not only in that they came to control an empire, but in that they also came to control its resources, such as land, trade routes, and productive forces.

This new position was very much like that of the Yemeni merchants of antiquity, but on a much larger scale. Control of land and of the agricultural surplus, which generated most of the state's revenue, increased commercial activity, since the politically dominant merchants now had access to a larger surplus and a wider market. Commerce was further facilitated, since the Islamic state did not neglect other forms of production. In fact, production should have increased to meet the demands of a growing urban population, especially at a time of ongoing distribution of wealth. Moreover, the Muslim merchants did not monopolize commercial activity, but allowed non-Muslim merchants to participate in the commercial dynamic of the empire. The latter were not politically dominant, however, and thus had to depend on their Muslim counterparts.

This relationship also typified the position of the non-Arab Muslims who were given the status of *mawali*. The *mawali* found that they could be included in the socioeconomic and political structure of the empire only by associating with an Arab. Their status depended on the status of their patrons. Although this relationship facilitated the integration of these elements, it, nevertheless, hindered their free participation and began to work to the disadvantage of the Arab merchants themselves toward the end of the Umayyad caliphate. Umar II attempted to remedy this situation during his short-lived reign but his efforts were not followed up by succeeding caliphs and the Umayyads began to give way to the Abbasids.

Mu'awiya made Damascus his capital. This choice was no doubt influenced by the fact that Damascus had been the seat of his power for the last twenty years and the place where he had established a solid foundation for an effective government. The removal of the capital to Damascus probably also reflects the transformation of Arab merchant capital and the alliance between Arab merchants and local merchants after the conquests. Damascus was an ancient city with an already-developed infrastructure that could support a politically and economically advanced merchant class much more easily than the newly created Basra, Kufa, and Fustat could. Also, Mecca and Medina could not adequately serve the interests of the triumphant merchants after the expansion transformed their political and economic position.

This much was recognized by 'Ali when he transferred his capital to Kufa, since, as he argued, manpower and capital were in Iraq. The non-Arab provinces of the empire assumed a greater political and economic significance than Arabia to the extent that they decided the course of Islamic history. Mecca and Medina, enjoying greater wealth and privileged status, the one as the object of pilgrimage and the other as the resting place of the Prophet, became important cultural centers. Thus, as Arab merchant capital was no longer politically confined to Arabia, the center that could control and regulate the affairs of the empire had to correspond to the new balance of power in favor of the provinces. Syria, with Damascus as its capital, filled these requirements. Damascus, furthermore, was strategically located near trade routes and was within easy access of the important provinces of the caliphate.

With the establishment of the Umayyad caliphate, the institution itself, created as an ad hoc decision at the time of Abu Bakr, went through several transformations. 'Umar introduced a new title, a salary for the officials, and the Diwan, which legitimized the economic and political gains of the New Segment. He, in effect, institutionalized a new social hierarchy dependent on Islamic precedence and in which the legitimate gains of the New Segment would be recognized. 'Uthman, however, began to undermine this legitimacy and proceeded to give the Traditional Segment the opportunity to monopolize the state structure as well as the greater share of the state's resources. The New Segment temporarily stopped this trend when members killed ʿUthman and chose ʿAli to serve their interests.

When Muʿawiya emerged from the civil war as the caliph of all the Muslims, he did not revert to the type of caliphate envisioned by ʿUthman or by ʿUmar. His was a compromise between the two types and reflected a more developed institution. Thus, when his power was consolidated and legitimized and when centralization of authority in the person of the caliph was finalized, Muʿawiya did not have to rely specifically on his relatives, as ʿUthman and ʿAli had done before him. Central authority was maintained in the Umayyad house and authority to govern was delegated to officials who were recruited from the wider range of Arab society. Selection of officials, therefore, rested on their qualifications and, primarily, on their loyalty to the Umayyads. Because the Umayyads had real political control, other officials could be recruited from anywhere as long as they served the interests of the state. Thus, like ʿUthman, Muʿawiya kept the Umayyads in control, and like ʿUmar, he allowed others to share in the political structure.

It is within this context that the *wufud* (tribal delegations) to Muʿawiya should be understood. He gave the state a popular dimension while Umayyad control remained unquestioned. This view of the caliphate is supported by Muʿawiya's statement that people could say and criticize whatever they pleased as long as they did not question or interfere in Umayyad rule.

The caliphate of the Umayyads was institutionalized as the functions of the state were organized in separate *diwans*. Aside from the already existing *diwans* (Diwan al-Jund and Diwan al-Kharaj), two more were added: Diwan al-Khatm and Diwan al-Barid. Diwan al-Khatm was instituted to provide secrecy and security in administrative communication; the government was beginning to separate itself from the people. Diwan al-Barid was instituted to facilitate communications. Gradually, each *diwan* was copied in the provinces so that by the time of ʿAbd al-Malik ([A.H. 65] A.D. 685), an administrative apparatus was already established. In addition to these bureaus, the *haras* (guards) and the office of *hajib* (chamberlain), as well as the *shurta* (police), were instituted.

Although Muʿawiya created a system of administration and followed policies that gave the impression of decentralization, power remained in the person of the caliph. This power manifested itself in several ways. For example, the building of the *maqsura* (a private prayer room in the mosque), which might have been inspired by reasons of security, is a visible symbol of the separateness of the ruler from his subjects. Similarly, the *minbar,* a raised platform, a pulpit on which the Khutba (the Friday sermon) was delivered, symbolized the caliph's power. Mu'awiya, moreover, introduced the practice of delivering the Khutba before the prayer rather than after it, a practice that is still followed. The Khutba, recited by the caliph or in his name, became an important symbol of political control and a forum from which new policies and directives were set in action. Reciting the Khutba before the prayer not only made the caliph's speech an intrinsic part of the prayer, but also gave his political position divine legitimacy.

Another important manifestation of this power was in the personal control of the economic resources of the state. This was most apparent in his claims of the *sawafi* land as his own. From this land, Mu'awiya distributed grants to his relatives, supporters, and to those he wished to recruit to his side. Land grants, as an instrument of the state, thus went through several changes. Muhammad gave land grants to many of his companions. These grants made the distribution of wealth a basic feature of Islam and helped to establish the new faith. Abu Bakr and 'Umar gave land grants in the newly won territories to consolidate and strengthen Medina's control. 'Uthman attempted to strengthen the power of the Traditional Segment with land grants, while 'Ali's policy favored the New Segment. With Mu'awiya, land grants were made to fortify Umayyad domination of the state.

Mu'awiya's power grew to the extent that he claimed the right to decide on the life and death of his political opponents. He was the first caliph to claim that power, a power that 'Uthman, with all his centralization, could not claim. Finally, institutionalizing the selection of his son Yazid as his successor was an embodiment of centralization of power, power that was to remain in the Umayyad family as the leader of the Arab merchant class.

Although Mu'awiya established a compromise caliphate, it worked, nonetheless, against the interests of the New Segment with all of its factions. The New Segment was relegated to the position of a fighting force directed against internal dissension as well as the expansion of the frontiers available for the merchant class. It now split into two definable factions: the Khawarij, who continued to remain outside of the state and opposed the Umayyads at every opportunity; and 'Ali's supporters, who became known as the Shi'a and who also continued to oppose the Umayyads but remained within the state. Mu'awiya utilized their differences for his own purposes when he insisted that the Kufans themselves should fight the Khawarij.

Muʿawiya also continued to undermine the economic interests of the New Segment, especially by placing the *sawafi* land at his disposal. With this income taken away from them, this faction of the New Segment was reduced further, despite objections that ended in the execution of Hujr ibn ʿAdi and some of his companions, the first political execution in Islam. The New Segment was thus forced into the service of the state and payment for military service became its only regular income.

In further consolidation of his caliphate, Muʿawiya turned his attention to the requirements of the merchants: the expansion of the frontiers of the state and the pacification of the internal opposition that came from three areas, the non-Arab inhabitants of the provinces, especially in Iran, the Khawarij, and the Shiʿa.

Expansion was carried to several fronts simultaneously, winning an area that was further expanded by succeeding Umayyad caliphs. In the east, Khurasan received fifty thousand families in A.H. 51 (A.D. 671) to become a new base for the expansion into central Asia. Muslim armies crossed the Oxus, took Kabul, and reached the Sind province. In the west, the Muslims built Qairawan in A.H. 50 (A.D. 670) and the Byzantines had to evacuate Ifriqya shortly afterward. ʿUqba ibn Nafiʿ pushed the frontiers farther west until he reached the Atlantic. The most spectacular, but least successful, were the naval attacks against Constantinople. The city was besieged several times, especially between A.D. 674 and 680. The expansion thus should not be regarded as an attempt merely to mask internal problems, but also to enlarge the territorial hegemony of the Arab merchants.

In dealing with the internal situation, Muʿawiya appointed al-Mughira ibn Shuʿba governor of Kufa, where he quietly worked to nurture Umayyad control. Al-Mughira did not pursue the opposition except when it threatened open revolt. ʿAbdallah ibn ʿAmir, meanwhile, reestablished Umayyad authority in the Sasanid territories that had revolted against Arab rule during the civil war. ʿAmr ibn al-ʿAs successfully integrated Egypt into the Umayyad realm so that fresh preparations could be made to expand from there into northern Africa.

The most successful policy in stamping out internal Arab opposition was to channel the frustrations of the Kufans against the Khawarij, who were blamed for the loss of the former's political power and the removal of the seat of the caliphate from their city. This was not an exploitation of mere tribal differences but a successful manipulation of different interests. Those who became Shiʿa felt justified in their vehement opposition to the Khawarij, since the latter were blamed for ʿAli's defeat and indeed for ʿAli's assassination. The most zealous in opposing the Khawarij were ʿAli's former supporters, such as ʿAdiyy ibn Hatim and especially SaʿSaʿa ibn Suhan. Active opposition was directed against the Khariji Farwa ibn Ashjaʿ, who declared his revolt near Kufa right after Muʿawiya was recognized by the Kufans. Al-Mughira applied the same tactics when he eliminated the Khariji revolt of al-Mustawrid two years later (A.H. 43 [A.D. 663]).

Other Khariji revolts during Muʿawiya's caliphate were treated in the same manner. In pursuing this policy, Muʿawiya secured ample room to consolidate his power while ʿAli's supporters were engaged in suppressing the Khawarij. It was while the Shiʿa were fighting the Khawarij that Muʿawiya was able to move against their interests and claim as his own the sawafi land, the very land that set off the revolt against ʿUthman. But by then the New Segment was powerless and its objections were crushed with unprecedented ruthlessness, as the execution of Hujr and his companions indicates.

In administering the capital cities of the provinces, Muʿawiya changed their cumbersome tribal arrangements and established a new and more effective system of government. In Iraq, this reorganization took place after Ziyad ibn Abi Sufyan, formerly Ibn Abihi, became the governor of Basra in A.H. 44 (A.D. 664) and of Kufa in A.H. 51 (A.D. 670). Much of the credit in governing Iraq is owed to his exceptional political acumen. In fact, his skill led Muʿawiya to adopt Ziyad as a brother, it being claimed that he was the offspring of Abu Sufyan from a slave woman in Taʾif named Sumayya. It was certainly an antitraditional move on the part of the caliph to claim an "illegitimate" as a brother. Indeed, Muʿawiya seems to have set traditions rather than followed them.

Basra and Kufa were rebuilt with bricks instead of straw and reeds. Kufa was divided into four quarters (instead of seven sections) where groups from different tribes were assembled together. Each quarter became an administrative unit divided into several subunits called ʿarafa. As each quarter had its government-appointed official, each ʿarafa had its own official called ʿarif. He was charged with maintaining order and discipline in his unit, distributing the stipends, reporting the additions and the subtraction of names to the Diwan, and making sure that members of the unit responded to the government's call for troops. Basra was similarly organized but had five sections instead of four. Removal of the tribal boundaries was still as relevant for effective government and a more inclusive social structure as when previous generations had dealt with the same issue by devising the *ilaf*, the *hilf*, and the institution of the Umma.

Mu'awiya's accomplishments were only the beginning. Before he died on 22 Rajab A.H. 60 (30 April A.D. 680), Mu'awiya laid a solid foundation on which his successors built and expanded. Coming out of another civil war after Yazid ibn Mu'awiya's short reign, the Umayyads were able to carry Mu'awiya's policies further. 'Abd al-Malik ibn Marwan (A.H. 65–86 [A.D. 685–705]), by establishing an "imperial army," pushed the frontiers even farther east and west and, at its peak, the Umayyad caliphate had become the largest empire the world had ever known. The predominant role of the Arab merchants reached its fullest during his reign and that of his son al-Walid. The reforms of 'Abd al-Malik were to reflect the Arab element's mastery of the social, economic, and political structure of the caliphate. He "Arabized" the bureaucracy (mainly Diwan al-Kharaj) and Arabic itself underwent a transformation to become the *lingua franca* for many centuries to come.

'Abd al-Malik introduced another far-reaching economic reform when he standardized the rate of exchange between gold and silver, integrating fully the economies of the eastern and western halves of the caliphate. The weights that determined this rate of exchange were the same weights that the Quraishi merchants had utilized in pre-Islamic Mecca. Merchants could travel in the wide regions of the empire and use either metal, without fear of economic loss. In fact, the merchants were the direct beneficiaries of this policy, especially when al-Hajjaj, governor of Iraq, minted new coins with Arabic characters for the first time. Coins bearing Arabic characters began to circulate, representing the economic power of the caliphate and of Arab merchants.

Furthermore, the building of the Dome of the Rock in Jerusalem and the Umayyad Mosque in Damascus, inaugurated by 'Abd al-Malik and continued by his son al-Walid, became the cultural and visible symbols of Umayyad power. These monumental buildings, among the numerous desert palaces, defied internal opposition with their massive presence and permanence. They were, furthermore, an expression of the cultural challenge to their external enemies.

By A.H. 100 (A.D. 720), when 'Umar II took office, the Arab merchant class had reached its peak. Further territorial expansion was stopped in favor of retrenchment. By then, consumer demands were too great and the markets too extensive to be satisfied by a dominant Arab merchant elite alone. Arab merchant capital thus reached another stage in its development and expansion. It could no longer operate successfully in such a

sprawling empire and Arab political hegemony could not be easily maintained over that area. The *mawali,* we have seen, were prevented from
participating fully by their status. By A.H. 100, this arrangement became
unsatisfactory in an empire that spanned three continents.

To remedy this situation, ʿUmar II attempted to change the relations of
power so as to remove any discrimination against the *mawali* and to give
them the opportunity to participate independently in the caliphate. Commercial activity and merchant capital would be reinvigorated by the new
social transformation. The reforms were designed to integrate the Arabs
and the *mawali* by making Islam, rather than ethnicity, the basis of social
relations.

His reforms, abruptly introduced and not in the interests of the dominant forces of the caliphate, were ignored by his successors. But it was
during his reign that a secret opposition movement, based on similar
principles, started to gather momentum. During the next thirty years, the
Umayyads, having failed to transform the ideology of the state to meet
their material needs, were confronted with several upheavals in various
parts of the caliphate. Social tension increased as the hour approached
for the Abbasids to declare their revolt. Rising in the eastern province of
Khurasan, the Abbasids finally succeeded in dislodging the Umayyads
from power in A.H. 133 (A.D. 750) when they Islamized the market and
merchant capital and ushered in an even greater commercial age by open-
ing up new markets, such as those in southeast Asia, west Africa, and the
east African coast.

Islam, Capitalism, or Feudalism

Merchant capital and its accumulation developed in Arabia before the
rise of Islam. Its development was easier than in neighboring states, even
though landowners were the governing class in all. Merchants in the non-
Arabian context (and this is true in the Sasanid and in the Roman states)
were competing with the state, as it represented an entrenched and powerful landed aristocracy. Although commerce existed and certain merchants prospered, they were to remain socially marginalized and politically weak.

Merchants in Arabia, on the other hand, were part of the power structure, whether secular (kings, city heads, tribal chiefs) or religious (temple
officials). The state was involved in exchange (the king's goods were sold
first), and it provided safe roads, rest stops, and laws to regulate business
(the Commercial Code of Qataban). Thus, the governing class consisted

of landowners who were also merchants. This may have been for geographical reasons: Arabia, especially the southern part, was surrounded by waterways used for commerce. And as a capital-producing activity, the governing class did not let trade slip out of its control. Another reason may have been the availability of agricultural land. Agriculture in southern Arabia was highly developed indeed (terracing, hybridization, dams, and so on). But in terms of the aggregate area cultivated, Arabia could not compare to what was available to, for example, the Sasanids or to the Roman world. This may have resulted in relatively fewer landlords and an ultimately weaker class of landed aristocracy, certainly much weaker than the senatorial class of Rome.

A third reason may have been the nature of agricultural products; other than foodstuffs, southern Arabia produced aromatic plants, especially frankincense, which was ceremonially and institutionally necessary in areas where it did not grow. Thus, those landlords (including the temple officials) who monopolized the production of frankincense were producing agricultural products destined for trade. All these factors combined produced a weak link in the ancient system.

This weakness, most readily apparent in the crises after the second half of the fifth century A.D., was exploited by Meccan merchants who initially owned no agricultural property. Starting with the institutional base of the sacred enclave, the *haram,* Meccan merchants continuously promoted practices and beliefs some of which were of a sacred nature and all of which increased the chances for the accumulation of capital and with it, political power. Accumulation did not necessarily depend on the selling of rare or luxury goods; any exchangeable commodity with a margin of profit would do, especially in a context in which food and water were not terribly abundant.

With practices and institutions that encouraged capital accumulation, Mecca's social formation gradually reached a critical stage in which several contradictions and obstacles appeared. Not being a landed aristocracy, Meccan merchants either had to develop additional institutions to ease them out of their condition, safeguard their wealth, and continue to accumulate capital, or had to stagnate and face social violence and economic loss.

This was the immediate background to the rise of Islam. Having emerged out of specific social conditions, Islam also contained answers to specific questions related to merchants' problems. In particular, the adoption of monotheism allowed for the establishment of a state with a divinely instituted authority through the Umma. It had the right to appropriate surplus wealth and to distribute it to the believers. It is true that monotheism, the concept of divinely constituted community, and the distribution of wealth are not specifically Islamic. In addition, pertinent pre-Islamic institutions and practices (for example, pilgrimage and *sadaqa*) were accommodated also in Islam. What Muhammad did was to place those institutional beliefs and practices in a monotheistic religious frame work instead of in tribal, pagan, or local frameworks.

Being the dominant social force and having been provided these institutions, merchants appropriated this ideological superstructure and rapidly dominated the state and the distribution of wealth. Their effective government was facilitated also by their historical training and experience to the extent that they defeated internal challenge, mainly that posed by the New Segment. Both segments challenged each other within the same framework and both used principles within Islam to legitimize their respective and often-conflicting interests. Externally, Arab merchants allied with local merchants and easily co-opted the lower echelons of the landed aristocracy (for instance, the *dihqans*) so that their newly formed empire was also secure against outside threats. Enjoying such power, Arab merchants began to acquire land as another avenue of investment and as an additional source of income. Land also helped them retain control of the state and its resources. Owing to pre-Islamic practice and to the fact that merchant capital was hegemonic and allowed other forms of production to co-exist, there was no conflict between the landlords and the merchants, especially since, at this time—a period of conquest and consolidation of political control—they had become one and the same class. The ongoing distribution of wealth allowed the landowners and the merchants to have similar interests, a situation that was to change in the future. The Umayyad state continued to articulate this hegemonic role and, when by the end of their century they failed to keep up with demands of merchant capital, they were swept aside by the Abbasids.

The contradictions began to disturb Arab merchants by the year A.H. 100 (A.D. 720). This is exemplified again by the relationship of the non-Arab Muslims to their Arab rulers. Non-Arab Muslims could be accommodated into the political/economic system rather poorly and only through association with an Arab. Their capital was not totally free, and part of it had to be given up as unproductive due to the associative relationship. Toward the end of the first century of Islamic history, the market and its demands were too extensive to be serviced by Arab merchants alone, even though some measures were provided for the inclusion of non-Arabs. To solve this dilemma, new ways had to be provided for the equal participation of all Muslims in the economy, and this is what Umar II attempted to do and what the Abbasids succeeded in doing. To remove the hurdle meant to abolish the distinction between the Arab and non-Arab, and at this time there was practically no distinction except for taxation. All subjects were to be taxed equally as Muslims, and Islam re-emerged as the new basis of the power structure under the Abbasids.

The Abbasids Islamized the market once again, as Muhammad and Abu Bakr had done in Arabia. But this time the Abbasids did it on a grand scale. It is no wonder, then, that capital accumulation increased to unprecedented levels, making the first century of the Abbasids the "golden age" of Islam.

Beginning with the third century A.H. and throughout the first half of it, new and far-reaching developments had a profound effect on the accumulation of capital. The details of this period are too complex to recount in an epilogue, but a few observations can be offered.

Peasant revolts, some of which were sustained for decades, broke out in various parts of the Abbasid Empire. These revolts constituted a direct threat to the state as well as to the landowners. Al-Ma'mun's victory in the civil war (A.H. 195–199 [A.D. 811–813]) brought another threat against the landowners when he adopted the Mu'tazili dogma and began to enforce their doctrine of the "Createdness of the Qur'an." He used the *mihna* (religious inquisition) to enforce his views. The most vehement opponent of the Mu'tazila and the doctrine of the Createdness of the Qur'an was Ahmad ibn Hanbal (d. A.H. 240 [A.D. 855]), himself a petty landlord. According to the instructions of the caliph, those who rejected the state doctrine were to be barred from any appointment in the government and were not to be appointed as judges or called on as witnesses. In fact, they were cast out of the political process and were discredited in the area through which they cultivated their power.

To fill the vacancies created by the dismissal of Ibn Hanbal and his associates, al-Ma'mun (A.H. 195–218 [A.D. 813–833]) and his immediate successors, al-Mu'tasim (A.H. 218–227 [A.D. 833–842]) and al-Wathiq (A.H. 227–233 [A.D. 842–847]), relied on Mu'tazili scholars, many of whom were merchants, to become confidants and advisers and to fill important positions in the government. Both the great Mu'tazili scholar Ibn Abi Daud and Muhammad ibn al-Zayyat, one of the wealthiest merchants in Baghdad and himself a member of the Mu'tazila school, were the vizirs of both al-Mu'tasim and al-Wathiq. In his capacity as a vizir, a post that he held for twelve years, Ibn al-Zayyat abolished the taxes collected from Basra, the most important commercial port in the

Abbasid realm, clear testimony to the alignment of interests between the state and the merchants.

It is also significant that Muʿtazili scholars, other than merchants, were artisans or were associated with artisans, as indicated by their names. This significance is made the more poignant when we analyze the principles of their school, because it becomes evident that their dispute with the Hanbalis was not merely a theological or doctrinal dispute, but a social conflict fought out on the ideological plane.

The Muʿtazila, and al-Maʾmun who adopted their doctrine, were hoping to change the ideological and legal structure. Rejecting Hadith—and therefore the Sunna—as a source of law, the Muʿtazila went on to say that the Qurʾan, as the infallible word of God, was the only valid source of law. But as it was created in time and place, it became temporal and subject to human interpretation through the use of reason. The ability to legislate outside the bounds of the Qurʾan and the Hadith/Sunna would have given the caliph the chance to transform his powers as well as those of his office and thus to acquire additional prerogatives, especially in the area of taxation. These powers were denied him by Ibn Hanbal and the other legal schools that were consolidating their principles at the time. Coupled with this, the Muʿtazila insisted that man had free will and therefore the ability to initiate and create acts. Man had the ability even to uncreate what God had created. In the face of man's power and ability, God's attributes were reduced to justice and unity.

Ahmad ibn Hanbal and his associates held contradictory views regarding the Qurʾan, the validity of the Hadith/Sunna, and the power of man. It is important that we not lose sight of the fact that, again, each side of the Muʿtazili-Hanbali dispute formulated its respective position and argued for it strictly within an Islamic framework. Passages in the Qurʾan were utilized to support the opposing views. Both being equally rooted in Islam, the balance of power in this dispute was in favor of the Muʿtazila as long as the caliph and his administration supported the school and enforced its doctrine. But with the accession of al-Mutawakkil to the caliphate (A.H. 233–247 [A.D. 847–861]), the balance of power shifted; the *mihna* was dropped, Ibn Hanbal was freed from prison, and the principles of the Muʿtazila were abandoned altogether.

As a true indicator of the nature of this conflict, al-Mutawakkil dismissed the Muʿtazili merchant vizir Ibn al-Zayyat and appointed in his place Abu al-Fadl al-Jarjaraʾi, a scion of a large landowning family. He brought along a team of administrators with similar landed interests. With this shift, the landed aristocracy visibly and effectively came to power. And with the landed aristocracy came the military; civilian rule began to give way to military rule. The military was recruited to keep the peasants on the land, intimidating them and making sure that they continued to produce for their landlords. In this alliance, the state could tax land, as visible wealth, more easily than it could tax merchant profits, and the landowners could keep their possessions intact. And by limiting the power of the caliph, landowners paid the Qur'anic taxes on agricultural surplus rather than any new tax that might be introduced by a more powerful caliph.

It is also significant that at this specific juncture, al-Mutawakkil initiated the use of *iqta*ᶜ (land grants) as a military administrative system, not because of lack of cash, but because it was a more effective system of control, since the military would be placed with the "troublesome" peasants.

The caliphate of al-Mutawakkil represents an important juncture in Abbasid history, if not in the history of Islam. Having failed to transform the powers of the caliph through Muᶜtazili doctrines, the caliph gradually lost power to the military, and civilian rule began to recede into the background. It is not so coincidental that al-Ashᶜari's (d. A.H. 330 [A.D. 942]) break with the Muᶜtazila to champion Hanbalism heralded the military dynasty of the Buyids (Baghdad, A.H. 334–447 [A.D. 945–1055]), with *amir al-umara*ʾ (commander of commanders) as the effective ruler. The *amir al-umara*ʾ made and unmade caliphs at will, and the caliphs, who once commanded a whole empire, were reduced to mere salaried officials of the Buyids and served only as legitimizing figureheads, as was outlined by al-Mawardi.

As a military elite, the Buyids used the *iqta*ᶜ system already in place and, despite some attempts to revive the economy early in their reign, abused their privilege (by excessive taxation and by neglect of the irrigation system and by using it in their military strategy), so that they were easily swept aside by another military dynasty, the Saljuks, who ruled in Baghdad from A.H. 447 to 591 (A.D. 1055 to 1194).

The Saljuks continued to use *iqta*ᶜ to the benefit of the military and their grand vizier, Nizam al-Mulk, regularized and legitimized the practice. Land grants became hereditary to the point that inheriting land became the only option as a system of governance. The caliphs, accorded a little more dignity under the Saljuks, continued to be figureheads in the shadow of the new military commander, now called the sultan. Trade continued, but the merchants no longer had a significant political role to play, even though some of them commanded great wealth.

The failure to transform the caliphate earlier brought with it another significant development: regionalization of the Abbasid realm. Regions with sufficient resources began to form semi-independent economic and political units that paid nominal allegiance to the caliph for the purpose of acquiring legitimacy. A plethora of petty dynasties cropped up to the point that any commander with a sufficient following could carve out a territory for himself. The Abbasid caliphate also ceased to be unique; there was the Fatimid caliphate (Cairo, A.H. 360–567 [A.D. 969–1171]), the Umayyad caliphate (in Spain until A.H. 432 [A.D. 1031]), and eventually other caliphates in northern Africa.

Political regionalization also meant regionalization of the market, which produced political/military as well as economic competition. Resources were slowly being depleted because of warfare and because of the abuses of *iqta'*, which made rebuilding increasingly difficult. Muslim merchants, who had contributed to the revival of a monetary economy in Europe, could no longer reach European shores. For the first time in several centuries, the Byzantines reoccupied the Syrian coast. Italian merchants set up *funduks* (warehouses), first in Alexandria, then in Cairo, then in 'Aidhab, on the Red Sea coast opposite Jedda. Muslim shipping and Muslim merchants could no longer meet the demands of the markets around them, as they had done when they successfully incorporated into their field of activity the markets of Asia and Mediterranean Europe. The knot that tied the two sides of the market was loosened and the Mongols and the Crusaders marched from opposite directions to meet on the shores of the Levant.

The Crusades and the Mongols were an obvious military threat to be challenged only through military means. Thus, the military, which was initially recruited to serve the landed aristocracy, now became a system unto itself and recruited individuals and groups to perpetuate itself. Its legitimacy was no longer questioned as it was the only force available to defend the "realm of Islam."

And where the knights in shining armor represented feudal Europe, the Mamluk knights represented the feudal Middle East. Building on Ayyubid *iqta'*, the Mamluks (A.H. 660–923 [A.D. 1260–1517]) entrenched the system even further. The military–landed aristocracy alliance was revived in the form of the Ottoman government system, a system that lasted, sometimes with the help of European powers, until the end of the First World War.

This system not only was legitimized by recourse to Islamic law and precedent but also had the advantage of being the basis of government. Enjoying this advantage, there was little incentive to change. Pockets of reform were closed by the weight of the Ottoman imperial system. And when change became necessary and desirable, it was either too late or was met by stiff institutional resistance. European industrial capital easily penetrated the Islamic world, especially during the nineteenth century, when the colonial powers destroyed, with varying degrees of success, the institutions and the economic infrastructure in the colonized areas that could have posed a serious obstacle to more effective colonial control. This inhibited local political and economic development. And with the absence of direct colonial rule after independence, the newly formed landed aristocracy under colonial rule came back with the military to dominate the state. The coercive power of the military remains the easier option in much of the Islamic world. But civilian rule, lost with the demise of the Mu'tazila, is slowly emerging, mainly where the formation of political parties is allowed.

In conclusion, Islam as a religion is neither oriented toward capitalism nor toward feudalism. As an ideological superstructure, it is sufficiently inclusive that it can be appropriated by the dominant social force. Thus, during its first two centuries, when the merchants were the dominant social force, they successfully appropriated institutional beliefs within Islam to advance their interests. As the infrastructure slowly changed during the first century of Abbasid rule, they attempted to formulate a supportive ideology based on Islamic arguments but they lost out to the landed aristocracy. As the latter became the dominant social force, they in turn appropriated institutions within Islam to safeguard their interests. And the maintenance of their interests required the presence of the military. Therefore, military *iqta'* became the more logical option. There were enough precedents in Islamic history and mechanisms within Islam to legitimize this practice. The military eventually became legitimate with the coming of the Mongols and especially the Crusades, and *iqta'* was normalized by the Mamluks.

Those who look at Islam as capitalist look at it during the first two centuries and select those institutions and practices that supported capital accumulation and project them onto the rest of Islamic history. They lose sight of the fact that social forces are dynamic and that they change. Similarly, those who contend that Islam is feudal look at it only after the rise of the landed aristocracy and most especially during the Mamluk and Ottoman periods. They too select specific institutions and mechanisms and project them onto other periods of Islamic history, thus also losing sight of the dynamism of social forces. This is the more reason to study history within a framework that focuses our attention on internal forces and dynamics. Only then do history and, in this case, Islamic history, become comprehensible instead of immutable and exotic.

Although this study was not intended to be part of the debate on the transition from feudalism to capitalism in Europe, some of my conclusions lend themselves to that question. Participants in this debate who focus on Europe and attempt to formulate a universal model have to take into account these conclusions, which do not fit their model of evolutionary stages. Yet, not all of the conclusions reached here contradict the findings pertinent to Europe. For example, a merchant state was founded and lasted for several centuries during a time when it was thought that a merchant state was theoretically impossible because merchants did not own the means of production. Commerce existed, and sometimes thrived, in the feudal Middle East (for example, the Karimi merchants), which is contrary to the European case. The destruction of the feudal system in Europe gave way to the growth of merchant capital and eventually industrial capital. In the Islamic world, and most notably in the Middle East, the opposite took place: merchant capital and its accumulation gave way to the growth of feudalism and military rule. This implies that other conditions must be analyzed to understand the transition from one system to another, not only in the Islamic world, but also in Europe. If a universal model is the object of comparative history, Islamic history, and that of the Middle East, should not be regarded only as a static backdrop to a dynamic drama played out in Europe.

Notes

Introduction

1. Martin Bernal, *Black Athena*, vol. 1, *The Fabrication of Ancient Greece*, pp. 189, 237. See also Edward W. Said, *Orientalism*, pp. 206–207, 231.

2. For a general critique of Orientalism, see, other than Bernal and Said, Bryan Turner, *Marx and the End of Orientalism*; Anwar Abdel Malik, "Orientalism in Crises," *Diogenes* 44 (1963): 103–140; Maxime Rodinson, "The Western Image and Western Studies of Islam," in *The Legacy of Islam*, ed. Joseph Schacht and C. E. Bosworth, pp. 9–62.

3. Patricia Crone, *Slaves on Horses*, p. 23.

4. See, for example, C. C. Torrey, *The Jewish Foundation of Islam*; Richard Bell, *The Origin of Islam in Its Christian Environment*.

5. Following Leon Catetani and Carl Becker, this view is expressed by, among others, E. Ashtor, *A Social and Economic History of the Near East in the Middle Ages*, pp. 10–11, and Philip K. Hitti, *History of the Arabs*, pp. 144–145.

6. See H. A. R. Gibb, "An Interpretation of Islamic History," *Journal of World History* 1 (1953): 39–62; F. M. Donner, *The Early Islamic Conquests*, in which it is claimed that the state wanted to control the nomads; M. A. Shaban, *Islamic History: A New Interpretation*, pp. 24, 56–57, in which he says that the caliph had no power.

7. Crone, *Slaves*, p. 5.

8. Patricia Crone and Michael Cook, *Hagarism: The Making of the Islamic World*.

9. Ibid., p. 75.

10. Ibid., pp. 33, 78, 125.

11. For an evaluation of Crone, *Slaves*, see Donner's review in *JAOS*, and Mahmood Ibrahim's review in *MW*.

12. Gustave E. von Grunebaum, *Medieval Islam*, p. 3. For a critique of von Grunebaum's cultural anthropology, see Abdallah Laroui, *La crise des intellectuels arabes: Traditionalisme ou historicisme*, pp. 59ff.

13. Thomas Kuhn, *The Structure of Scientific Revolutions*.

14. See, for example, Henri Lammens, "La Mecque à la veille de l'hégire"; *Mélange de l'Université Saint-Joseph* (Beirut), 1924, pp. 97–439; idem, "La république marchande de la Mecque vers l'an 600 de notre ère," *Bulletin de l'Institut Egyptien* 5th ser., no. 4 (1910): 23–54; C. C. Torrey, *The Commercial-Theological Terms in the Koran;* W. M. Watt, *Muhammad at Mecca;* Maxime Rodinson, *Islam and Capitalism;* idem, *Muhammad;* Eric Wolf, "The Social Organization of Mecca and the Origins of Islam." *Southwest Journal of Anthropology* 7 (1951): 329–356. For studies on merchants and commerce in later Islamic history, see S. D. Goitein, *Studies in Islamic History and Institutions;* idem, *Mediterranean Society;* Peter Gran, *Islamic Roots of Capitalism: Egypt, 1760–1840;* Maurice Lombard, *The Golden Age of Islam;* Abraham Udovitch, *Partnership and Profit in Medieval Islam.* Patricia Crone, in *Meccan Trade,* has tried to minimize Meccan trade by rejecting the idea that Meccans traded in spices, but she is unable to reject Meccan merchant activity. The notion that merchant capital is accumulated only by exchanging luxury goods is largely self-serving, since her efforts are an attempt to justify the notions put forth in her previous publications (e.g., that Islam was a nativist movement in reaction to outside interference).

15. Rodinson, *Islam and Capitalism*, pp. 6–7.

16. Michael Tigar and Madeleine Levy, *Law and the Rise of Capitalism*, p. 4.

17. Ibid., pp. 72–73.

18. Basing his work largely on Crone and Cook, Sulaiman Bashir produced another "static and sterile" reading of the sources and of Islamic history in *Al-Tarikh al-Akhar*. For an evaluation of this book, see Mahmood Ibrahim, "The Petrification of Islam," *Birzeit Research Review* 4 (1987): 64–73, 150–161.

19. See, for example, Lawrence Conrad, "Abraha and Muhammad: Some Observations Apropos of Chronology and Literary Topoi in the Early Arabic Historical Tradition," *Bulletin of the School of Oriental and African Studies* 50 (1987): 225–240; idem, "Seven and Tasbi': On the Implications of Numerical Symbolism for the Study of Medieval Islamic History," *JESHO* 31 (1988): 42–73.

20. See Abdallah Laroui, *Al-'Arab wa al-Fikr al-Tarikhi*, pp. 84–85.

1. Pre-Islamic Arabia

1. The most detailed account, based on archaeological, epigraphic, and literary sources, of the history of pre-Islamic Arabia is found in Jawad 'Ali, *Al-Mufassal fi Ta'rikh al-'Arab Qabl al-Islam*. See also Hitti, *History*, pp. 14–86; De Lacy O'Leary, *Arabia before Muhammad*.

2. Abu M. Hasan al-Hamdani, *Sifat Jazirat al-'Arab*, p. 50; idem, *Al-Iklil*, Pts. 1, 2, p. 7.

3. I. Karachkovsky, *Ta'rikh al-Adab al-Jughrafi al-'Arabi*, 1:170.

4. For a discussion of inscriptions found in northern Arabia, see F. V. Winnett and W. L. Reed, *Ancient Records from North Arabia*, esp. p. 117. Taima, in this area, was under the control of the Assyrians and the Babylonians and was the

provincial residence of the last king of Babylonia: see S. Langdon, "The Shalamians of Arabia," *JRAS*, 1927, pp. 529–533.

5. See Jacques Ryckmans, *Les Institutions monarchiques en Arabie meridional avant l'Islam (Ma'in et Saba')*.

6. *'Ali, Al-Mufassal*, 1:122–123.

7. M. Rostovetzeff, *Caravan Cities*, pp. 21, 57.

8. Ryckmans, *Institutions*, pp. 20–28.

9. *'Ali, Al-Mufassal*, 1:109–110.

10. Most of these inscriptions were published in *Corpus Inscriptionum Arabicum*; G. Ryckmans, "Inscriptions Sud-Arabes," *Le Muséon* 40 (1927): 161–200; Albert Jamme, *Sabaen Inscriptions from Mahram Bilqis (Ma'rib)*; idem, *Classification descriptive général des inscriptions sud-arabes*.

11. Jamme, *Sabaen Inscriptions*, p. 54.

12. Ibid., p. 55.

13. Ibid., pp. 18–19.

14. Ibid., p. 44.

15. Ibid., pp. 90, 98, 102, 114, 119, 172, 218, passim.

16. Ibid., pp. 68–70, 77–79, 92, 93, 97, 137, passim.

17. Ibid., pp. 155–156, 163, 165.

18. G. W. van Beek, "Frankincense and Myrrh in Ancient South Arabia," *JAOS* 78 (1958): 141–153.

19. A. T. Wilson, *The Persian Gulf*, p. 45.

20. For a divergent view on this, see A. F. L. Beeston, "Kingship in South Arabia," *JESHO* 15 (1972): 256–268.

21. *'Ali, Al-Mufassal*, 2:132–134; H. St. J. B. Philby, "Three New Inscriptions from Hadhramaut," *JRAS*, 1945, pp. 124–133. For ports and shipping lanes, see van Beek, "Frankincense," p. 146; *Periplus of the Erythrean Sea*, trans. W. H. Schoff; J. I. Miller, *Spice Trade of the Roman Empire*; E. Warmington, *Commerce between the Roman Empire and India*. On Arab seafaring, see G. F. Hourani, *Arab Seafaring in the Indian Ocean*.

22. A. Jamme, *The al-'Uqla Texts*, pp. 17, 25.

23. Richard Bowen, "Irrigation in Ancient Qataban," in *Archeological Discoveries in South Arabia*, 2:43.

24. *Periplus*, p. 35.

25. On the importance of Aden, see Warmington, *Commerce*, p. 11, passim; *Periplus*, pp. 8, 32; al-Hamdani, *Sifat*, p. 53; Abu Ali al-Marzuqi, *Al-Azmina wa al-Amkina*, 2:164.

26. *'Ali, Al-Mufassal*, 2:192–193; J. Ryckmans, "Ritual Meals in the Ancient South Arabian Religion," *PSAS*, 1972, p. 38; F. Stark, "Notes on the Southern Incense Route of Arabia," *IC* 10 (1936): 199.

27. *'Ali, Al-Mufassal*, 1:199, 202–203.

28. Ibid., pp. 189–190.

29. A. F. L. Beeston, *Qahtan Studies in Old South Arabian Epigraphy: The*

Mercantile Code of Qataban, pp. 11–13, passim; A. G. Lundin, "Le régime citadin de l'Arabi du Sud aux IIe–IIIe siècle de notre ère," *PSAS,* 1972, p. 27.

30. Warmington, *Commerce,* pp. 13, 187.

31. Ibid., pp. 192–193; Miller, *Spice Trade,* p. 21.

32. An account on the history of Himyar may be found in H. von Wissman, "Himyar, Ancient History." *Le Muséon* 77 (1964): 429–497. Reference to Strabo, who accompanied Gallus, may be found in Hitti, *History,* p. 46.

33. Von Wissman, "Himyar," pp. 446, 463; ʿAli, *Al-Mufassal,* 1:368, 520–521. For the problem of chronology, see A. F. L. Beeston, "The Problem of South Arabian Chronology," *BSOAS* 16 (1954): 39–42; H. St. J. B. Philby, "South Arabian Chronology," *Le Muséon* 62 (1949): 229–249.

34. *Periplus,* pp. 30–31.

35. Hitti, *History,* p. 57.

36. G. Levi Della Vida, "Pre-Islamic Arabia," in *The Arab Heritage,* ed. N. Faris, p. 33.

37. H. Ingrams, "From Cana to Shabwa: The South Arabian Incense Road," *JRAS,* 1944–45, p. 179.

38. See Ryckmans, "Ritual Meals," and Stark, "Notes."

39. ʿAli, *Al-Mufassal,* 7:53–54, 202, 205; Irfan Shahid, "Pre-Islamic Arabia," in *Cambridge History of Islam,* vol. 1, ed. P. M. Holt, p. 7.

40. Lundin, "Le régime citadin," p. 27.

41. Ibid., p. 28. See also G. E. M. de Ste. Croix, *The Class Struggle in the Ancient Greek World,* esp. chaps. 3 and 4.

42. Shahid, "Pre-Islamic Arabia," p. 7.

43. Ahmad Khan, "The Tanning Cottage Industry in Pre-Islamic Arabia," *JPHS* 19 (1971): 85–100.

44. For a brief history of Petra, see Hitti, *History,* pp. 67–74.

45. Ibid., p. 70; Rostovetzeff, *Caravan Cities,* pp. 19, 31, 34; Levi Della Vida, "Pre-Islamic Arabia," p. 32; Warmington, *Commerce,* p. 12.

46. For a brief history of Palymyra, see Rostovetzeff, *Caravan Cities,* pp. 120–150; Hitti, *History,* pp. 74–78; Warmington, *Commerce,* pp. 99–100.

47. G. F. Hourani, "Did Roman Competition Ruin South Arabia?" *JNES* 11 (1952): 294; Levi Della Vida, "Pre-Islamic Arabia," p. 37.

48. Warmington, *Commerce,* pp. 160, 170, 211. On cotton, see A. M. Watson, "The Rise and Spread of Old World Cotton," in *Studies in Textile History in Memory of Harold Burnham,* ed. V. Gervers, pp. 355–368; idem, *Agricultural Innovation in the Early Islamic World,* pp. 31–41. The silk industry flourished in the Near East after the silkworm was introduced in Byzantium around A.D. 553. It spread to such cities as Beirut, Tyre, and Antioch: see R. S. López, "Silk Industry in the Byzantine Empire," *Speculum* 20 (1945): 12, 20.

49. See notes 65 and 66, chap. 4.

50. ʿAli, *Al-Mufassal,* 2:567–568. On the spread of Christianity to Yemen, see J. S. Trimingham, *Christianity among the Arabs in Pre-Islamic Times,* pp. 287–

303; F. V. Winnett, "Reference to Jesus in Pre-Islamic Arabian Inscriptions," *Muslim World* 31 (1941): 314–353.

51. Walter Dostal, "The Evolution of Bedouin Life," in *L'Antica Società Bedouina*, ed. F. Gabrielli, p. 3.

52. See, for example, Nushwan ibn Saʿid al-Himyari, *Khulasat al-Sira al-Jamiʿa Li ʿajaʾib Akhbar al-Muluk al-Tababiʿa*.

53. H. St. J. B. Philby and Tritton, "Najran Inscription," *JRAS*, 1944, pp. 119–129; Sidney Smith, "Events in Arabia in the Sixth Century A.D.," *BSOAS* 16 (1954): 442. For more information on Najran, see N. Pigulevskaja, "Les rapports sociaux à Nedjran au début du VI⁰ siècle de l'ère chrétienne," *JESHO* 4 (1961): 1–14.

54. For information on Najran, see Yaqut, *Muʿjam al-Buldan*, 4:751–757. For the treaty with Najran, see Abu Yusuf, *Kitab al-Kharaj*, p. 78; al-Baladhuri, *Futuh*, p. 77.

55. Ibn Hawqal, *Surat al-Ard*, pp. 25, 36. See also al-Hamdani, *Sifat*, p. 67; Khan, "Cottage Industry," p. 89.

56. Yaqut, *Muʿjam*, 3:388–390; Ibn Jaʿfar, *Kitab al-Kharaj*, p. 189; al-Maqdisi, *Ahsan al-Taqasim fi Maʿrifat al-Aqalim*, pp. 87, 98.

57. Al-Baladhuri, *Futuh*, p. 74; Yaqut, *Muʿjam*, 3:420–426; al-Marzuqi, *Al-Azmina*, 2:164; Ibn Hawqal, *Surat*, p. 37.

58. Ibn Adam, *Kitab al-Kharaj*, p. 147.

59. Nichola Ziyadeh, "Tatuwwur al-Turuq al-Bahriyya wa al-Tijariyya," *Majallat Dirasat al-Khalij waʾl-Jazira al-ʿArabiyya* 1 (1975): 69, 79; Wilson, *The Persian Gulf*, p. 27. For the commercial importance of this region, see al-Marzuqi, *Al-Azmina*, 2:163; al-Maqdisi, *Ahsan al-Taqasim*, pp. 92, 97; Ibn Hawqal, *Surat*, p. 38. Duba was another port in this region: see al-Marzuqi, *Al-Azmina*, 2:168.

60. *Periplus*, p. 36; see also van Beek, "Frankincense," pp. 144, 146.

61. Adballah ibn Humyyid al-Salimi, *Tuhfat al-Aʿyan fi Sirat Ahl Uman*, pp. 17ff.

62. Al-Marzuqi, *Al-Azmina*, 2:164–165; Ibn Hawqal, *Surat*, p. 38. Rabia was another important port in Hadramawt: see al-Marzuqi, *Al-Azmina*, 2: 165; al-Baghdadi, *Al-Muhabbar*, p. 267. There were other settlements, such as Samhar, which were started by migrants from Yemen: see A. F. L. Beeston, "The Settlement at Khor Reir," *JOS* 2 (1976): 39–42.

63. Al-Salimi, *Tuhfat*, p. 37; see also J. C. Wilkinson, "Arab-Persian Relations in Late Sasanid Oman," *PSAS*, 1972, pp. 40–51; Ibn Ruzaiq, *Imams and Sayyids of Oman*, pp. 3ff.

64. On the Banu Julanda, see J. C. Wilkinson, "The Julanda of Oman," *JOS*, 1975: 97–108; on their mercantile activities, see al-Marzuqi, *Al-Azmina*, 2:163; Yaqut, *Muʿjam*, 3:368–369.

65. Yaqut, *Muʿjam*, 4:1024–1031; ʿAli, *Al-Mufassal*, 2:273–275.

66. See H. St. J. B. Philby, "Motor Tracks and Sabaen Inscriptions in Najd,"

GJ 116 (1950): 214; idem, "Two Notes from Central Arabia," *GJ* 113 (1949): 86–93.

67. On the Banu Kinda, see G. Olinder, *Kings of Kinda of the Family of Akil al-Murar.*

68. ʿAli, *Al-Mufassal,* 3 : 321. The Banu Kinda were related by marriage to the Lakhmids of Hira: see Olinder, *Kings,* p. 49; on their relationship to the Banu Taghlib, p. 95.

69. Van Beek, "Frankincense," p. 145.

70. Smith, "Events," p. 442. Taxes on silk were an important source of gold for the Sasanids from Byzantium: G. Ostrogorsky, *History of the Byzantine State,* p. 75; Archibald Lewis, *Naval Power and Trade in the Mediterranean: 500– 1000 A.D.,* pp. 33ff.; Irfan Kawar, "The Arabs in the Peace Treaty of 561 A.D.," *Arabica,* 1956, p. 187.

71. Al-Marzuqi, *Al-Azmina,* 2 : 162–163. Pearls were an important commodity: Ibn Hawqal, *Surat,* p. 47; al-Maqdisi, *Ahsan al-Taqasim,* p. 101; Warmington, *Commerce,* p. 167.

72. Olinder, *Kings,* pp. 72ff.; Smith, "Events," p. 461; ʿAli, *Al-Mufassal,* 2 : 548, 3 : 193.

73. Gustave von Grunebaum, "Nature of Arab Unity," *Arabica* 10 (1963): 17, 70.

74. On this situation, see O'Leary, *Arabia,* p. 119; al-Marzuqi, *Al-Azmina,* 2 : 162, 165, says that during this period tribes began to demand money for access to the markets.

75. Ibn Qutaiba, *Kitab al-Maʿarif,* p. 636; al-Muqaddasi, *Al-Badʾ wa al-Taʾrikh,* 3 : 180, where he says that dhu Shanatir was a qayel; al-Tabari, *Taʾrikh,* 2 : 117ff.

76. Al-Tabari, *Taʾrikh,* p. 124; al-Muqaddasi, *Al-Badʾ,* 3 : 183; Ibn Qutaiba, *Kitab al-Maʿarif,* p. 637. For more about dhu Nuwwas's attack on Najran, see J. Ryckmans, *La persecution des Chrétiens Himyarites au sixième siécle.*

77. This intervention was also carried out with the blessings of the Byzantines, who were approached first by Dhu Thaʿlaban: see al-Tabari, *Taʾrikh,* 2 : 124; for references that speak of the Byzantine connection, see Smith, "Events"; Kawar, "Peace Treaty," p. 87; Lewis, *Naval Power,* pp. 33–34.

78. ʿAli, *Al-Mufassal,* 3 : 488.

79. Al-Tabari, *Taʾrikh,* 2 : 128.

80. Ibid., p. 130.

81. ʿAli, *Al-Mufassal,* 3 : 485–487.

82. Ibid.

83. For a discussion and references to this inscription, see M. J. Kister, "The Campaign of Huluban," *Le Muséon* 78 (1965): 425ff.; Smith, "Events."

84. For a divergent view, that the collapse of the dam caused the bedouinization of Arabia, see C. W. Caskell, "Bedouinization of Arabia," in *Studies in Islamic Cultural History,* ed. G. von Grunebaum, pp. 36–46.

85. Al-Tabari, *Taʾrikh*, 2:130ff.; see also M. J. Kister, "Some Reports concerning Mecca from Jahiliyya to Islam," *JESHO* 15 (1972): pp. 61ff.

86. For a brief history of Hira, see Hitti, *History*, pp. 81–84; Irfan Shahid, "Hira." More details may be found in G. Rothstein, *Die Dynastie der Lahmiden in al-Hira*.

87. Smith, "Events," pp. 442, 461; ʿAli, *Al-Mufassal*, 2:548, 3:193.

88. M. J. Kister, "Hira: Some Notes on Its Relations with Arabia," *Arabica* 15 (1968): 145–148.

89. On the Ghassanids and their relationship to the Lakhmids, see ʿAli, *Al-Mufassal*, 3:347; Theodor Nöldeke, *Die Ghassanischen Fursten aus dem Hause Gafna's*, pp. 1–63; Ismaʿil Khalidi, "The Arab Kingdom of Ghassan," *MW* 65 (1956): 193–206; Irfan Kawar, "Arethas, son of Jabalah," *JAOS* 75 (1955): 205–216; Irfan Shahid, "Ghassan," in *Encyclopedia of Islam*.

90. See Kawar, "Peace Treaty"; Hitti, *History*, p. 83; ʿAli, *Al-Mufassal*, 3: 220, 406.

91. For the organization of the army, see ʿAli, *Al-Mufassal*, 3:198–199; Kister, "Hira," p. 149. For Hira's administrative divisions, see Michael G. Morony, *Iraq after the Muslim Conquest*, p. 152.

92. Kister, "Hira," pp. 150–151; other tribal chiefs are mentioned in Olinder, *Kings*, p. 170.

93. Al-Marzuqi, *Al-Azmina*, 2:191; Kister, "Hira," p. 153.

94. Ibn ʿAbd Rabbihi, *Al-ʿIqd al-Farid*, 2:10.

95. Economic cooperation determined this relationship, such as that with the Salim and the Hawazin: see Kister, "Hira," pp. 149–157; Ibn ʿAbd Rabbihi, *Al-ʿIqd*, 5:133, 135.

96. Irfan Shahid, "Arabic Literature," in *Cambridge History of Islam*, p. 659; von Grunebaum, "Arab Unity," p. 18.

97. Christianity was already practiced by many of the subjects of the Lakhmids: see Trimingham, *Christianity*, pp. 178–202, esp. pp. 198–199.

98. See F. M. Donner, "The Bakr b. Waʾil Tribes and Politics in Northeastern Arabia on the Eve of Islam," *SI* 51 (1980): 5–38.

2. The Development of Merchant Capital in Mecca

1. The Kaʿba existed before the creation of the universe and represents the center of the universe: al-Azraqi, *Akhbar Mecca*, pp. 22–27. For the significance of the sacred area and sacred time, see Mircea Eliade, *The Sacred and the Profane*, chaps. 1 and 2; Philip K. Hitti, *Capital Cities of Arab Islam*, pp. 3–13; Mahmood Ibrahim, "Social and Economic Conditions in Pre-Islamic Mecca, *IJMES* 14 (1982): 243–258.

2. Al-Azraqi, *Akhbar*, pp. 47, 54–56.

3. This process is described in, among others, ibid., pp. 60–63; al-Baghdadi, *Kitab al-Munammaq*, pp. 82–84, 349–351, where he says that a disease caused many of the Khuzaʿa to die and thus weakened them and allowed Qusayy to

take over. See also M. al-Tabari, *Ta'rikh Al-Rusul wa'l Muluk*, 2:254–258; Ibn Hisham, *Al-Sira al-Nabawiyya*, 1:109.

4. Jamme, *Uqla*.

5. See, for example, Ibn Hazm, *Jamharat Ansab al-ʿArab*, pp. 12–13.

6. Ibid., pp. 13–14; Ibn Qutaiba, *Kitab al-Maʿarif*, pp. 68–70.

7. See al-Azraqi, *Akhbar*, p. 63; al-Tabari, *Ta'rikh*, 2:258.

8. Al-Azraqi, *Akhbar*, pp. 85, 134–135.

9. Ibid., pp. 66, 107, 135; al-Tabari, *Ta'rikh*, 2:260; Ibn Hisham, *Al-Sira*, 1:120; al-Baghdadi, *Munammaq*, pp. 19, 222; ʿAli, *Al-Mufassal*, 4:144.

10. Al-Azraqi, *Akhbar*, pp. 69, 436–441.

11. Ibid., p. 66; Ibn Hisham, *Al-Sira*, 1:116; M. Hamidullah, "The City State of Mecca," *IC* 12 (1938): 254–277.

12. Al-Thaʿalibi, *Thimar al-Qulub fi al-Mudaf wa al-Mansub*, p. 16.

13. Ibid., p. 116; al-Baghdadi, *Kitab al-Muhabbar*, p. 157; M. J. Kister, "Mecca and Tamim," *JESHO* 8 (1965): 141–144.

14. Al-Qurtubi, *Al-Jamiʿ Li Ahkam al-Qur'an*, 2:204ff., 20:209.

15. Al-Thaʿalibi, *Thimar*, p. 115; al-Baghdadi, *Al-Munammaq*, pp. 31–32.

16. Al-Qurtubi, *Al-Jamiʿ*, 2:205; Kister, "Mecca and Tamim," p. 124.

17. Al-Qurtubi, *Al-Jamiʿ*, 2:205.

18. Al-Baghdadi, *Al-Munammaq*, p. 32.

19. Ibid., p. 33. For a modern discussion of the *ilaf*, see Kister, "Mecca and Tamim," pp. 116ff.; M. Hamidullah, "Al-Ilaf ou les rapport économico-diplomatique de la Mecque pré-Islamique," in *Mélanges Louis Massingnon*, p. 293; R. Simon, "Hums et ilaf ou commerce sans guerre," in *Acta Hungaricae*, 1970, pp. 204–232.

20. Al-Baghdadi, *Al-Muhabbar*, pp. 162–163; idem, *Al-Munammaq*, pp. 35–36, 123, 147, 163, 171, 173, 180, 246, 359, 441.

21. Kister, "Mecca and Tamim," p. 121. For tribal and clan leaders who came to Mecca and settled, see al-Baghdadi, *Al-Munammaq*, pp. 295, 297, passim.

22. Al-Baladhuri, *Ansab al-Ashraf*, 4A:1. For other well-connected Meccans, see Kister, "Mecca and Tamim," pp. 158–160; al-Baghdadi, *Al-Muhabbar*, pp. 55, 62ff.

23. Al-Baghdadi, *Al-Munammaq*, p. 276; al-Baladhuri, *Ansab*, 1:52; W. M. Watt, *Muhammad at Medina*, pp. 154–157.

24. Al-Marzuqi, *Al-Azmina*, 2:165; al-Baghdadi, *Al-Muhabbar*, p. 267.

25. Al-Baghdadi, *Al-Munammaq*, pp. 277, 288.

26. Kister, "Mecca and Tamim," esp. pp. 146ff.

27. Al-Baghdadi, *Al-Muhabbar*, pp. 264, 265.

28. Ibid., p. 264. For a discussion of this and additional references, see Kister, "Mecca and Tamim," pp. 128–130.

29. Kister, "Mecca and Tamim," pp. 126–127.

30. Al-Baghdadi, *Al-Munammaq*, p. 280.

31. Ibid., pp. 280–281; see also M. J. Kister, "Some Reports concerning Ta'if," *Jerusalem Studies in Arabic and Islam*, 1979, pp. 1–18.

32. About al-ʿAs ibn Waʾil, see al-Baladhuri, *Ansab*, 1:139; about Abu Uhaiha, p. 142, and al-Baghdadi, *Al-Munammaq*, p. 360; about ʿAbd al-Muttalib, al-Baladhuri, *Ansab*, 1:74, al-Baghdadi, *Al-Munammaq*, p. 99. See also al-Baladhuri, *Futuh*, p. 66.

33. Al-Baghdadi, *Al-Munammaq*, pp. 124–126.

34. Ibid., pp. 126–128; al-Baladhuri, *Ansab*, 1:75.

35. Al-Baghdadi, *Al-Munammaq*, pp. 68, 76, where he says that the army was afflicted with measles also. For a discussion of this expedition, see Kister, "Mecca," pp. 67–73.

36. Al-Azraqi, *Akhbar*, p. 97.

37. Kister, "Hira," pp. 145–148. The Meccans, nevertheless, renewed their contacts with Yemen, and a delegation came to congratulate Saif ibn Dhi Yazan and to ask him for a safe conduct; see Ibn ʿAbd Rabbihi, *Al-ʿIqd*, 2:23–28.

38. Al-Baghdadi, *Al-Munammaq*, pp. 178–181; Ibn Bakkar, *Jamharat Nasab Quraish*, pp. 428–430.

39. Al-Fasi, *Shafaʾ al-Gharam bi Akhbar al-Balad al-Haram*, pp. 143–144; Watt, *Muhammad at Mecca*, p. 15.

40. Ibn al-Athir, *Al-Kamil fi al-Taʾrikh*, 2:588–594; al-Baghdadi, *Al-Munammaq*, p. 190.

41. Al-Baladhuri, *Ansab*, 1:101; al-Baghdadi, *Al-Munammaq*, pp. 192–193, 195–196; for the significance of this war, see Watt, *Muhammad at Mecca*, pp. 12ff.

42. Al-Baghdadi, *Al-Munammaq*, pp. 198–208.

43. Ibid., pp. 209–211.

44. Watt, *Muhammad at Mecca*, p. 11; al-Baghdadi, *Al-Munammaq*, pp. 45–49, 170, 186; al-Baladhuri, *Ansab*, 1:128.

45. Al-Azraqi, *Akhbar*, p. 120.

46. Ibid., pp. 120–121; al-Baghdadi, *Al-Munammaq*, p. 143.

47. For the connection between the *hums* and Abraha's expedition, see al-Azraqi, *Akhbar*, p. 120; al-Athir, *Al-Kamil*, 1:452.

48. Al-Azraqi, *Akhbar*, p. 121; al-Baghdadi, *Al-Munammaq*, p. 144.

49. Ibn Al-Athir, *Al-Kamil*, 1:452; al-Azraqi, *Akhbar*, p. 120; al-Baghdadi, *Al-Munammaq*, p. 143.

50. Al-Azraqi, *Akhbar*, p. 121; al-Baghdadi, *Al-Muhabbar*, p. 178.

51. Al-Azraqi, *Akhbar*, pp. 121–122; al-Baghdadi, *Al-Munammaq*, pp. 144–145, 424.

52. Kister, "Mecca," p. 76.

53. Al-Marzuqi, *Al-Azmina*, 2:165, 168. On Hakim, see Ibn Bakkar, *Jamharat*, pp. 355, 446.

54. On the *muʿallaqat*, see R. A. Nicholson, *A Literary History of the Arabs*, pp. 101ff.; H. A. R. Gibb, *Arabic Literature*, pp. 22ff.

55. Al-Baghdadi, *Al-Munammaq*, pp. 190, 275; idem, *Al-Muhabbar*, p. 267; al-Marzuqi, *Al-Azmina*, 2 : 166.

3. Merchant Capital and Mecca's Internal Development

1. Al-Baghdadi, *Al-Munammaq*, pp. 238, 286, 288, 294, 295, 297, 299.

2. Ibid., pp. 277, 280; al-Azraqi, *Akhbar*, pp. 436—441.

3. Al-Baghdadi, *Al-Munammaq*, pp. 331—332.

4. Ibid., p. 285.

5. Ibid., p. 285; see also al-Azraqi, *Akhbar*, p. 447.

6. Al-Baghdadi, *Al-Munammaq*, pp. 290—291.

7. Ibid., p. 292.

8. Wolf, "Social Organization of Mecca," p. 334. Stratification was also noted by Barbara Aswad, "Social and Ecological Aspects in the Formation of Islam," in *Peoples and Cultures of the Middle East*, Louis Sweet, 1 : 58. For a more sustained analysis, see Watt, *Muhammad at Mecca*, esp. chap. 1; idem, "Social and Economic Aspects in the Rise of Islam," *IQ* I (1954): 90—103.

9. ʿAli, *Al-Mufassal*, 4 : chaps. 4 and 7, passim, esp. p. 370.

10. Legal books are full of references to the status of *mawali* and the mechanisms by which they could unbond themselves. See, for example, al-Qastalani, *Irshad as-Sari fi Sahih al-Bukhari*, 4 : 315ff.; Ibn Anas, *Muwattaʾ*, pp. 392, 555; al-Baghdadi, *Al-Muhabbar*, pp. 344ff.

11. Al-Baghdadi, *Al-Munammaq*, p. 322.

12. Some, such as ʿAbdallah ibn Salul, Safwan ibn Umayya, al-ʿAs ibn Waʾil, and Suhail ibn ʿAmr forced their slave women into prostitution. See al-Nisaburi, *Asbab Nuzul al-Qurʾan* (1968), pp. 211, 220; idem, *Asbab Nuzul* (1969), pp. 326—328, 339. Others were smiths: al-Qastalani, *Irshad*, 4 : 32. The B. Makhzum owned many slaves: al-Isfahani, *Kitab al-Aghani*, 1 : 65; al-Masʿudi, *Muruj adh-Dhahab wa Maʿadin al-Jawhar*, 4 : 155, where ʿAbdalla ibn Jadʿan is mentioned as a slave dealer. See also Ibn al-Athir, *Al-Kamil*, 2. : 66, 67, 68, 70.

13. Ibn Anas, *Muwattaʾ*, pp. 369, 392; al-Qastalani, *Irshad*, 4 : 292, 326, 327, 332.

14. Al-Qastalani, *Irshad*, pp. 300—307, 316; Ibn Hisham, *Al-Sira*, 2 : 223; Saʿid ibn al-ʿAs and Hind bint ʿAbdal-Muttalib also freed slaves: ʿAli, *Al-Mufassal*, 4 : 198.

15. Al-Baghdadi, *Al-Munammaq*, p. 37; idem, *Al-Muhabbar*, p. 164; al-Malik, *Al-Sira*, 1 : 113; al-Baladhuri, *Ansab*, 1 : 60.

16. Marshall Sahlins, *Tribesmen*, pp. 36—37.

17. Al-Nisaburi, *Asbab* (1968), pp. 59, 87, 88; see also Kister, "Mecca," p. 78; ʿAli, *Al-Mufassal*, 3 : 363; Ibn Saʿd, *Kitab al-Tabaqat*, 3 : 23; Lammens, *La Mecque*, p. 257.

18. Al-Baladhuri, *Ansab*, 1 : 57; al-Nisaburi, *Asbab* (1969), pp. 87, 88; Lammens, *La Mecque*, pp. 235—240; ʿAli, *Al-Mufassal*, 4 : 61.

19. ʿAli, *al-Mufassal*, p. 61.

20. Lammens, *La Mecque,* p. 237; Rodinson, *Muhammad,* p. 36; Wolf, "Social Organization," p. 335; Ibn al-Athir, *Al-Kamil,* 2:88; al-Baladhuri, *Ansab,* 1:193.

21. Ibn Qutaiba, *Al-Maʿarif,* pp. 575–576; Ibn Rusta, *Al-Aʿlaq al-Nafisa,* p. 215; al-Qastalani, *Irshad,* 4:29, 33, 35.

22. Al-Baghdadi, *Al-Munammaq,* pp. 52, 53, 241, 424; al-Azraqi, *Akhbar,* p. 97; al-Baghdadi, *Al-Muhabbar,* pp. 190–191.

23. See, for example, al-Azraqi, *Akhbar,* pp. 65–66.

24. Al-Baghdadi, *Al-Munammaq,* pp. 42–43, 222, 331–332; Ibn Hisham, *Al-Sira,* 1:20; Ibn Al-Athir, *Al-Kamil,* 2:22; al-Baghdadi, *Al-Muhabbar,* pp. 166–167.

25. Al-Baghdadi, *Al-Munammaq,* p. 223; al-Baladhuri, *Ansab,* 1:56–57; al-Maqrizi, *Kitab al-Nizaʿ wa al-Takhasum,* p. 8; Ibn Hisham, *Al-Sira,* 1:124.

26. Al-Baghdadi, *Al-Munammaq,* pp. 80–82.

27. Ibid., pp. 40–41; al-Azraqi, *Akhbar,* p. 453; al-Maqrizi, *Al-Nizaʿ,* p. 10.

28. Al-Maqrizi, *Al-Nizaʿ,* p. 11; Al-Baghdadi, *Al-Munammaq,* pp. 94–98; al-Baladhuri, *Ansab,* 1:73; al-Athir, *Al-Kamil,* 2:15.

29. Al-Baghdadi, *Al-Munammaq,* pp. 85–88; al-Baladhuri, *Ansab,* 1:69. For questions about the B. al-Najjar connection, see al-Tabari, *Taʾrikh,* 2:248; Ibn al-Athir, *Al-Kamil,* 2:11.

30. Al-Baladhuri, *Ansab,* 1:71.

31. Ibid., pp. 71–72; al-Baghdadi, *Al-Munammaq,* pp. 88–91.

32. Al-Baghdadi, *Al-Munammaq,* pp. 98–102.

33. Ibid., pp. 130–133, also pp. 112–114.

34. Ibid., pp. 55–57.

35. Ibid., pp. 57–67.

36. Ibid., p. 206.

37. Ibid., p. 218; see also al-Masʿudi, *Muruj,* 4:122–123, in which he says that the *hilf* was formed a few months later; Ibn Hisham, *Al-Sira,* 1:122–124.

38. See, for example, Watt, *Muhammad at Mecca,* p. 13.

39. Al-Baghdadi, *Al-Munammaq,* pp. 47, 341; see also al-Yaʿaqubi, *Taʾrikh,* 2:18.

40. Al-Baladhuri, *Ansab,* 1:136; al-Baghdadi, *Al-Munammaq,* pp. 234–236, 241.

41. Al-Baghdadi, *Al-Munammaq,* pp. 241, 244, 245, 246.

4. Merchant Capital and the Rise of Islam

1. Al-Azraqi, *Akhbar,* p. 363; Ibn Anas, *Muwattaʾ,* p. 451. References to famine abound: al-Baghdadi, *Al-Munammaq,* pp. 37, 103, 124, 166, 167, 263, 424; idem, *Al-Muhabbar,* p. 164; Ibn Hisham, *Sira,* 1:113; al-Baladhuri, *Ansab,* 1:58, 60, 101.

2. The boycott lasted two or three years: Ibn Hisham, *Al-Sira,* 2:17–18; al-Tabari, *Taʾrikh,* 2:336, 342; Watt, *Muhammad at Medina,* pp. 121–122.

3. Al-Tabari, *Ta'rikh*, 2:343–346; Ibn Hisham, *Al-Sira*, 2:44, 47–48.

4. On his way back to Mecca, Muhammad stopped at Nakhla, the abode of al-Uzza, and prayed: al-Tabari, *Ta'rikh*, 2:346. To enter Mecca, he sought the *jiwar* of al-Akhnas ibn Shuraiq, but the latter could not give it because he was a *halif* in Mecca (p. 347). Other Muslims who returned to Mecca, especially from Abyssinia, had to seek the *jiwar* of a Meccan, and their status was tenuous (p. 340; Ibn Hisham, *Al-Sira*, 2:216).

5. See Watt, *Muhammad at Mecca*, pp. 20ff.; idem, *Islam and the Integration of Society;* idem, "Social and Economic Aspects"; idem, "Ideal Factors in the Origin of Islam." *IQ* 2 (1955): 161–174.

6. For studies on Muhammad, see Watt, *Muhammad at Mecca* and *Muhammad at Medina;* Rodinson, *Muhammad;* Martin Lings, *Muhammad;* Ibn Hisham, *Al-Sira*, trans. Alfred Guillaum as *The Life of Muhammad.*

7. There were others in Mecca who did not worship idols: al-Baghdadi, *Al-Munammaq*, pp. 176–178. For the significance of the incident at Ghar Hira' (*tahanauf*) in Muhammad's relationship to Khadija, see Leila Ahmad, "Women and the Advent of Islam," *Signs* 2 (1986): 665–691.

8. For references to red stone and white stone deities, see Gustave von Grunebaum, *Classical Islam*, p. 24; for other sacred centers, see al-Kalbi, *Kitab al-Asnam*, pp. 45, 48, 56, 61, passim.

9. M. G. S. Hodgson, *The Venture of Islam: The Classical Age of Islam*, 1:128–134.

10. Ibid., p. 130.

11. This connection is discussed by Max Weber, *The Sociology of Religion*, esp. pp. 35ff.

12. Watt, *Muhammad at Mecca*, pp. 72–74; Rodinson, *Muhammad*, p. 98.

13. Al-Tabari, *Ta'rikh*, 2:347–348.

14. Ibid., p. 350; Ibn Kathir, *Al-Sira al-Nabawiyya*, 2:358; ibn al-Athir, *Al-Kamil*, 2:93; Ibn Hisham, *Al-Sira*, 2:51.

15. Ibn Hisham, *Al-Sira*, 2:56–64.

16. Al-Samhudi, *Wafa' al-Wafa'*, 1:152ff.; Ibn Hisham, *Al-Sira*, 2:91; al-Isfahani, *Aghani*, 17:116–130.

17. Fredrick Denny, "Umma in the Constitution of Medina," *JNES* 36 (1977): 39–47. The Jews of Medina were originally members of the Umma but were later cast out. For Muhammad's relations with the Jews, see Watt, *Muhammad at Medina*, pp. 192–220.

18. Al-Samhudi, *Wafa'*, 1:62, 72; A. al-Baladhuri, *Futuh*, pp. 6–7.

19. For a discussion of the Constitution, see R. B. Serjeant, "The Constitution of Medina," *IQ* 3 (1964): 3–16; idem, "The Sunna Jami'ah, Pacts with Yathrib Jews, and the Tahrim of Yathrib: An Analysis and Translation of the Documents comprised in the So-called Constitution of Medina," *BSOAS* 41 (1978): 1–48; Moshe Gil, "The Constitution of Medina: A reconsideration," *Israel Oriental*

Studies 4 (1974): 44–66; an excellent discussion appears in Watt, *Muhammad at Medina*, pp. 221–250.

20. Qur'an, 2:213, 5:48, 6:38, 7:34, 10:47, 40:5, 45:28.

21. Ibn Hisham, *Al-Sira*, 2:106, 108.

22. Qur'an, 10:47; Ibn Hisham, *Al-Sira*, 2:107.

23. Ibn Anas, *Muwatta'*, pp. 426, 429, 430, 501, 502; al-Qastalani, *Irshad*, 4:51, 188; *Sahih Muslim* (on the margins of *Irshad*), 6:400.

24. Al-Qastalani, *Irshad*, 4:175–177, 187; Ibn Anas, *Muwatta'*, p. 494.

25. Al-Qastalani, *Irshad*, 4:177.

26. Ibid., pp. 131–134.

27. Ibid., pp. 175, 192.

28. Ibid., pp. 170, 183; al-Baladhuri, *Futuh*, p. 9; Ibn Sallam, *Kitab al-Amwal*, p. 363. Many tracts of land were developed by Salman al-Farisi: al-Samhudi, *Wafa'*, 2:154. In anticipation of further development, many began to enclose dead lands by demarcating them with stones, a process called *tahjir*: Ibn Adam, *Kitab al-Kharaj*, p. 65.

29. Al-Samhudi, *Wafa'*, 1:189–190; al-Qastalani, *Irshad*, 4:184. 'Umar followed the rule that if anyone abandoned the land for three consecutive years, he or she forfeited it: see al-Maqrizi, *Al-Kitat*, 1:176.

30. See al-Samhudi, *Wafa'*, 1:539; Saleh el-Ali, "The Topography of Medina," *IC* 35 (1961): 65–92; M. J. Kister, "The Market of the Prophet," *JESHO* 8 (1965): 272–276. The Prophet refused to fix prices: Abu Yusuf, *Kitab al-Kharaj*, pp. 52–53. 'Umar did not allow merchants to undersell other merchants: Ibn Anas, *Muwatta'*, p. 451. The activity in the market and opportunities for commerce distracted the Muslims from Muhammad's sermon: Qur'an, 62:10, 11.

31. Ibn Kathir, *Al-Sira*, 2:249; Ibn 'Abd al-Birr, *Al-Isti'ab fi Ma'rifat al-Ashab*, 2:514, 761.

32. Al-Qastalani, *Irshad*, 4:156. Another case concerns a certain al-Hajjaj al-Sullami: al-Tabari, *Ta'rikh*, 3:17–18.

33. Al-Azraqi, *Akhbar*, p. 456; al-Maqrizi, *Al-Niza'*, p. 20; Ibn 'Abd al-Birr, *al-Isti'ab*, 2:729; ibn Hisham, *Al-Sira*, 2:104–105.

34. I. Lichtenstadter, "Fraternization in Early Islam," *IC* 6 (1942): 47–53; al-Baghdadi, *Al-Muhabbar*, p. 71; al-Baladhuri, *Ansab*, 1:270–271.

35. Al-Nisaburi, *Asbab Nuzul*, p. 56.

36. That social status was taken into consideration is implied in al-Jahiz, *Al-'Uthmaniyya*, pp. 121–122. For various fraternizations, see entries in Ibn Sa'd, *Kitab Al-Tabaqat al-Kabir*. Ibn 'Abd al-Birr, *Isti'ab*, 1:94, 194, 229, 2:567, 651, 801, 4:1418; Ibn Hisham, *Al-Sira*, 2:108; al-Baghdadi, *Al-Muhabbar*, p. 72.

37. See, for example, the raids on Qararat al-Kudr and Dawmat al-Jandal, which were led by 'Abd al-Rahman ibn 'Awf, and the one against the Banu Sulaim: al-Baladhuri, *Ansab*, 1:310–311. In the raid on Badr al-Maw'id, the Mus-

lims stayed for the duration of the market and doubled their capital: al-Waqidi, *Kitab al-Maghazi,* 1:338. On the raid on al-Abwaʾ, where the Muslims concluded a nonaggression treaty with the Banu Damra, see ibid., p. 12.

38. Al-Waqidi, *Al-Maghazi,* 1:13–16.

39. Ibid., pp. 16–18; al-Qastalani, *Irshad,* 4:31; al-Baladhuri, *Ansab,* 1:372; al-Nisaburi, *Asbab Nuzul,* p. 42. For the Qurʾanic justification, see, besides 2:217, 6:41. On the significance of the distribution of wealth in winning adherents to Islam, see al-Baladhuri, *Futuh,* p. 283.

40. On the battle of Badr, see ibn Hisham, *Al-Sira,* 2:182ff.; Watt, *Muhammad at Medina,* p. 19.

41. Ibn Hisham, *Al-Sira,* 3:14ff.; Watt, *Muhammad at Medina,* p. 21.

42. Al-Waqidi, *Al-Maghazi,* 2:490–491.

43. Ibn Al-Athir, *Al-Kamil,* 2:184.

44. Al-Waqidi, *Al-Maghazi,* 2:553–554.

45. Ibid., pp. 555ff. For more information about Dihya, see A. H. Harley, "Dihya al-Kalbi," *JPASB* 18 (1922): 273–285.

46. Al-Waqidi, *Al-Maghazi,* 2:492; al-Yaʿaqubi, *Taʾrikh,* 2:57, 90; Ibn Sallam, *Al-Amwal,* p. 366; al-Baihaqi, *Dalaʾil al-Nubuwwa,* 2:90–91.

47. Ibn Hisham, *Al-Sira,* 3:196; al-Waqidi, *Al-Maghazi,* 2:593; for the negotiations, see ibid., pp. 604ff.

48. The text of the treaty can be found in al-Waqidi, *Al-Maghazi,* 2:611–612; see also Watt, *Muhammad at Medina,* pp. 46–55; al-Waqidi, *Al-Maghazi,* p. 801.

49. Al-Waqidi, *Al-Maghazi,* 2:606, 610–611.

50. Ibid., p. 612.

51. See, for example, al-Tabari, *Taʾrikh,* 2:648–649, 3:30; Ibn al-Athir, *Al-Kamil,* 2:204, 211–213; Ibn Saʿd, *Al-Tabaqat,* 2:18.

52. Al-Waqidi, *Al-Maghazi,* 2:608–609; al-Tabari, *Taʾrikh,* 2:635.

53. Al-Waqidi, *Al-Maghazi,* 2:625–627, 629.

54. Ibid., pp. 741–746; Ibn ʿAbd al-Birr, *al-Istiʿab,* 1:62, 3:1034.

55. For a divergent view, see F. M. Donner, "The Food Boycott and Muhammad's Policy," *JESHO* 20 (1977): 249–266.

56. Al-Waqidi, *Al-Maghazi,* 2:780, 792, 798, 815, 822; Ibn Saʿd, *Al-Tabaqat,* 1:39. For the conquest of Mecca, see also Watt, *Muhammad at Medina,* pp. 64ff.

57. On the battle of Hunain, see al-Waqidi, *Al-Maghazi,* 3:885ff.; ibn Hisham, *Al-Sira,* 4:101, 103.

58. Al-Waqidi, *Al-Maghazi,* 3:922, 924, 925, 928, 929, 931.

59. Abu Yusuf, *Kitab al-Kharaj,* p. 19; Ibn Anas, *Muwattaʾ,* p. 302; al-Qastalani, *Irshad,* 4:39.

60. Al-Waqidi, *Al-Maghazi,* 3:890; ibn Hisham, *Al-Sira,* 4:62; Ibn ʿAbd al-Birr, *al-Istiʿab,* 2:720; al-Baladhuri, *Ansab,* 1:362–363.

61. Al-Baghdadi, *Al-Munammaq,* pp. 532–533; al-Waqidi, *Al-Maghazi,* 3:944; Watt, *Muhammad at Medina,* pp. 348–353.

62. Ibn Hisham, *Al-Sira*, 4:152, 158, 162, 165, 170, 172, 180; al-Tabari, *Ta'rikh*, 3:130, 133, 136, 138–139.

63. On the tax officials, their destinations, and their instructions, see Ali ibn Husayn al-Ahmadi, *Makatib al-Rasul;* M. Hamidullah, *Majmuʿ at al-Watha'iq al-Siyasiyya.*

64. Ibn Hisham, *Al-Sira*, 4:174; al-Ahmadi, *Makatib*, pp. 117, 187.

65. The full text of the treaty and detailed references can be found in Hamidullah, *Al-Watha'iq*, pp. 140–142, 144–145, 153–158.

66. Ibn ʿAbd al-Birr, *al-Istiʿab*, 4:1404–1405.

67. Al-Ahmadi, *Makatib*, p. 147; Hamidullah, *Al-Watha'iq*, pp. 121, 128, 129, 130.

68. Hamidullah, *al-Watha'iq*, pp. 112, 114, 115, 116, 117, 119, 126.

69. Ibid., pp. 123, 124; ibn Hisham, *Al-Sira*, 4:183.

5. Islamic Expansion and the Establishment of the Islamic State

1. De Ste. Croix, *Class Struggle*, p. 409, also pp. 78, 95, 124, 125, 126, 129, 340.

2. Donner, *Early Conquests*, p. 172.

3. Ibid., p. 170.

4. De Ste. Croix, *Class Struggle*, p. 483.

5. Ibid., pp. 483, 484; Hitti, *History*, p. 165.

6. A. N. Stratos. *Byzantium in the Seventh Century*, 2:92ff.; Hitti, *History*, pp. 153ff.; de Ste. Croix, *Class Struggle*, pp. 489ff.

7. F. Gabrieli, *Muhammad and the Conquests of Islam*, p. 110.

8. Shaban, *History*, pp. 24–25. Other theories are briefly evaluated by Donner, *Early Conquests*, pp. 3–7.

9. Donner, *Early Conquests*, pp. 51–90.

10. Al-Baladhuri, *Futuh*, p. 128; Al-Waqidi, *Kitab Futuh al-Sham*, p. 1.

11. Albrecht Noth, "Die Literarisch Uberlieferten Vertrage der Eroberungszeit als Historische Quellen für die Behandlung der Unterworfenen Nicht-Muslims durch Iher Neun Muslimischen Oberherren," in *Studien Zum Minderheiten-problem im Islam*, ed. Tilman Nagel et al., 1:282–314.

12. Ibid., pp. 229ff.

13. Ibid., p. 313.

14. For an excellent account on the *Ridda* War, see Elias Shoufani, *Al-Riddah and the Muslim Conquest of Arabia;* Wathima ibn Musa, *Kitab al-Ridda;* Ahmad Ghunaim, *Hurub al-Ridda: Four Manuscripts from al-Iktifa fi Maghazi al-Mustafa wa al-Thalatha al-Kulafa.*

15. For an evaluation of Musailama's movement, see Dale Eikelman, "Musailama," *JESHO* 10 (1967): 17–52; al-Tabari, *Ta'rikh*, 2:284–285.

16. Al-Baladhuri, *Futuh*, p. 118; Ibn al-Athir, *Al-Kamil*, 2:353–357; al-Nuwayri, *Nihayat al-Irab*, p. 19; Ghunaim, *Hurub*, pp. 81–82.

17. For a short biography of Khalid and the battles in which he was involved, see Ibn ʿAbd al-Birr, *al-Istiʿab*, 2:426–431.

18. For Khalid's encounter with the Banu Asad, see Ibn Khayyat, *Taʾrikh*, 1:81; Ghunaim, *Hurub*, pp. 45–56; Wathima, *Al-Ridda*, pp. 2–5. For his encounter with the Banu Hanifa, especially Hadiqat al-Mawt, see Ghunaim, *Hurub*, pp. 107–111; Wathima, *Al-Ridda*, p. 16; al-Tabari, *Taʾrikh*, 3:289; al-Baladhuri, *Futuh*, pp. 106–107.

19. Al-Tabari, *Taʾrikh*, 3:301, 303–304, 311; al-Baladhuri, *Futuh*, p. 101; Ibn Aʿtham, *Kitab al-Futuh*, 1:45–48, 52, 54.

20. Ibn Al-Athir, *Al-Kamil*, 2:372–373; al-Baladhuri, *Futuh*, p. 92; al-Tabari, *Taʾrikh*, 3:315–316; Ibn Aʿtham, *Al-Futuh*, 1:75.

21. Al-Tabari, *Taʾrikh*, 3:185, 229–230; al-Baladhuri, *Futuh*, p. 125.

22. Al-Tabari, *Taʾrikh*, 3:232; al-Baladhuri, *Futuh*, p. 126; al-Yaʿaqubi, *Taʾrikh*, 2:131.

23. Al-Tabari, *Taʾrikh*, 3:323–324; Ibn al-Athir, *Al-Kamil*, 2:326.

24. Al-Tabari, *Taʾrikh*, 3:330ff.; al-Muqaddasi, *Al-Badʿ*, 5:109; al-Yaʿaqubi, *Taʾrikh*, 2:123; Ibn Aʿtham, *Al-Futuh*, 1:86–87.

25. Donner, *Early Conquests*, pp. 101–111. Negotiations for leadership positions and the planning of the campaign during the month of Muharram are implied in al-Waqidi, *Futuh*, pp. 2–3.

26. The Syrian campaign is amply documented by Donner, *Early Conquests*, pp. 111–155; Gabrieli, *Muhammad*, pp. 143ff.; D. C. Dennet, *Conversion and Poll Tax in Early Islam*, pp. 49ff.; Stratos, *Byzantium*, vol. 2.

27. Shaban, for example, says that the army was split into three contingents to gain the most booty: *History*, p. 25.

28. For example, Abu Bakr did not appoint Saʿid ibn Al-ʿAs, because he did not give his oath of allegiance to Abu Bakr as readily as others did; see al-Tabari, *Taʾrikh*, 3:387.

29. Treaties concluded during the course of the early Islamic expansion are documented in D. R. Hill, *Termination of Hostilities in the Early Arab Conquest*. For Busra, see ibid., p. 71; al-Baladhuri, *Futuh*, p. 134.

30. Al-Baladhuri, *Futuh*, p. 155. Hims became the storehouse of the wheat and oil from the coastal areas and other places, p. 159.

31. Ibid., pp. 144–146; al-Tabari, *Taʾrikh*, 3:438–443.

32. Al-Baladhuri, *Futuh*, pp. 60, 162; Dennet, *Conversion*, pp. 56–57. For the Yarmuk battle, see al-Tabari, *Taʾrikh*, 3:396ff.; Ibn al-Athir, *Al-Kamil*, 2:411ff.

33. Al-Baladhuri, *Futuh*, pp. 138–139.

34. Al-Baladhuri, *Futuh*, pp. 164–169; Dennet, *Conversion*, p. 63.

35. Al-Baladhuri, *Futuh*, p. 150–152.

36. Ibid., p. 145; Dennet, *Conversion*, p. 55; Hill, *Termination*, p. 72.

37. Abu Yusuf, *Kitab al-Kharaj*, pp. 143, 146, 203, 204; Ibn Sallam, *Al-Amwal*, p. 87; Ibn Adam, *Kitab al-Kharaj*, pp. 10, 11, 32, 34, 49–51.

38. The markets were set up for Abu ʿUbaida's army: see Abu Yusuf, *Kitab al-Kharaj*, p. 151. Hims set up the market: see al-Baladhuri, *Futuh*, p. 155; Edessa set up the market for the Muslims: p. 205. Busra set up the market for the Muslims: see al-Azdi, *Taʾrikh Futuh al-Sham*, p. 81.

39. For more information on Antioch, see John H. Liebeschuetz, *Antioch: City and Imperial Administration in the Late Roman Empire*, pp. 44–48, 52–53, 73–77; Georges Tchalenko, *Villages antiques de la Syrie du Nord*.

40. Al-Baladhuri, *Futuh*, p. 175; Yaqut, *Muʿajam*, 1:382.

41. Such was the case of ʿUmair ibn Saʿid, *mawla* of ʿAbd al-Rahman ibn ʿAwf. See al-Waqidi, *Futuh al-Shaʾm*, p. 192. ʿUmair, as a *mawla* himself, had a *mawla* of his own.

42. Dennet, *Conversion*, p. 44.

43. Al-Baladhuri, *Futuh*, p. 169.

44. Ibid., p. 167; Hill, *Termination*, p. 63.

45. Al-Baladhuri, *Futuh*, p. 168.

46. For developments in the Hijaz, see Saleh el-Ali, "Muslim Estates in the Hijaz," *JESHO* 2 (1959): 247–261. Having wealth and prisoners of war, the Muslims in Medina embarked on an ambitious reclamation program. For example, Abu Huraira and ʿUrwa ibn al-Zubair had orchards developed and dug wells, and many others built palaces: al-Samhudi, *Wafaʾ*, 1:141, 195, 196, 197, 199; see pp. 162, 164, 166ff. for the mosques that were built and the areas that were developed between Mecca and Medina.

47. Stratos, *Byzantium*, 2:127.

48. Dennet, *Conversion*, pp. 57–64.

49. Al-Dinawari, *Al-Akhbar al-Tiwal*, pp. 112–113, 116; al-Tabari, *Taʾrikh*, 3:344ff.; al-Baladhuri, *Futuh*, p. 295.

50. For Khalid's major activities before his transfer to Syria, see al-Tabari *Taʾrikh*, 3:353, 355, 376, 378; al-Baladhuri, *Futuh*, pp. 296–306; F. M. Donner, "*The Arab Tribes in the Muslim Conquest of Iraq*"; idem, *Early Conquests*, pp. 176–185; Morony, *Iraq*, pp. 223–226.

51. Ibn Al-Athir, *Al-Kamil*, 2:449; al-Tabari, *Taʾrikh*, 3:478–479.

52. Shaban, *History*, p. 28.

53. Provisions were sent by ʿUmar, and others were captured locally: al-Baladhuri, *Futuh*, pp. 314, 316. For the battle of Qadisiyya, see Donner, *Early Conquests*, pp. 202–209. It seems that some Arabs were still hesitant about supporting the Muslims, as they waited to see which side would win the battle. After the Muslims won, these Arabs joined them: al-Tabari, *Taʾrikh*, 3:582.

54. Al-Tabari, *Taʾrikh*, 4:13ff., 17. Each share of the booty was 12,000 dirhams after the Fifth was sent to the treasury. A royal carpet, sixty square cubits with jewels, was sent to Medina as part of the Fifth (p. 21), a piece that was ʿAli's share was worth 20,000 dirhams, "and that was not the best of the jewels" (p. 22).

55. For a chronology of the Muslim conquest of the Sasanid territories, see

A. H. Zarinkub, "The Arab Conquest of Iran and Its Aftermath," in *Cambridge History of Iran,* ed. R. N. Frey, 4 : 1–56; Gabrieli, *Muhammad,* pp. 118ff.

56. The share at Nihawand was 6,000 dirhams for the horsemen and 2,000 for the footmen: al-Tabari, *Ta'rikh,* 4 : 132; the Rawadif were the most anxious to go to Nihawand so that they could "fight well for the sake of religion and to get some fortune" (p. 127).

57. For the treaties of Nihawand, Isfahan, Rayy, and Qumis, see al-Tabari, *Ta'rikh,* 4 : 136–137, 141, 151, 152.

58. Ibid., p. 32; al-Baladhuri, *Futuh,* pp. 327, 329; Dennet, *Conversion,* pp. 41–42.

59. For a discussion of the position of peasants and the land, see Abd al-Aziz al-Duri, "Landlord and Peasant in Early Islam"; P. G. Forand, "The Status of the Land and the Inhabitants of the Sawad during the First Two Centuries of Islam," *JESHO* 14 (1971): 25–37; J. M. Judeh, *Al-ʿArab wa al-Ard fi al-Iraq.*

60. Saleh el-Ali, *Al-Tanzimat al-Ijtimaʿiyya wa al-Iqtisadiyya fi al-Basra;* idem, "Khitat al-Basra," *Summer* 8 (1952): 72–83, 281–302; M. H. al-Zubaidi, *al-Haya al-Ijtimaʿiyya wa al-Iqtisadiyya fi al-Kufa.*

61. Al-Tabari, *Ta'rikh,* 4 : 45, 46, 47, 5 : 60, 368, 369, 6 : 240.

62. See, for example, al-Baladhuri, *Futuh,* pp. 351, 356, 358, 439, 440, 441, 442, 443.

63. For example, ʿAbdallah ibn Masʿud was *sahib al-aqbad* in Syria: al-Tabari, *Ta'rikh,* 3 : 397; al-Saʾib in Nihawand, 4 : 116. See also al-Dinawari, *Al-Akhbar,* p. 138.

64. P. Grierson, "The Financial Reforms of Abd al-Malik," *JESHO* 3 (1960): 241–264; al-Baladhuri, *Futuh,* p. 575.

65. ʿAmr traded in leather and perfumes in Alexandria; see al-Kindi, *Al-Wulat wa al-Qudat,* p. 7; Ibn ʿAbd al-Hakam, *Futuh Misr wa Akhbaruha,* pp. 53–54; al-Maqrizi, *Al-Khitat,* 1 : 540, 570.

66. For a chronology of the conquest of Egypt, see Alfred Butler, *The Arab Conquest of Egypt and the Last Thirty Years of the Roman Dominion;* Ibn ʿAbd al-Hakam, *Futuh Misr,* pp. 57–58; Gabrieli, *Muhammad,* pp. 167ff.

67. It was agreed that the market would be set up between Fustat and Alexandria: Ibn ʿAbd al-Hakam, *Futuh Misr,* pp. 70, 72, 73; al-Maqrizi, *Al-Khitat,* 1 : 550.

68. Ibn ʿAbd al-Hakam, *Futuh Misr,* p. 74; Butler, *Arab Conquest,* pp. 320–321.

69. Mahmud Abuswa, "The Arabization and Islamization of the Maghrib: A Social and Economic Reconstruction of the History of the Maghrib during the First Two Centuries of Islam," pp. 107–108.

70. See, for example, Shaban, *History,* pp. 31–32.

71. W. Kubiak, *Al-Fustat: Its Foundation and Early Urban Development.* Although Kubiak provides excellent information, his conclusions are the us-

ual clichés regarding the expansion and the foundation of cities; see Mahmood Ibrahim's review in *Ufahamu* 13 (1983): 165–168.

72. Ibn Sa'd, *Al-Tabaqat*, 4:81; al-Tabari, *Ta'rikh*, 4:100.

73. Ibn 'Abd al-Hakam, *Futuh Misr*, p. 165; al-Tabari, *Ta'rikh*, 4:100.

74. Al-Tabari, *Ta'rikh*, p. 100; Ibn 'Abd al-Hakam, *Futuh Misr*, p. 163.

75. *Futuh Misr*, p. 163.

76. Ibn Anas, *Muwatta' Malik*, p. 442; Ibn 'Abd al-Hakam, *Futuh Misr*, p. 166.

6. The Emergence of the New Segment

1. Al-Tabari, *Ta'rikh*, 4:116–117, 6:48; al-Baladhuri, *Futuh*, p. 374; al-Dinawari, *Al-Akhbar*, pp. 137–138; Ibn 'Abd al-Birr, *Al-Isti'ab*, 4:1172.

2. Ibn 'Abd al-Birr, *al-Isti'ab*, p. 1403.

3. Al-Tabari, *Ta'rikh*, 4:220.

4. Ibn Anas, *Muwatta'*, p. 479; al-Ya'aqubi, *Ta'rikh*, 2:157.

5. See, for example, the case of Hind, wife of Abu Sufyan, al-Tabari, *Ta'rikh*, 4, p. 221; the case of Sa'd ibn Abi Waqqas, p. 251; al-Baladhuri, *Futuh*, p. 474, for the case of Abu Bakrah.

6. See Ibn 'Abd al-Hakam, *Futuh Misr*, pp. 147–148; Ya'aqubi, *Ta'rikh*, 2:157; al-Baladhuri, *Futuh*, pp. 474–475, supplies the names of at least twenty officials who were similarly treated; see also al-Tabari, *Ta'rikh*, 4:68, for the case of Khalid.

7. Al-Tabari, *Ta'rikh*, 3:367; al-Baladhuri, *Futuh*, pp. 298–299. Khalid did not allow Khuraim to ask for more money.

8. Al-Tabari, *Ta'rikh*, 3:596.

9. Ibid.; al-Dinawari, *al-Akhbar*, p. 117, for the case of Nafi'. Madh'ur ibn 'Adiyy al-'Ijli went from Iraq to Syria then to Egypt, where he acquired land: al-Azdi, *Futuh al-Sham*, p. 81. Anas ibn Malik, the Prophet's servant, lived in Basra, where he was able to accumulate a considerable amount of wealth: al-Maqdisi, *Al-Istibsar ti Nasab al-Sahaba min al-Ansar*, p. 33. 'Uthman ibn Abi al-'As lived in Basra, where he developed land near al-Ubulla: Ibn Sa'd, *Al-Tabaqat*, 7, pt. 1: 27. Al-Hajjaj ibn 'Atik became a stonecutter and made a lot of money: al-Baladhuri, *Futuh*, pp. 340; Simak became the first iron smith, p. 348.

10. The Prophet first abolished *hilf* (al-Baghdadi, *Al-Munammaq*, p. 316) and then 'Umar abolished *wala'* (Ibn Sallam, *Al-Amwal*, pp. 177ff).

11. Al-Tabari, *Ta'rikh*, 4:209; al-Baladhuri, *Futuh*, p. 552; Puin Gerd-Rudiger, *Der Diwan von 'Umar Ibn al-Hattab*, pp. 94–115. Abu Bakr distributed stipends equally to the Muslims (Judeh, *Al-'Arab*, p. 187). Abu Sufyan was concerned that people would abandon commerce once they were assigned stipends (al-Baladhuri, *Futuh*, p. 560).

12. Al-Baladhuri, *Futuh*, pp. 553, 562; Martin Hinds, "Kufan Political Alignments and Their Background in the Mid-Seventh Century A.D.," *IJMES* 2 (1971): 349.

13. Al-Tabari, *Ta'rikh*, 4:191; Ibn al-Athir, *Al-Kamil*, 3:49; Ibn Aʿtham, *Al-Futuh*, 2:83.

14. Al-Tabari, *Ta'rikh*, 4:227ff.; al-Baladhuri, *Ansab*, 5:15ff.

15. Al-Baladhuri, *Ansab*, pp. 16–17.

16. Ibid., pp. 18, 19; for an account of the wealth of members of the *shura*, see al-Masʿudi, *Muruj*, 4:253–255.

17. El-Ali, "Muslim Estates," p. 257.

18. Al-Tabari, *Ta'rikh*, 4:231.

19. Ibid., pp. 232–233.

20. Ibid., pp. 238–239; al-Baladhuri, *Ansab*, 5:22.

21. Al-Baladhuri, *Ansab*, p. 20; al-Tabari, *Ta'rikh*, 4:234.

22. Shaban, *History*, p. 62.

23. Ibid., p. 62, where he also describes the new caliph as "conservative." He goes on to say that the caliph went from failure to failure (pp. 67, 69).

24. Ibn Al-Athir, *Al-Kamil*, 3:31.

25. Al-Baladhuri, *Futuh*, pp. 150–152, 158, 175, 211.

26. Ostrogorsky, *Byzantine State*, p. 116; Lewis, *Naval Power*, pp. 54–55.

27. Al-Tabari, *Ta'rikh*, 4:260; al-Baladhuri, *Futuh*, p. 152.

28. Ibn Aʿtham, *Al-Futuh*, 2:118–119; al-Baladhuri, *Futuh*, p. 150; al-Tabari, *Ta'rikh*, 4:304; Ostrogorsky, *Byzantine State*, p. 116.

29. Ibn Aʿtham, *Al-Futuh*, 2:126.

30. Al-Baladhuri, *Ansab*, 5:25, 58.

31. Al-Tabari, *Ta'rikh*, 3:616.

32. Shaban, *History*, p. 56.

33. Al-Baladhuri, *Ansab*, 5:30–31. ʿUthman's view of the treasury is contrasted with that of Ibn Masʿud, who declared upon resigning, "Rather, I thought that I was the keeper of the treasury of the Muslims."

34. Abu Suwa, *Arabization*, p. 211.

35. Al-Baladhuri, *Futuh*, pp. 335, 336, 355, 442, 445; Abu Yusuf, *Kitab al-Kharaj*, pp. 62, 63, 67; Ibn Sallam, *Al-Amwal*, pp. 399, 400. Thus, of the New Segment, ʿAmmar ibn Yasir, Khabbab ibn al-Art, ʿAbdallah ibn Masʿud, and Usama ibn Zaid received land grants that were at times whole villages.

36. Al-Tabari, *Ta'rikh*, 4:280.

37. Ibid., pp. 280–281, 398; Ibn Sallam, *Al-Amwal*, p. 360, 361; al-Baladhuri, *Futuh*, pp. 335, 445; al-Maqrizi, *Al-Khitat*, 1:178; see also Judeh, *Al-ʿArab*, pp. 128–129.

38. Al-Tabari, *Ta'rikh*, 4:318, 323; al-Baladhuri, *Ansab*, 5:40–41; Ibn al-Athir, *Al-Kamil*, 3:188.

39. Shaban, *History*, pp. 51, 63.

40. Ibid., p. 68.

41. Martin Hinds, "The Murder of the Caliph Uthman," *IJMES* 3 (1972): 450–469.

42. Ibid., pp. 450–451.

43. Al-Tabari, *Taʾrikh*, 3:496, 511, 512, 537, 4:27, 115, 130.

44. Ibid., 4:129.

45. Al-Baladhuri, *Ansab*, 5:57.

46. Ibn Saʿd, *Al-Tabaqat*, 4, pt. 1:161–175.

47. Al-Baladhuri, *Ansab*, 5:52–56; al-Tabari, *Taʾrikh*, 4:283–285.

48. Ibn al-Athir, *Al-Kamil*, 3:114–115, 134; al-Tabari, *Taʾrikh*, 4:309.

49. ʿAbdallah did not receive his stipend for two years on orders from ʿUthman. For more information, see Ibn Saʿd, *Al-Tabaqat*, 3, pt. 1:106–114.

50. For the whole incident, see al-Baladhuri, *Ansab*, 5:30–36.

51. Al-Baladhuri, *Ansab*, 1:156–175, 5:163; Ibn Saʿd, *Al-Tabaqat*, 6, pt. 1: 167–189.

52. Al-Baladhuri, *Futuh*, p. 559.

53. Al-Baladhuri, *Ansab*, 5:36–37.

54. Ibid., p. 41. Another letter was sent from people in Medina, p. 49.

55. Ibid., p. 42.

56. Al-Tabari, *Taʾrikh*, 4:279.

57. Ibid., pp. 317–318; al-Baladhuri, *Ansab*, 5:43ff.; Ibn al-Athir, *Al-Kamil*, 3:139.

58. Ibn Aʿtham, *Al-Futuh*, 2:174; al-Tabari, *Taʾrikh*, 4:319.

59. Al-Tabari, *Taʾrikh*, 4:319–320; Ibn al-Athir, *Al-Kamil*, 3:140.

60. Ibn al-Athir, *Al-Kamil*, 3:143; al-Tabari, *Taʾrikh*, 4:324.

61. Al-Tabari, *Taʾrikh*, pp. 333–335.

62. Ibid., p. 331; al-Athir, *Al-Kamil*, 3:148.

63. Al-Baladhuri, *Ansab*, 5:45.

64. Ibid., p. 46.

65. For the development of the Egyptian opposition, see Hinds, "Murder of Uthman," pp. 452–457; al-Baladhuri, *Ansab*, 5:49ff.; al-Kindi, *Al-Wulat*, pp. 14–15.

66. Al-Baladhuri, *Ansab*, 5:50; al-Tabari, *Taʾrikh*, 4:292.

67. Al-Baladhuri, *Ansab*, 5:51.

68. Hinds, "Murder of Uthman," p. 455; al-Kindi, *Al-Wulat*, pp. 15, 17.

69. Al-Baladhuri, *Ansab*, 5:59.

70. Al-Tabari, *Taʾrikh*, 4:348; al-Baladhuri, *Futuh*, 5:64.

7. The Civil War and the Struggle for Power

1. Al-Tabari, *Taʾrikh*, 4:433.

2. Ibn Aʿtham, *Al-Futuh*, 2:245; al-Tabari, *Taʾrikh*, 4:434; Ibn al-Athir, *Al-Kamil*, 3:192; Hinds, "Murder of Uthman," p. 468.

3. Al-Tabari, *Taʾrikh*, 4:434; Ibn al-Athir, *Al-Kamil*, 3:193; Ibn Aʿtham, *Al-Futuh*, 2:245.

4. Al-Tabari, *Taʾrikh*, 4:429, 431, 433–435; Ibn al-Athir, *Al-Kamil*, 3:191, 192, 194, 211; Ibn Aʿtham, *Al-Futuh*, 2:256–259; al-Dinawari, *Al-Akhbar*, pp. 142–143.

5. Al-Tabari, *Ta'rikh*, 4:439, 440, 441; Ibn Muzahim, *Kitab Waq'at Siffin*, pp. 11–12; see also al-Mas'udi, *Muruj*, 5:296, where he says that 'Ali took back land given out by 'Uthman.

6. Al-Tabari, *Ta'rikh*, 4:442, 443; al-Dinawari, *Al-Akhbar*, p. 141.

7. Ibn A'tham, *Al-Futuh*, 2:246; Ibn al-Tiqtaqa, *Al-Fakhri*, p. 87.

8. Al-Tabari, *Ta'rikh*, 4:437; al-Athir, *Al-Kamil*, 3:195.

9. Ibn A'tham, *Al-Futuh*, 2:374–375.

10. Ibn al-Athir, *Al-Kamil*, 3:203–204; al-Tabari, *Ta'rikh*, 4:444.

11. Al-Mas'udi, *Muruj*, 5:304–305; Ibn A'tham, *Al-Futuh*, 2:279; Ibn Qutaiba, *Al-Imama wa al-Siyasa*, pp. 99–100; al-Tabari, *Ta'rikh*, 4:443, 444, 451; Ibn al-Athir, *Al-Kamil*, 3:209, where he says that they tried to give the caliphate to 'Uthman's son.

12. Ibn Qutaiba, *Al-Imama*, pp. 101–102.

13. 'Abdallah ibn 'Amir was one of the largest landlords in Basra. See Judeh, *Al-'Arab*, p. 242. He joined Talha and Zubair and gave them money: al-Tabari, *Ta'rikh*, p. 452; Marwan joined, p. 454, Ibn al-Athir, *Al-Kamil*, 3:208.

14. Ibn A'tham, *Al-Futuh*, 2:268; al-Dinawari, *Al-Akhbar*, p. 143. For the reluctance of al-Ansar to leave with 'Ali, see Ibn al-Athir, *Al-Kamil*, 3:205–206, 221.

15. Al-Ya'aqubi, *Ta'rikh*, 2:179; Ibn al-A'tham, *Al-Futuh*, 2:250; al-Dinawari, *Al-Akhbar*, p. 145.

16. Ibn Khayyat, *Ta'rikh*, pp. 199ff.; al-Tabari, *Ta'rikh*, 4:488, 535–536, 541. For 'Ali's insulting address, see al-Dinawari, *Al-Akhbar*, pp. 151. At least nine tribes were on both sides of the conflict, ibid., pp. 146–147; Morony, *Iraq*, pp. 244, 249–250.

17. Al-Tabari, *Ta'rikh*, 4:562; Ibn Muzahim, *Siffin*, pp. 82ff.; Ibn A'tham, *Al-Futuh*, 2:397.

18. Ibn Muzahim, *Siffin*, pp. 44, 60; Ibn A'tham, *Al-Futuh*, 3:21–22, 43.

19. Al-Ya'aqubi, *Ta'rikh*, 2:184; al-Tabari, *Ta'rikh*, 4:558; Ibn Muzahim, *Siffin*, pp. 37–40.

20. Ibn Muzahim, *Siffin*, pp. 44, 47; Ibn A'tham, *Al-Futuh*, 2:397; al-Dinawari, *Al-Akhbar*, p. 159.

21. See, for example, Ibn A'tham, *Al-Futuh*, 2:p. 401.

22. Ibn Muzahim, *Siffin*, p. 49; Ibn Qutaiba, *Al-Imama*, p. 134; al-Dinawari, *Al-Akhbar*, p. 160.

23. Ibn Muzahim, *Siffin*, pp. 55–56, 60; Ibn A'tham, *Al-Futuh*, 2:404–405.

24. Al-Tabari, *Ta'rikh*, 4:562; al-Dinawari, *Al-Akhbar*, p. 161; Ibn Muzahim, *Siffin*, pp. 56, 60.

25. See, for example, Ibn A'tham, *Al-Futuh*, 3:28, 98, 207, 260; Ibn Muzahim, *Siffin*, p. 29, 85–89, 105, 109, 319, passim; Ibn Qutaiba, *Al-Imama*, pp. 185, 209.

26. For an analysis of the traditions that circulated around Mu'awiya, see

E. L. Petersen, *'Ali and Mu'awiya in Early Arabic Tradition;* al-Dhahabi, *Siyar A'lam al-Nubala'*, pp. 85–86.

27. Ibn Muzahim, *Siffin*, p. 128.

28. Ibid., pp. 115–116.

29. Ibid., pp. 133, 134, 135.

30. Al-Tabari, *Ta'rikh*, 4:566.

31. Ibn Muzahim, *Siffin*, p. 151; al-Tabari, *Ta'rikh*, 4:565.

32. Al-Tabari, *Ta'rikh*, 4:569–572; Ibn Muzahim, *Siffin*, p. 161.

33. Ibn Muzahim, *Siffin*, pp. 185, 193.

34. Ibid., pp. 196ff. For correspondence and negotiations, see also Ibn Qutaiba, *Al-Imama*, pp. 149, 151, 162, and passim.

35. Ibn Muzahim, *Siffin*, pp. 187, 198; al-Tabari, *Ta'rikh*, 4:573.

36. Ibn Muzahim, *Siffin*, pp. 200–201.

37. Ibid., p. 202; Ibn A'tham, *Al-Futuh,* 3:29.

38. Ibn A'tham, *Al-Futuh*, p. 95; Ibn Muzahim, *Siffin*, p. 86.

39. Ibn Muzahim, *Siffin*, p. 477; al-Tabari, *Ta'rikh*, 5:48.

40. See Ibn Qutaiba, *Al-Imama*, pp. 193, 194, 195, 197; al-Dinawari, *Al-Akhbar*, pp. 190–191; Ibn Muzahim, *Siffin*, pp. 482ff.

41. Ibn Qutaiba, *Al-Imama*, p. 205.

42. Ibn Muzahim, *Siffin*, p. 21; Ibn A'tham, *Al-Futuh*, 2:367, 370.

43. Al-Dinawari, *Al-Akhbar*, p. 192; al-Tabari, *Ta'rikh*, 5:51; Ibn Muzahim, *Siffin*, p. 500.

44. Ibn Muzahim, *Siffin*, p. 499; al-Tabari, *Ta'rikh*, 5:51–52.

45. Al-Tabari, *Ta'rikh*, pp. 52–53; Ibn Muzahim, *Siffin*, p. 508.

46. Ibn Muzahim, *Siffin*, p. 510; see also Martin Hinds, "The Siffin Arbitration Agreement," *JSS* 17 (1972):93–129.

47. The text of the treaty makes it explicit that the arbitration was between 'Ali and Mu'awiya, and since the issue that separated them was the death of 'Uthman, it became the issue of the arbitration. See also W. M. Watt, *The Formative Period of Islamic Thought*, p. 13.

48. Al-Tabari, *Ta'rikh*, 5:55, 56; Ibn Muzahim, *Siffin*, pp. 512–513.

49. See, for example, Watt, *Formative Period*, p. 20; idem, "Kharijite Thought in the Umayyad Period," *Der Islam* 36 (1961):215–232, where he says that the Khawarij were seeking a divinely constituted community. But the rest of the Muslims were also members of a divinely constituted community. That the struggle was between northern Arabs and southern Arabs is typified by Fazlur Rahman, *Islam*, pp. 162–169, 172. On the formation of the Khawarij and the Shi'a, see J. Wellhausen, *Religio-Political Factions in Early Islam.*

50. Hinds, "Kufan Alignments," p. 347.

51. Al-Tabari, *Ta'rikh*, 5:75.

52. Al-Kindi, *Al-Wulat*, p. 20.

53. Ibid., pp. 21–22; al-Tabari, *Ta'rikh*, 4:457.

54. Al-Kindi, *Al-Wulat*, pp. 28–29; al-Tabari, *Ta'rikh*, 5:557; Ibn al-Athir, *Al-Kamil*, 3:356–358.

55. Ibn al-Athir, *Al-Kamil*, 3:360–364; al-Tabari, *Ta'rikh*, 5:110.

56. Ibn al-Athir, *Al-Kamil*, 3:375.

57. Ibid., p. 376; Ibn A'tham, *Al-Futuh*, 4:48–49.

58. Ibn al-Athir, *Al-Kamil*, 3:376; al-Tabari, *Ta'rikh*, 5:135.

59. Ibn al-Athir, *Al-Kamil*, 3:377; al-Tabari, *Ta'rikh*, 5:136; Ibn A'tham, *Al-Futuh*, 4:37.

60. Ibn al-Athir, *Al-Kamil*, 3:378; Ibn Qutaiba, *Al-Imama*, p. 253; Ibn A'tham, *Al-Futuh*, 1:226; al-Tabari, *Ta'rikh*, 5:136.

61. Ibn al-Athir, *Al-Kamil*, 3:380; Ibn A'tham, *Al-Futuh*, 4:45–47.

62. See al-Tawhidi, *Al-Imta' wa al-Mu'anasa*, 2:63.

63. Ibn al-Athir, *Al-Kamil*, 3:381.

64. Ibid., p. 380.

65. Ibid., pp. 383–385; Ibn A'tham, *Al-Futuh*, 4:53, 56, 58, 62–64; al-Tabari, *Ta'rikh*, 5:139–140.

66. Ibn Muzahim, *Siffin*, pp. 61, 96; Ibn A'tham, *Al-Futuh*, 4:67, 78, 100–101; Ibn al-Athir, *Al-Kamil*, 3:358, 364.

67. Al-Tabari, *Ta'rikh*, 5:140; Ibn al-Athir, *Al-Kamil*, 3:385.

68. Ibn al-Athir, *Al-Kamil*, 3:405–407. Notables from Kufa asked Mu'awiya to come to their city: al-Baladhuri, *Ansab*, 3:p. 31.

Bibliography

Traditional Arabic Sources

Abu Yusuf, Yaʿqub ibn Ibrahim. *Kitab al-Kharaj.* 5th ed. Ed. Muhibb ad-din al
Khatib. Cairo: Al-Matbaʿa al-Salafiyya, 1976.

al-Azdi, M. ibn ʿAbdallah. *Taʾrikh Futuh al-Sham.* Cairo: Sijill al-ʿArab, 1970.

al-Azraqi, Abu al-Walid Muhammad. *Akhbar Mecca.* Ed. F. Wüstenfeld. 1857.
Reprint. Beirut: Dar Khayyat, 1964.

al-Baghdadi, M. ibn Habib. *Kitab al-Muhabbar.* Ed. I. Lichtenstadter. Beirut:
Al-Maktab al-Tijari Li al-Ttibaʿah Wa al-Nashr, 1943.

———. *Kitab al-Munammaq fi Akhbar Quraish.* Ed. M. Khorshid. Hyderabad:
Daʾirat al-Maʿarif al-ʿUthmaniyya, 1965.

al-Baihaqi, Ibrahim ibn M. *Dalaʾil al-Nubuwwa.* Ed. A. R. M. Uthman. Medina:
Al-Maktaba al-Salafiyya, 1969.

al-Baladhuri, Ahmad ibn Yahya. *Ansab al-Ashraf.* Vol. 1. Ed. M. Hamidallah.
Cairo: Dar al-Maʿarif, 1959.

———. *Ansab al-Ashraf.* Vol. 3. Ed. M. Baqir al-Mahmudi. Beirut: Dar al-
Taʾrafuf, 1977.

———. *Ansab al-Ashraf.* Vol. 4A. Ed. M. J. Kister. Jerusalem: The University
Press, 1975.

———. *Ansab al-Ashraf.* Vol. 5. Ed. S. D. Goitein. Jerusalem: The University
Press, 1936.

———. *Futuh al-Buldan.* Ed. Salah ad-Din al-Munajjid. Cairo: Maktabat Nahdat Misr, 1956. Translated as *The Origins of the Islamic State,* trans. Philip K.
Hitti and Frances Murgotten. New York: Columbia University Press, 1916,
1924.

Al-Dhahabi, M. ibn Ahmad. *Siyar Aʿlam al-Nubalaʾ.* Ed. M. A. Talas. Cairo: Dar
al-Maʿarif, 1962.

———. *Taʾrikh al-Islam.* Ed. H. al-Qudsi. Cairo: Matbaat al-Madani, 1974.

al-Dinawari, Abu Hanifa Ahmad. *Al-Akhbar al-Tiwal.* Ed. ʿAbd al-Munʿim
ʿAmir and G. al-Shayyal. Cairo: Dar Ihyaʾ al-Kutub, 1960.

al-Fasi, M. ibn Ahmad. *Shafaʾ al-Gharam bi Akhbar al-Balad al-Haram*. Ed. F. Wüstenfeld. 1857. Reprint. Beirut: Dar Khayyat, 1964.

al-Hamdani, Abu M. Hasan. *Al-Iklil*. Parts 1 and 2. Upsala: Almquist & Wiksells, 1953.

———. *Al-Iklil*. Vol. 2. Ed. M. A. al-Akwa. Cairo: Matbaʿat as-Sunna al-Muhammadiyya, 1967.

———. *Sifat Jazirat al-ʿArab*. Ed. D. H. Muller. Leiden: Brill, 1884.

al-Himyari, Nushwan ibn Saʿid. *Khulasat al-Sira al-Jamiʿa Li-ʿajaʾib Akhbar al-Muluk at-Tababiʿa*. Ed. A. al-Muʾayyad and I. al-Jarafi. Cairo: Qusay M. D. al-Khatib, 1975.

Ibn ʿAbd al-Birr, Yusuf ibn ʿAbdallah. *Al-Istiʿab fi Maʿrifat al-Ashab*. Ed. Ali M. al-Bajawi. Cairo: Maktabat Nahdat Misr, n.d.

Ibn ʿAbd al-Hakam, ʿAbd al-Rahman ibn ʿAbdallah. *Futuh Misr wa Akhbaruha*. Ed. Charles Torrey. New Haven: Yale University Press, 1920.

Ibn ʿAbd Rabbihi, Ahmad ibn Muhammad. *Al-ʿIqd al-Farid*. Ed. Ahmad Amin et al. Cairo: Matbaʿat Lajnat at-Taʾlif, 1948.

Ibn Adam, Yahya. *Kitab al-Kharaj*. Ed. A. M. Shakir. Cairo: Al-Matbaʿa al-Salafiyya, 1964.

Ibn Anas, Malik. *Muwattaʾ*. Ed. A. R. Amrush. Beirut: Dar al-Nafaʾis, 1971.

Ibn Aʿtham, Ahmad Abu Muhammad. *Kitab al-Futuh*. Ed. M. Khan. Hyderabad: Daʾirat al-Maʿarif al-ʿUthmaniyya, 1968.

Ibn al-Athir, ʿIzz al-Din. *Al-Kamil fi al-Taʾrikh*. Ed. C. J. Tornberg. 1897. Reprint. Beirut: Dar Sadir, 1965.

Ibn Bakkar, Zubair. *Jamharat Nasab Quraish*. Ed. M. Shakir. Cairo: Maktabat Dar al-ʿUruba, 1961.

Ibn Hawqal, Abu al-Qasim. *Surat al-Ard*. Ed. M. de Goeje. Leiden: Brill, 1873.

Ibn Hazm, Ali ibn Ahmad. *Jamharat Ansab al-ʿArab*. Ed. Abd al-Salam M. Harun. Cairo: Dar al Maʿarif, 1971.

Ibn Hisham, M. ibn ʿAbd al-Malik. *Al-Sira al-Nabawiyya*. Ed. Abd al-Salam M. Harun. Cairo: Al-Maktaba al-Azhariyya. 1974. Translated as *The Life of Muhammad*, trans. Alfred Guillaum. London: Oxford University Press, 1955.

Ibn Jaʿfar, Qudama. *Kitab al-Kharaj*. Ed. M. de Goeje. Leiden: Brill, 1889.

Ibn Kathir, Ismaʿil ibn ʿUmar. *Al-Sira al-Nabawiyya*. Ed. M. Abdel Wahid. Cairo: Isa al-Halabi, 1964.

Ibn Khayyat, Khalifa. *Taʾrikh*. Ed. Suhail Zakkar. Damascus: Wazarat ath-Thaqafa waʾl-Irshad al-Qawami, 1968.

Ibn Muzahim, Nasr. *Kitab Waqʿat Siffin*. 2nd ed. Ed. Abd al-Salam M. Harun. Cairo: Al-Muʾassasa al-ʿArabiyya al-Haditha, 1962.

Ibn Qutaiba, Abdallah ibn Muslim. *Al-Imama wa al-Siyasa*. Ed M. M. al-Rafiʿi. Cairo: Matbaʿat al-Nil, 1937.

———. *Kitab al-Maʿarif*. Ed. T. Ukasha. Cairo: Dar al-Maʿarif, 1969.

Ibn Rusta, Ahmad ibn ʿUmar. *Al-Aʿlaq an-Nafisa*. Ed. M. J. de Goeje. Leiden: Brill, 1891.

Ibn Ruzaiq, Salil. *Imams and Sayyids of Oman.* Trans. G. P. Badger. London: Hakluyt Society, 1871.

Ibn Saʿd, Muhammad. *Kitab al-Tabaqat al-Kubra.* Ed. Edward Sachau. 1917. Reprint. Beirut: Dar Beirut, 1978.

Ibn Sallam, Abu ʿUbaid al-Qasim. *Kitab al-Amwal.* Ed. M. Khalil Haras. Cairo: Dar al-Fikr, 1975.

Ibn al-Tiqtaqa, M. ibn Ali ibn Tabatiba. *Al-Fakhri.* Ed. M. A. Ibrahim and A. al-Jarim. Cairo: Matbaʿat al-Maʿarif, 1923.

al-Isfahani, Abu al-Faraj. *Kitab al-Aghani.* Cairo: Al-Maktaba al-ʿArabiyya, 1970.

al-Jahiz, ʾAmr ibn Bahr. *Al-ʿUthmaniyya.* Ed. Abd al-Salam M. Harun. Cairo: Dar al-Kitab al-Arabi, 1955.

al-Kalbi, Hisham ibn Muhammad. *Kitab al-Asnam.* Ed. Ahmad Zaki. Cairo: Al-Dar al-Qawmiyya, 1955 (photocopy of Dar al-Kutub ed., 1924).

al-Kilaʾi, Sulaiman ibn Musa. *Al-Iktifa fi Maghazi al-Mustafa wa al-Thalalatha al-Khulafa.* Ed. Ahmad Ghunaim. Cairo: Dal al-Ittihad, 1974.

al-Kindi, Muhamad ibn Yusuf. *Al-Wulat wa al-Qudat.* Ed. Rhuvon Guest. Leiden: Brill, 1912.

al-Maqdisi, al-Mutahhar ibn Tahir. *Al Badʾ wa al-Taʾrikh.* Ed. C. Huart. 1899. Reprint. Baghdad.

al-Maqdisi, Ibn Qudama ʿAbdallah. *Al-Istibsar fi Nasab al-Sahaba min al-Ansar.* Ed. Ali Nuwaihid. Beirut: Dar al-Fikr, 1971.

al-Maqrizi, Taqiyy al-Din. *Al-Khitat.* Cairo: Dar al-Tahrir (photocopy of Bulaq ed., 1850).

———. *Kitab al-Nizaʿ wa al-Takhasum.* Leiden: Brill, 1882.

al-Marzuqi, Abu Ali. *Al-Azmina wa al-Amkina.* Hyderabad: Daʾirat al-Maʿarif, 1912.

al-Masʿudi. *Muruj adh-Dhahab wa Maʿadin al-Jawhar.* Ed. and trans. Barbier de Meynard. Paris: Imprimerie Imperiale, 1861.

al-Muqaddasi, Shams al-Din Muhammad ibn Ahmad. *Ahsan al-Taqasim fi Maʿrifat al-Aqalim.* Ed. M. J. de Goeje. Leiden: Brill, 1906.

al-Nawawi, Muhyyi ad-Din ibn Saharaf. *Sahih Muslim.* 1886. Reprint. Beirut: Dar Sader.

al-Nisaburi, Ali ibn Ahmad. *Asbab Nuzul al-Quʾran.* Cairo: Muʾassassat al-Halabi, 1968.

———. *Asbab Nuzul al-Quʾran.* Ed. A. Saqr. Cairo: Dar al-Kitab al-Jadid, 1969.

al-Nuwairi, Shihab ad-Din Ahmad. *Nihayat al-Irab.* Vols. 19 and 20. Ed. M. Abu al-Fadl Ibrahim. Cairo: al-Hayʾa al-Misriyya al-ʿAmma li al-Kitab, 1975.

al-Qastalani, Shihab al-Din Ahmad. *Irshad as-Sari fi Sahih al-Bukhari.* 1886. Reprint. Beirut: Dar Sader.

al-Qurtubi, M. ibn Ahmad. *Al-Jamiʿ Li Ahkam al-Qurʾan.* Cairo: Dar al-Qalam, 1966.

al-Samhudi, Nur al-Din ʿAli. *Wafaʾ al-Wafaʾ.* Cairo: Matbaʿat al-Adab, 1908.

al-Tabari, Muhammad ibn Jarir. *Ta'rikh al-Rusul wa al-Muluk*. Ed. M. Abu al-Fadl Ibrahim. Cairo: Dar al-Ma'arif, 1970.

al-Tawhidi, Abu Hayyan. *Al-Imta' wa al-Mu'anasa*. Ed. A. Amin and Ahmad al-Zayn. Beirut: Maktabat al-Hayat, 1965.

al-Tha'alibi, Abu Mansur Abd al-Malik. *Thimar al-Qulub fi al-Mudaf wa al-Mansub*. Ed. M. Abu al-Fadl Ibrahim. Cairo: Dar Nahdat Misr, 1965.

al-Waqidi, M. ibn 'Umar. *Kitab Futuh al-Sham*. Cairo: Al-Matba'ah al-Maymuniya, 1891.

———. *Kitab al-Maghazi*. Ed. Marsden Jones. London: Oxford University Press, 1966.

Wathima ibn Musa, Abu Yazid. *Kitab al-Ridda*. Mainz: Verlag der Akademie der Wissenschaften und der Literatur, 1951.

al-Ya'aqubi, Ahmad ibn Abi Ya'qub. *Ta'rikh*. Beirut: Dar Sader, 1960.

Yaqut, Abu 'Abdallah al-Hamawi. *Mu'ajam al-Buldan*. Ed. F. Wüstenfeld. 1866. Reprint. Tehran: n.p., 1965.

Modern Studies

Abdel Malik, Anwar. "Orientalism in Crisis." *Diogenes* 44 (1963): 103–140.

Abuswa, Mahmud. "The Arabization and Islamization of the Maghrib: A Social and Economic Reconstruction of the History of the Maghrib during the First Two Centuries of Islam." Ph.D. dissertation, University of California, Los Angeles, 1984.

Ahmad, Leila. "Women and the Advent of Islam." *Signs* 2 (1986): 665–691.

al-Ahmadi, Ali ibn Husayn. *Makatib ar-Rusul*. Beirut: Dar al-Muhjir, n.d.

'Ali, Jawad. *Al-Mufassal fi Ta'rikh al-'Arab Qabl al-Islam*. Beirut: Dar al-'Ilm li al-Malayin, 1968.

el-Ali, Saleh. "Khitat al-Basra." *Summer* 8 (1952): 72–83, 281–302.

———. "Muslim Estates in the Hijaz." *Journal of the Economic and Social History of the Orient* 2 (1959): 247–261.

———. *Al-Tanzimat al-Ijtima'iyya wa al-Iqtisadiyya fi al-Basra*. 2d ed. Beirut: Dar al-Tali'ah, 1969.

———. "The Topography of Medina." *Islamic Culture* 35 (1961): 65–92.

Ashtor, E. *A Social and Economic History of the Near East in the Middle Ages*. Berkeley & Los Angeles: University of California Press, 1976.

Aswad, Barbara. "Social and Ecological Aspects in the Formation of Islam." In *Peoples and Cultures of the Middle East*, ed. Louis Sweet, I: 53–73. Garden City: Natural History Press, 1970.

Bashir, Sulaiman. *Al-Tarikh al-Akhar*. Jerusalem: n.p., 1984.

Beeston, A. F. L. "Kingship in South Arabia." *Journal of the Economic and Social History of the Orient* 15 (1972): 256–268.

———. "The Problem of South Arabian Chronology." *Bulletin of the School of Oriental and African Studies* 16 (1954): 39–42.

———. *Qahtan Studies in Old South Arabian Epigraphy: The Mercantile Code of Qataban*. London: Luzac, 1959.

———. "The Settlement at Khor Reir." *Journal of Oman Studies* 2 (1976): 39–42.

Bell, Richard. *The Origin of Islam in Its Christian Environment*. London: Macmillan, 1926.

Bernal, Martin. *Black Athena*. Vol. 1: *The Fabrication of Ancient Greece*. New Brunswick: Rutgers University Press, 1987.

Bowen, Richard. "Irrigation in Ancient Qataban." In *Archaeological Discoveries in South Arabia*, 2: 43–131. Baltimore: Johns Hopkins University Press, 1958.

Butler, Alfred. *The Arab Conquest of Egypt and the Last Thirty Years of the Roman Dominion*. Oxford: Clarendon Press, 1902.

Caskell, C. W. "Bedouinization of Arabia." In *Studies in Islamic Cultural History*, ed. G. von Grunebaum, pp. 36–46. Menosha: American Anthropological Association, 1954.

Conrad, Lawrence. "Abraha and Muhammad: Some Observations Apropos of Chronology and Literary Topoi in Early Arabic Historical Tradition." *Bulletin of the School of Oriental and African Studies* 50 (1987): 225–240.

———. "Seven and Tasbiʿ: On the Implications of Numerical Symbolism for the Study of Medieval Islamic History." *Journal of the Economic and Social History of the Orient* 31 (1988): 42–73.

Crone, Patricia. *Meccan Trade*. Princeton: Princeton University Press, 1987.

———. *Slaves on Horses*. Cambridge: Cambridge University Press, 1980.

Crone, Patricia, and Michael Cook. *Hagarism: The Making of the Islamic World*. Cambridge: Cambridge University Press, 1977.

Dennet, D. C. *Conversion and Poll Tax in Early Islam*. Cambridge, Mass.: Harvard University Press, 1950.

Denny, Fredrick. "Umma in the Constitution of Medina." *Journal of Near Eastern Studies* 36 (1977): 26–59.

de Ste. Croix, G. E. M. *The Class Struggle in the Ancient Greek World*. London: Duckworth, 1981.

Donner, F. M. "The Arab Tribes in the Muslim Conquest of Iraq." Ph.D. dissertation, Princeton University, 1975.

———. "The Bakr b. Waʾil Tribes and Politics in Northeastern Arabia on the Eve of Islam." *Studia Islamica* 51 (1983): 5–38.

———. *The Early Islamic Conquests*. Princeton: Princeton University Press, 1981.

———. "The Food Boycott and Muhammad's Policy." *Journal of the Economic and Social History of the Orient* 20 (1977): 249–266.

———. Review of Patricia Crone, *Slaves on Horses*. *Journal of the American Oriental Society*, 1982, pp. 367–371.

Dostal, Walter. "The Evolution of Bedouin Life." In *L'Antica Società Bedouina*, ed. F. Gabrielli, pp. 11–34. Rome: Instituto di Studi Orientali Università, 1959.

al-Duri, Abd al-Aziz. "Landlord and Peasant in Early Islam." *Der Islam* 56 (1979): 97–105.

Eicklemen, Dale. "Musailama." *Journal of the Economic and Social History of the Orient* 10 (1967): 17–52.

Eliade, Mircea. *The Sacred and the Profane*. Trans. W. Trask. New York: Harcourt, Brace & World, 1959.

Encyclopedia of Islam. 4 vols. 2d ed. Ed. H. A. R. Gibb et al. Leiden: Brill, 1960–.

Forand, P. G. "The Status of the Land and the Inhabitants of the Sawad during the First Two Centuries of Islam." *Journal of the Economic and Social History of the Orient* 14 (1971): 25–37.

Gabrieli, F. *Muhammad and the Conquests of Islam*. Trans. V. Luling and R. Linell. New York: McGraw-Hill, 1968.

Gerd-Rudiger, Puin. *Der Diwan von ʿUmar Ibn al-Hattab*. Bonn: Friedrich Wilhelm Universität, 1970.

Ghunaim, Ahmad. *Hurub al-Ridda: Four Manuscripts from al-Iktifa fi Maghazi al-Mustafa wa al-Thalatha al-Khulafa*. Cairo: Dar al-Ittihad, 1974.

Gibb, H. A. R. *Arabic Literature*. Oxford: Clarendon Press, 1963.

———. "An Interpretation of Islamic History." *Journal of World History* 1 (1953): 39–62.

Gil, Moshe. "The Constitution of Medina: A Reconsideration." *Israel Oriental Studies* 4 (1974): 44–66.

Goitein, S. D. *Mediterranean Society*. 3 vols. Berkeley & Los Angeles: University of California Press, 1967–1978.

———. *Studies in Islamic History and Institutions*. Leiden: Brill, 1965.

Gran, Peter. *Islamic Roots of Capitalism: Egypt, 1760–1840*. Austin: University of Texas Press, 1979.

Grierson, P. "The Financial Reforms of Abd al-Malik." *Journal of the Economic and Social History of the Orient* 3 (1960): 241–264.

Hamidullah, M. "The City State of Mecca." *Islamic Culture* 12 (1938): 254–277.

———. "Al-Ilaf ou les rapports économic-diplomatiques de la Mecque pré-Islamique." In *Mélanges Louis Massignon*, pp. 293–311. Damas: Institut Français de Damas 2 [1957].

———. *Majmuʿat al-Watha ʾiq al-Siyasiyya*. Beirut: Dar al-Irshad, 1969.

Harley, A. H. "Dihya al-Kalbi." *Journal of the Proceedings of the Asiatic Society of Bengal* 18 (1922): 273–285.

Hill, D. R. *Termination of Hostilities in the Early Arab Conquest*. London: Luzac, 1971.

Hinds, Martin. "Kufan Political Alignments and Their Background in the Mid-Seventh Century A.D." *International Journal of Middle Eastern Studies* 2 (1971): 346–367.

———. "The Murder of the Caliph Uthman." *International Journal of Middle Eastern Studies* 3 (1972): 450–469.

———. "The Siffin Arbitration Agreement." *Journal of Semitic Studies* 17 (1972): 93–129.

Hitti, Philip K. *Capital Cities of Arab Islam.* Minneapolis: University of Minnesota Press, 1970.

———. *History of the Arabs.* 10th ed. New York: St. Martin's Press, 1970.

Hodgson, M. G. S. *The Venture of Islam: The Classical Age of Islam.* Chicago: University of Chicago Press, 1974.

Hourani, G. F. *Arab Seafaring in the Indian Ocean.* Princeton: Princeton University Press, 1951.

———. "Did Roman Competition Ruin South Arabia?" *Journal of Near Eastern Studies* 11 (1952): 291–295.

Ibrahim, Mahmood. Review of Crone, *Slaves on Horses. Muslim World* 73 (1983): 287–290.

———. Review of Kubiak, *Al-Fustat: Its Foundation and Early Urban Development. Ufahamu* 13 (1983): 165–168.

———. "Social and Economic Conditions in Pre-Islamic Mecca." *International Journal of Middle Eastern Studies* 14 (1982): 343–358.

———. "The Petrification of Islam." *Birzeit Research Review* 4 (1987): 64–73, (English) 150–161.

Ingrams, H. "From Cana to Shabwa: The South Arabian Incense Road." *Journal of Royal Asiatic Society,* 1945, pp. 169–185.

Jamme, Albert. *Classification descriptive général des inscriptions sud-arabes.* Tunis: Institut des Belles Lettres Arabe, 1948.

———. *Sabaen Inscriptions from Mahram Bilqis (Maʾrib).* Baltimore: Johns Hopkins University Press, 1962.

———. *The al-ʿUqla Texts.* Washington, D.C.: Catholic University Press, 1963.

al-Janabi, K. *Takhtit Madinat al-Kufa.* Baghdad: Dar al-Jumhuriyya, 1967.

Judeh, J. M. *Al-ʿArab wa al-Ard fi al-Iraq.* Amman: Amman University Press, 1977.

Karachkovsky, I. *Taʾrikh al-Adab al-Jughrafi al-ʿArabi.* Trans. Salah al-Din H. Uthman. Cairo: Arab League, 1963.

Kawar, Irfan. "Arethas, Son of Jabalah." *Journal of the American Oriental Society* 75 (1955): 205–216.

———. "The Arabs in the Peace Treaty of 561 A.D." *Arabica,* 1956, pp. 181–213.

Khalidi, Ismaʿil. "The Arab Kingdom of Ghassan." *Muslim World* 65 (1965): 193–206.

Khan, Ahmad. "The Tanning Cottage Industry in Pre-Islamic Arabia." *Journal of Pakistan Historical Society* 19 (1971): 85–100.

Kister, M. J. "The Campaign of Huluban." *Le Muséon* 78 (1965): 425–436.

———. "Hira: Some Notes on Its Relations with Arabia." *Arabica* 15 (1968): 145–169.

———. "The Market of the Prophet." *Journal of the Economic and Social History of the Orient* 8 (1965): 272–276.

————. "Mecca and Tamim." *Journal of the Economic and Social History of the Orient* 8 (1965): 113–163.

————. "Notes on an Account of the Shura of Umar." *Journal of Semitic Studies* 9 (1964): 320–326.

————. "Some Reports concerning Mecca from Jahiliyya to Islam." *Journal of the Economic and Social History of the Orient* 15 (1972): 61–93.

————. "Some Reports concerning Ta'if." *Jerusalem Studies in Arabic and Islam* (1979): 1–18.

Kubiak, W. *Al-Fustat: Its Foundation and Early Urban Development.* Warsaw: Wydawn, Universytetu Warszawskiego, 1982.

Kuhn, Thomas. *The Structure of Scientific Revolutions.* 2d ed. Chicago: University of Chicago Press, 1972.

Lammens, Henri. *La cité arabe de Taif à la veille de l'hégire.* Beirut: Imprimerie Catholique, 1922.

————. *La Mecque à la veille de l'hégire.* Beirut: Imprimerie Catholique, 1924.

————. "La Mecque à la veille de l'hégire." *Mélange de l'Université Saint-Joseph* (Beirut), 1924, pp. 97–439.

————. "La république marchande de la Mecque vers l'an 600 de notre ère." *Bullétin de l'Institut Egyptien* 5th ser., no. 4 (1910): 23–54.

Langdon, S. "The Shalamians of Arabia." *Journal of the Royal Asiatic Society,* 1927, pp. 529–533.

Laroui, Abdallah. *Al-ʿArab wa al-Fikr al-Tarikhi.* Casablanca: Arab Cultural Center, 1983.

————. *La crise des intellectuels arabes: Traditionalisme ou historicisme.* Paris: Librairie Françoise Maspero, 1974. Translated as *The Crises of the Arab Intellectuals: Traditionalism or Historicism,* trans. Diarmid Cammel. Berkeley & Los Angeles: University of California Press, 1976.

Levi Della Vida, G. "Pre-Islamic Arabia." In *The Arab Heritage,* ed. N. Faris, pp. 25–57. Princeton: Princeton University Press, 1934.

Lewis, Archibald. *Naval Power and Trade in the Mediterranean: 500–1000 A.D.* Princeton: Princeton University Press, 1951.

Liebeschuetz, John H. *Antioch: City and Imperial Administration in the Late Roman Empire.* Oxford: Clarendon Press, 1972.

Lichtenstadter, I. "Fraternization in Early Islam." *Islamic Culture* 6 (1942): 47–53.

Lings, Martin. *Muhammad.* New York: Inner Traditions International, 1983.

Lombard, Maurice. *The Golden Age of Islam.* Trans. Joan Spenser. Amsterdam & Oxford: North Holland, 1975.

López, R. S. "Silk Industry in the Byzantine Empire." *Speculum* 20 (1945): 1–42.

Lundin, A. G. "Le régime citadin de l'Arabi du Sud aux IIᵉ–IIIᵉ siècle de notre ère." *Proceedings of the Seminar for Arabian Studies,* 1972, pp. 26–29.

Miller, J. I. *Spice Trade of the Roman Empire.* Oxford: Oxford University Press, 1969.

Morony, Michael G. *Iraq after the Muslim Conquest.* Princeton: Princeton University Press, 1984.

Nicholson, R. A. *A Literary History of the Arabs.* 1907. Reprint. Cambridge: Cambridge University Press, 1969.

Noldeke, Theodor. *Die Ghassanischen Fursten aus dem Hause Gafna's.* Berlin: Akademie der Wissenschaften, 1887.

O'Leary, De Lacy. *Arabia before Muhammad.* London: K. Paul, Trench, Trubner, 1927.

Olinder, Gunner. *Kings of Kinda of the Family of Akil al-Murar.* Lund: Trubner, 1927.

Ostrogorsky, G. *History of the Byzantine State.* New Brunswick: Rutgers University Press, 1969.

Periplus of the Erythrean Sea. Trans. W. H. Scohff. New York: Longman Green, 1912.

Petersen, E. L. *'Ali and Mu'awiya in Early Arabic Tradition.* Odense: Odense University Press, 1974.

Philby, H. St. J. B. "Motor Tracks and Sabaen Inscriptions in Najd." *Geographical Journal* 116 (1950): 211–215.

———. "South Arabian Chronology." *Le Muséon* 62 (1949): 229–249.

———. "Three New Inscriptions from Hadhramout." *Journal of the Royal Asiatic Society,* 1945, pp. 124–133.

———. "Two Notes from Central Arabia." *Geographical Journal* 113 (1949): 86–93.

Philby, H. St. J. B., and Tritton. "Najran Inscriptions." *Journal of the Royal Asiatic Society,* 1944, pp. 119–129.

Pigulevskaja, N. "Les rapports sociaux à Nedjran au début du VIᵉ siècle de l'ère chrétienne." *Journal of the Economic and Social History of the Orient* 4 (1961): 1–14.

Poliak, A. N. *Feudalism in Egypt, Syria, Palestine, and the Lebanon, 1250–1900.* London: Royal Asiatic Society, 1939.

———. "La feudalité islamique." *Revue des Etudes Islamique,* 1936, pp. 247–265.

Rahman, Fazlur. *Islam.* 2d ed. Chicago: University of Chicago Press, 1979.

Rodinson, Maxime. *Islam and Capitalism.* Trans. Brian Pearce. Austin: University of Texas Press, 1978.

———. *Muhammad.* Trans. Ann Carter. New York: Vintage Press, 1974.

———. "The Western Image and Western Studies of Islam." In *The Legacy of Islam,* ed. Joseph Schacht and C. E. Bosworth, pp. 9–62. 2d ed. Oxford: Clarendon Press, 1974.

Rostovetzeff, M. *Caravan Cities.* Trans. D. Rice and T. Talbot Rice. Oxford: Oxford University Press, 1932.

Rothstein, G. *Die Dynastie der Lahmiden in al-Hira.* Berlin: Reuther, 1899.

Ryckmans, G. "Inscriptions Sud-Arabes (septième serie)." *Le Muséon* 40 (1927): 161–200.

Ryckmans, J. *L'Institutions monarchiques en Arabie meridionale avant l'Islam (Ma'in et Saba')*. Louvain: Publications Universitaires, 1951.

——. *La persecution des Chrétiens Himyarites au sixième siècle*. Istanbul: Nederlands Historisch-Archaeologisch Institut, 1956.

——. "Ritual Meals in the Ancient South Arabian Religion." *Proceedings of the Seminar for Arabian Studies*, 1971, pp. 36–39.

Sahlins, Marshall. *Tribesmen*. Englewood Cliffs: Prentice-Hall, 1968.

Said, Edward W. *Orientalism*. New York: Vintage Books, 1979.

al-Salimi, Adballah ibn Humyyid. *Tuhfat al-A'yan fi Sirat Ahl Uman*. Cairo: Matba'ut al-Sha'b, 1931.

Serjeant, R. B. "The Constitution of Medina." *Islamic Quarterly* 3 (1964): 3–16.

——. "The Sunna Jami'ah Pacts with Yathrib Jews, and the Tahrim of Yathrib: An Analysis and Translation of the Documents comprised in the So-called Constitution of Medina." *Bulletin of the School of Oriental and African Studies* 41 (1978): 1–48.

Shaban, M. A. *Islamic History: A New Interpretation*. Cambridge: Cambridge University Press, 1970.

Shahid, Irfan. "Arabic Literature." *Cambridge History of Islam,* ed. P. M. Holt et al., 2:657–671. Cambridge: Cambridge University Press, 1970.

——. "Ghassan." In *Encyclopedia of Islam*. 2d ed. 2:1020–1021.

——. "Hira." In *Encyclopedia of Islam*. 2d ed., 3:462–463.

——. "Pre-Islamic Arabia." In *Cambridge History of Islam,* ed. P. M. Holt et al., 1:3–29. Cambridge: Cambridge University Press, 1970.

Shoufani, Elias. *Al-Riddah and the Muslim Conquest of Arabia*. Toronto: University of Toronto Press, 1973.

Simon, R. "Hums et ilaf ou commerce sans guerre." *Acta Hungaricae* (Budapest), 1970, pp. 204–232.

Smith, Sidney. "Events in Arabia in the Sixth Century A.D." *Bulletin of the School of Oriental and African Studies* 16 (1954): 425–468.

Stark, F. "Notes on the Southern Incense Route of Arabia." *Islamic Culture* 10 (1936): 193–210.

Stratos, A. N. *Byzantium in the Seventh Century*. Vol. 2. Trans. Harry T. Hionides. Amsterdam: Adolf M. Hakkert, 1972.

Tchalenko, Georges. *Villages antiques de la Syrie du Nord*. Paris: P. Geuthner, 1953–1958.

Tigar, Michael, with the assistance of Madeleine Levy. *Law and the Rise of Capitalism*. New York: Monthly Review Press, 1977.

Torrey, C. C. *The Commercial-Theological Terms in the Koran*. Leiden: Brill, 1892.

——. *The Jewish Foundation of Islam*. New York: Jewish Institute of Religion Press, 1933.

Trimingham, J. S. *Christianity among the Arabs in Pre-Islamic Times*. London: Longman, 1979.

Turkhan, Ibrahim Ali. *Al-Nuzum al-Iqtaʿiyya fi al-Sharq al-Awsat fi al-ʿUsur al-Wusta*. Cairo: Al-Kitab al-ʿArabi, 1968.

Turner, Bryan. *Marx and the End of Orientalism*. London: George Allen & Unwin, 1978.

Udovitch, Abraham. *Partnership and Profit in Medieval Islam*. Princeton: Princeton University Press, 1970.

van Beek, G. W. "Frankincense and Myrrh in Ancient South Arabia." *Journal of the American Oriental Society* 78 (1958): 141–153.

von Grunebaum, Gustave. *Classical Islam*. Chicago: Aldine, 1970.

———. *Medieval Islam*. Chicago: University of Chicago Press, 1971.

———. "Nature of Arab Unity." *Arabica* 10 (1963): 5–23.

von Wissman, H. "Himyar, Ancient History." *Le Muséon* 77 (1964): 429–497.

Warminton, E. *Commerce between the Roman Empire and India*. 2d ed. London: Curzon Press, 1974.

Watson, A. M. *Agricultural Innovation in the Early Islamic World*. Cambridge: Cambridge University Press, 1983.

———. "The Rise and Spread of Old World Cotton: In *Studies in Textile History in Memory of Harold Birnham,* ed. V. Gervers, pp. 355–368. Toronto: Royal Ontario Museum, 1977.

Watt, W. M. *The Formative Period of Islamic Thought*. Edinburgh: Edinburgh University Press, 1973.

———. "Ideal Factors in the Origin of Islam." *Islamic Quarterly* 2 (1955): 161–174.

———. *Islam and the Integration of Society*. London: Routledge & Kegan Paul, 1961.

———. "Kharijite Thought in the Umayyad Period." *Der Islam* 36 (1961): 215–232.

———. *Muhammad at Mecca*. Oxford: Oxford University Press, 1953.

———. *Muhammad at Medina*. Oxford: Oxford University Press, 1956.

———. "Social and Economic Aspects in the Rise of Islam." *Islamic Quarterly* 1 (1954): 90–103.

Weber, Max. *The Sociology of Religion*. Trans. E. Ficshoff, intro. T. Parsons. Boston: Beacon Press, 1964.

Wellhausen, J. *Die religios-politischen Oppositonspartteien im alten Islam*. Gottingen, 1901. Translated as *The Religio-Political Factions in Early Islam.*, trans. R. C. Costle & S. M. Walzer. Amsterdam & London: North Holland, 1975.

Wilkinson, J. C. "Arab-Persian Relations in the Late Sasanid Oman." *Proceedings of the Seminar for Arabian Studies,* 1972, pp. 40–51.

———. "The Julanda of Oman." *Journal of Oman Studies,* 1975, pp. 97–108.

Wilson, A. T. *The Persian Gulf*. Oxford: Oxford University Press, 1928.

Winnett, F. V. "Reference to Jesus in Pre-Islamic Arabian Inscriptions." *Muslim World* 31 (1941): 314–353.

Winnett, F. V., and W. L. Reed. *Ancient Records from North Arabia*. Toronto: University of Toronto Press, 1970.

Wolf, Eric. "The Social Organization of Mecca and the Origins of Islam." *Southwest Journal of Anthropology* 7 (1951): 329–356.

Zarinkub, A. H. "The Arab Conquest of Iran and Its Aftermath." In *Cambridge History of Iran,* ed. R. N. Frey, 4:1–56. Cambridge: Cambridge University Press, 1975.

Ziyadeh, Nichola. "Tatuwwur al-Turuq al-Bahriyya wa al-Tijariyya." *Majallat Dirasat al-Khalij waʾl-Jazira al-ʿArabiyya* 1 (1975): 69–94.

al-Zubaidi, M. H. *Al-Haya al-Ijtimaʿiyya wa al-Iqtisadiyya fi al-Kufa.* Cairo: Al-Matbaʿah al-ʿAlmiyya, 1970.

Index